AF575936

JULIE STEINER

BIRDS IN THE BARNES FOUNDATION

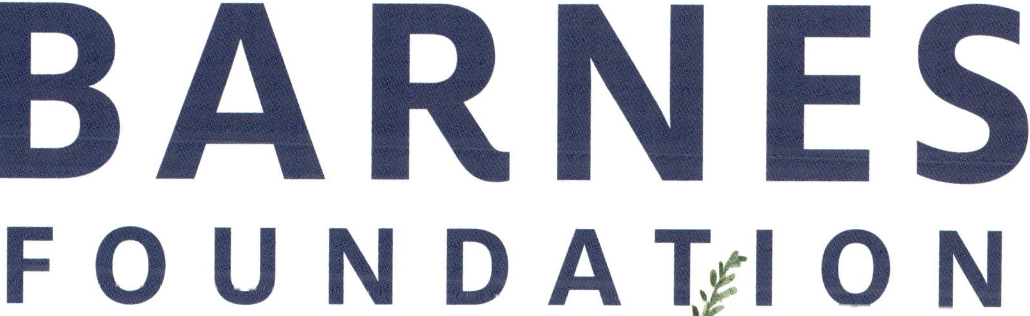

Legend says Dr. Barnes put a bird in every room of his collection... can you find them?

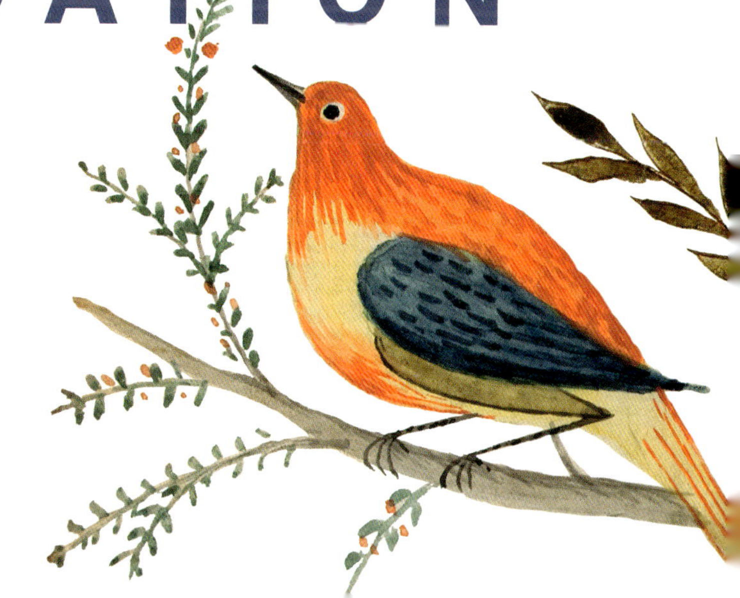

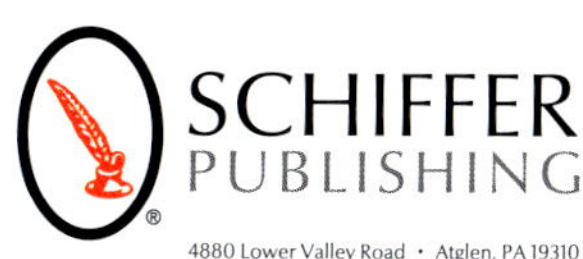

4880 Lower Valley Road • Atglen, PA 19310

Library of Congress Control Number: 2019946886

Designed by Molly Shields
Front cover design by Olivia Verdugo
Gallery photography by Sean Murray
Type set in MiloOT/ZapfEllipt BT

ISBN: 978-0-7643-5905-7
Printed in China

Published by Schiffer Publishing, Ltd.
4880 Lower Valley Road
Atglen, PA 19310
Phone: (610) 593-1777; Fax: (610) 593-2002
E-mail: Info@schifferbooks.com
Web: www.schifferbooks.com

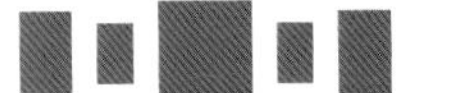

THE BARNES FOUNDATION

Contents

5 *A Bird in Every Room?*

6 Gallery 1: A Conventional Beginning
10 Gallery 2: Strange Arrangements
16 Gallery 3: Hardware on the Walls
18 Gallery 4: Storytelling without Words
24 Gallery 5: Dragons and Birds
30 Gallery 6: A Distinctly American Collection
34 Gallery 7: Form over Function
40 Gallery 8: Close Connections
44 Gallery 9: The Mystery Deepens
48 Gallery 10: The Art in Everyday Life
52 Gallery 11: Motion and Stillness
56 Gallery 12: Friends and Family
62 Gallery 13: Lush Green Landscapes
66 Gallery 14: Art History Flyby
76 Gallery 15: Flying around the World
86 Gallery 16: Home and Away
92 Gallery 17: Pennsylvania Roots
106 Gallery 18: Reflections and Repetitions
112 Balcony: A Dividing Line
124 Gallery 19: Size and Scale
128 Gallery 20: The Process of Making Art
132 Gallery 21: The Legend of the Birds
136 Gallery 22: Interwoven Cultures
140 Gallery 23: Bringing It All Together

150 *The More We Look, the More We See*
153 *Author's Note*
154 *Image Credits*
157 *Bibliography*
158 *Acknowledgments*

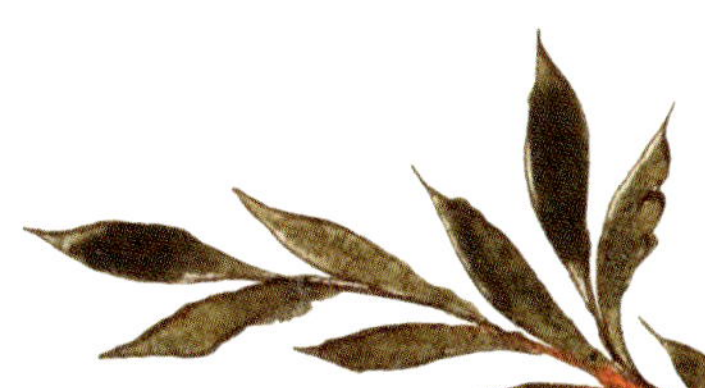

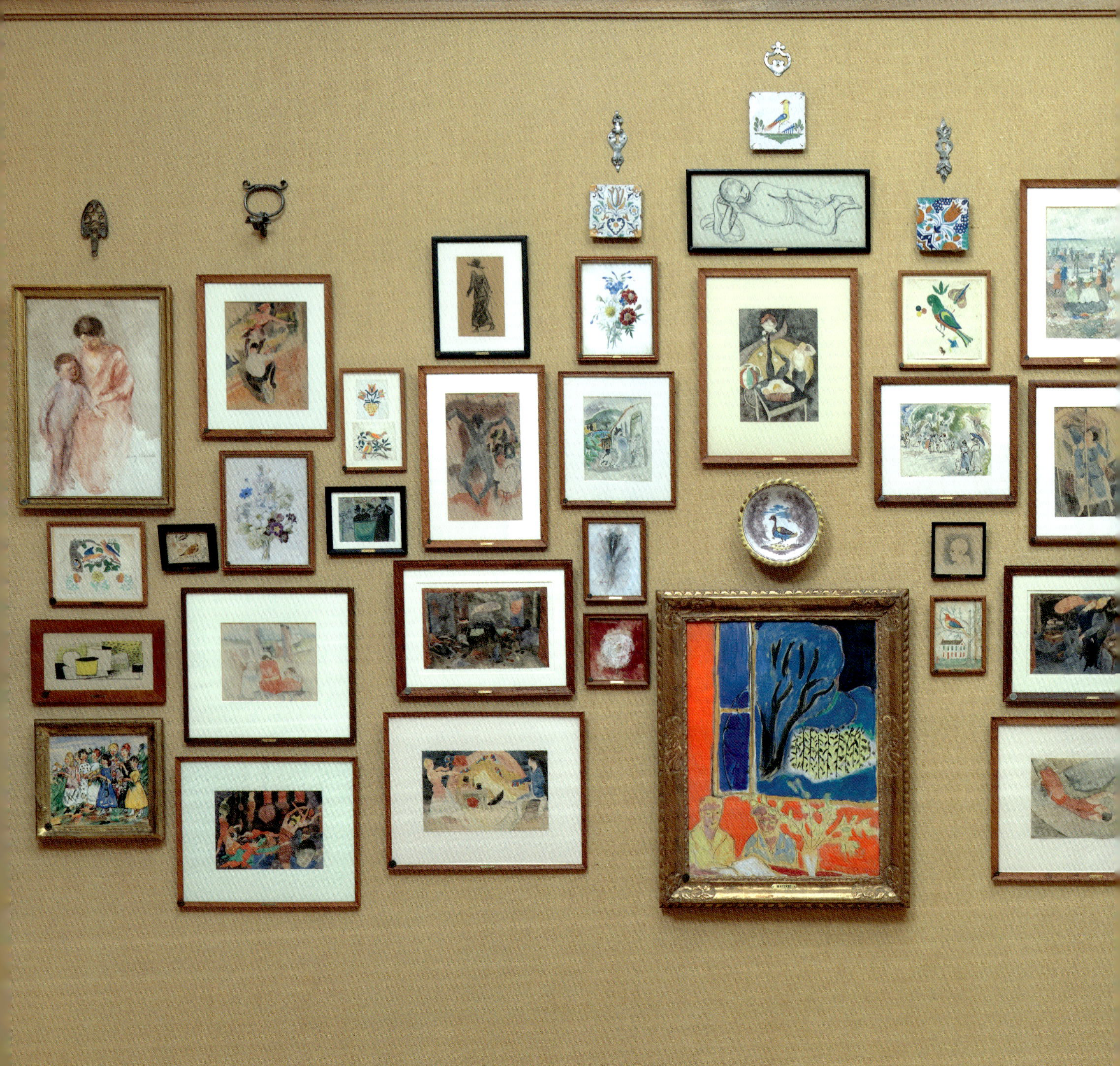

A Bird in Every Room?

Many people come to the Barnes Foundation looking for artistic masterworks: vast numbers of post-impressionist and early modern paintings for which the collection is best known. But all around and in between the paintings on the walls are odd keys, hinges, and metal hardware, and surrounding those are chairs, trunks, pottery, and candlesticks: a confounding array of art and objects unlike that in any other museum. You might ask, "What are all these things doing here together?"

In addition to the diverse collection and the unconventional arrangements, the Barnes is filled with legends and folklore, including conjectures about why each item was chosen, and why it was placed where it is. Included in those legends is a hitherto unsubstantiated rumor that the founder, Dr. Albert C. Barnes (1872–1951), placed a bird in every room of his collection. Did he? And, if so, why?

Dr. Barnes used his galleries as a teaching collection, encouraging students to look at art and draw conclusions based on direct observation. He wanted visitors to his collection to appreciate the artwork not on the basis of their artistic education or knowledge, but on what they saw while investigating each room.

We invite you to come see the Barnes Foundation's collection in a new way, looking past the masterworks and into the corners of the collection, investigating the smaller drawings and odd objects. Come with us on a playful, room-by-room tour of the Barnes collection, looking for birds. Along the way we'll find some notable names but also self-taught artists, and furniture, textiles, ironwork, and things many would hesitate to call "fine art" at all. If you are a newcomer to the collection, this "birdwatching" in the galleries can be a starting point to take in this large and comprehensive collection. If you are already knowledgeable about the artistic movements and artists represented here, searching for birds offers a new perspective and a fresh way to see. Along the way, we will endeavor to answer this question: Is there really a bird in every room of the Barnes Foundation?

Ensemble view, Room 17, north wall.

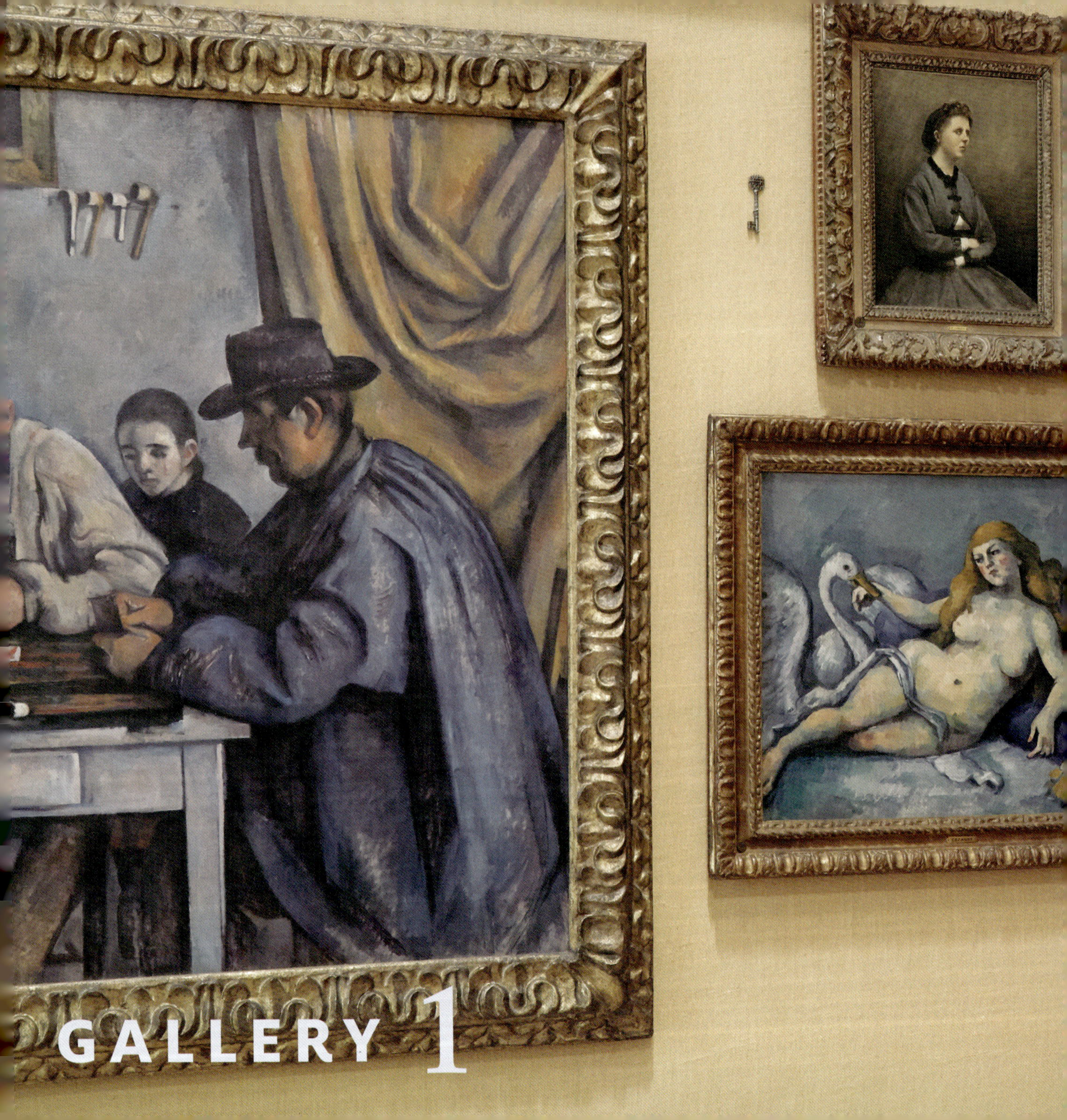

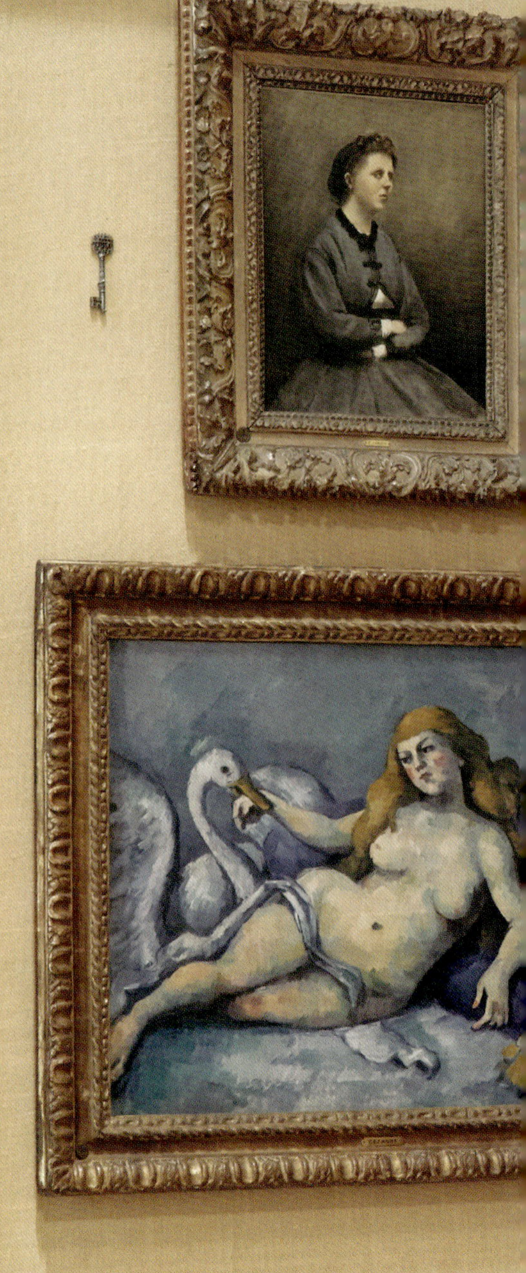

GALLERY 1

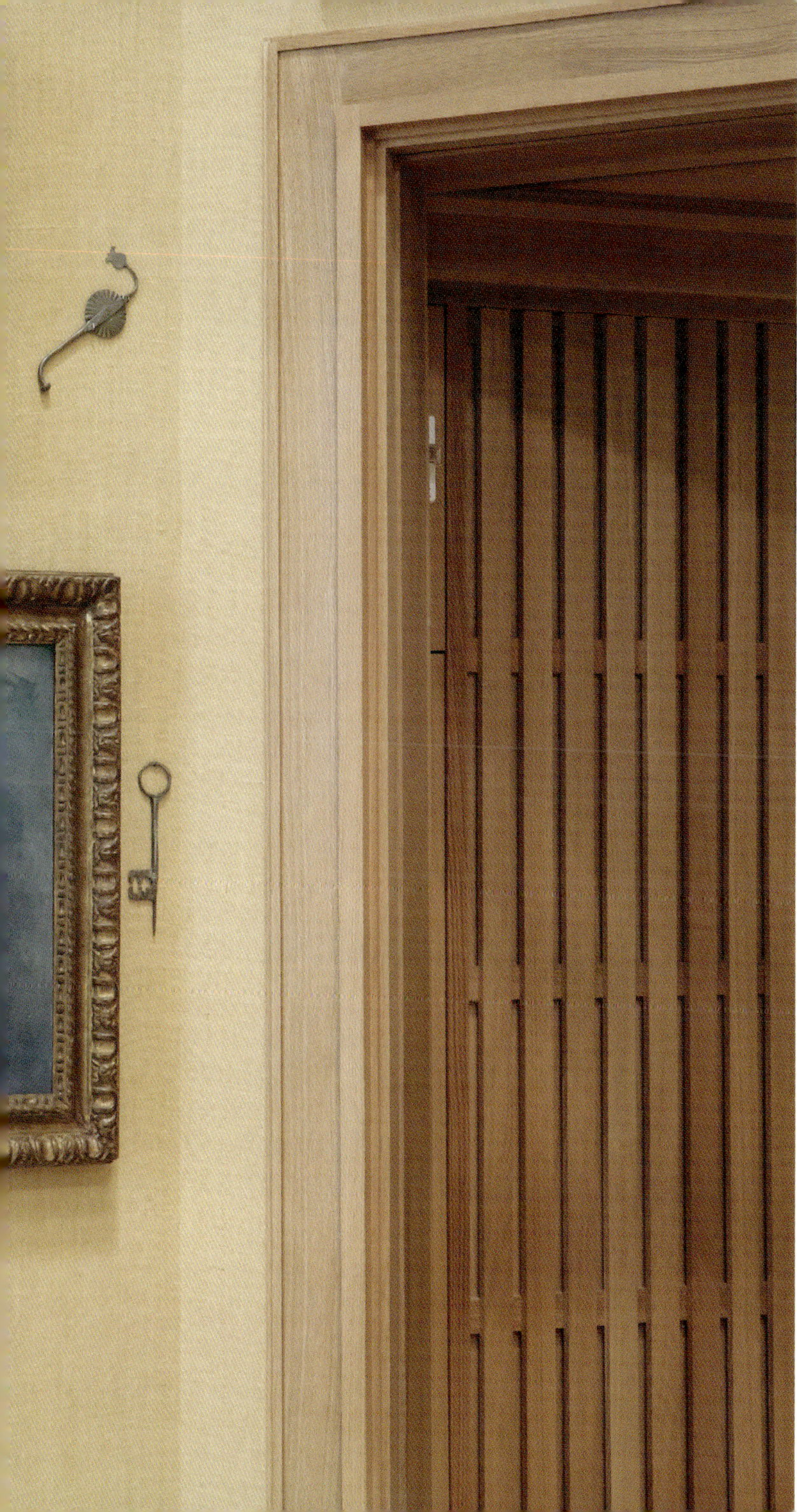

Ensemble view, Room 1, west wall.

A Conventional Beginning

Let us begin our search in the first and largest central gallery. Here we see only one feathered creature in the room: the swan in Paul Cézanne's *Leda and the Swan*, a grand and formal bird, portraying the Greek god Zeus taking animal form to seduce the mortal woman Leda. This story from classical mythology was also depicted by artists such as da Vinci, Michelangelo, Correggio, and Rubens. Cézanne figured among Dr. Barnes's favorite painters, and the collection holds a total of sixty-nine of his works.

While Gallery 1 starts with a painting whose enjoyment benefits from an education in classical literature, this is not typical of the collection or Barnes's taste in art, or the way the collection is presented, which will become more evident in the very next room.

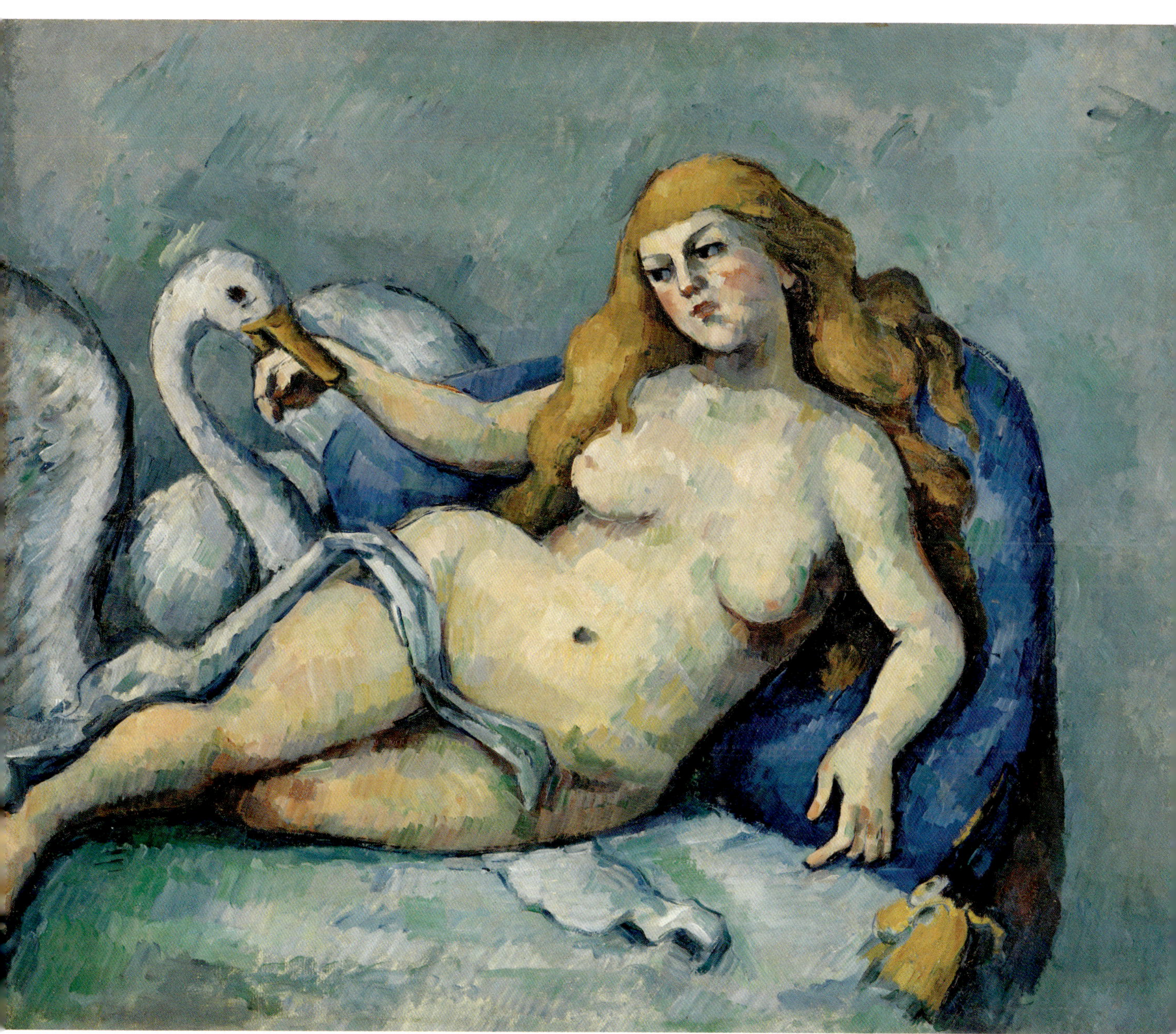

Paul Cézanne. *Leda and the Swan*, c. 1880 (possibly later).

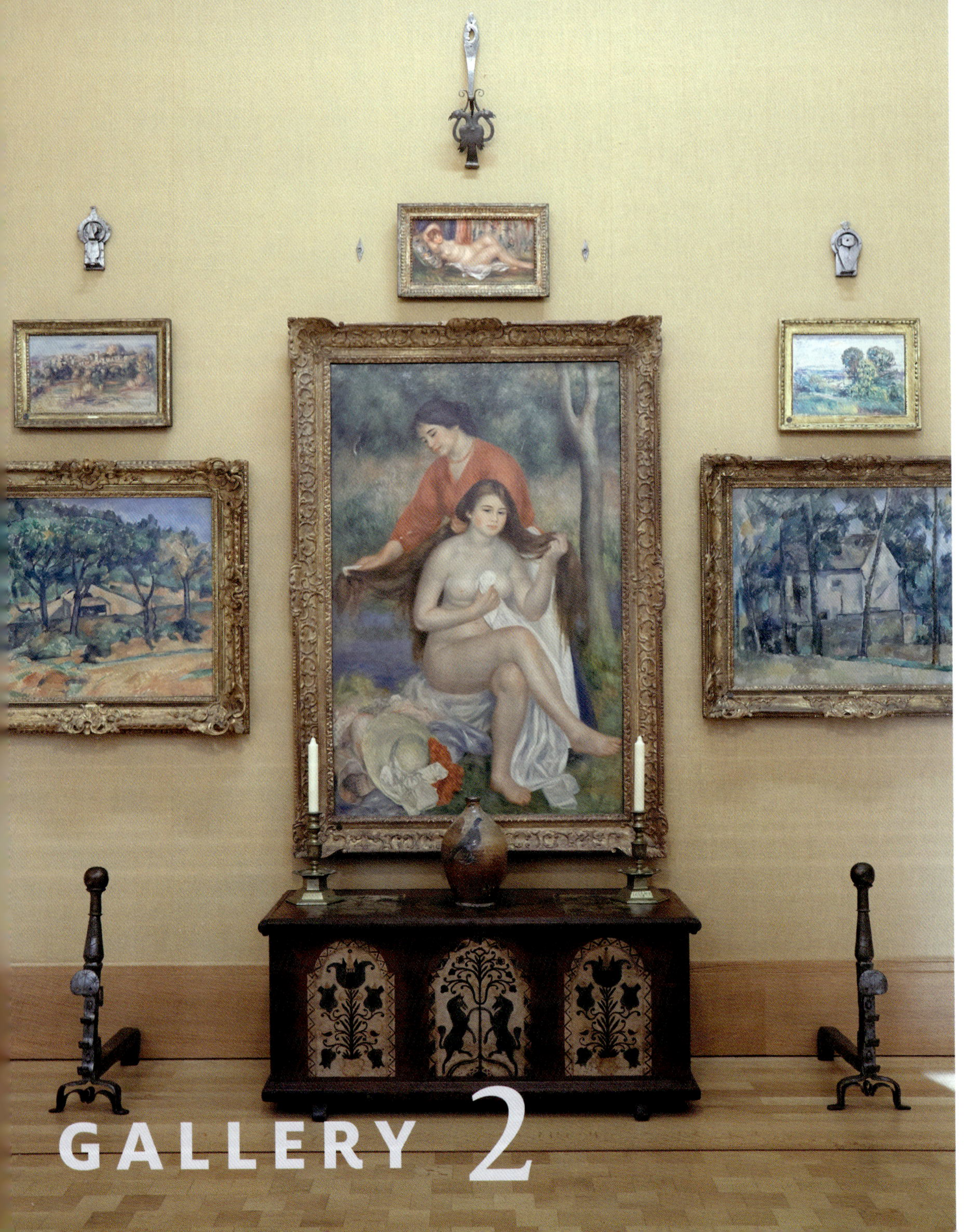

GALLERY 2

Strange Arrangements

Dr. Barnes hung the art in his collection in groupings that include not only paintings, but furniture, candlesticks, pottery, household objects, and tapestries, as well as metal hinges, locks, keys, and other ironwork pieces hanging on the walls. Dr. Barnes called these groupings "ensembles," like musical ensembles of varying instruments, and these arrangements were essential to the way Dr. Barnes taught art appreciation at the Foundation. Through the ensembles, Dr. Barnes encouraged the viewer to find visual connections between disparate objects and to study the relations of works from different artists, cultures, and eras on the same wall.

The birds in Gallery 2 show the repetition of subjects in Barnes's ensembles: a metal doorknocker with a pair of birds hangs over the Renoir painting *Bather and Maid*, matched with another bird drawn in the glaze of the jug just below it. Functional objects by anonymous makers play as essential a role in this collection as large-scale works by notable names in art history.

Ensemble view, Room 2, north wall.

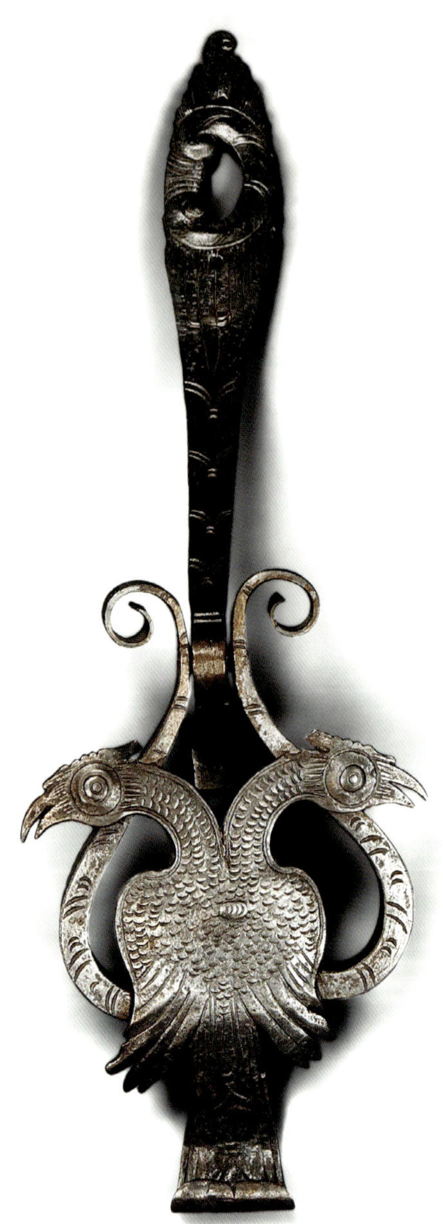

Door Knocker, 18th century.

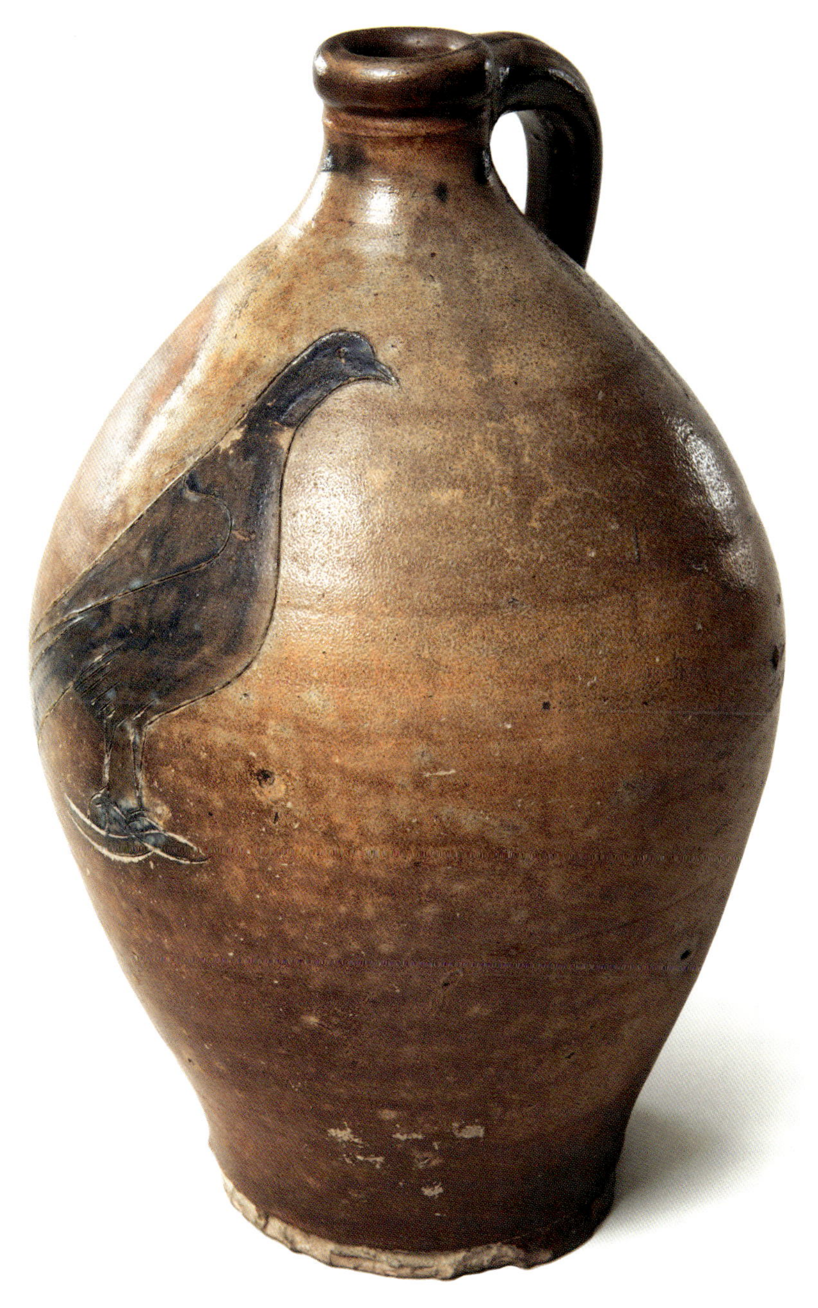

Jug, 1830–1850.

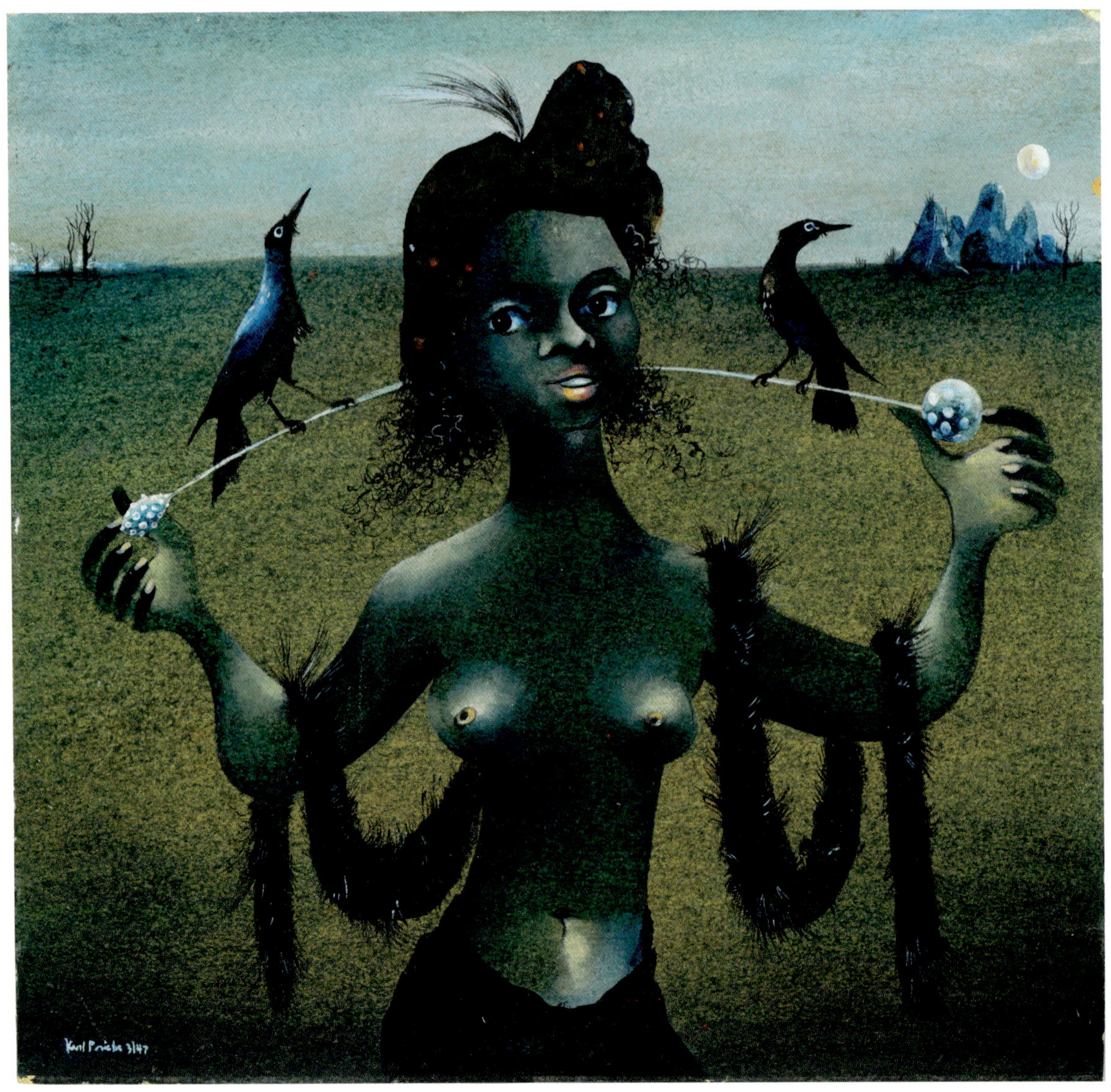

 Karl Priebe. *Miss Chalfont*, 1947.

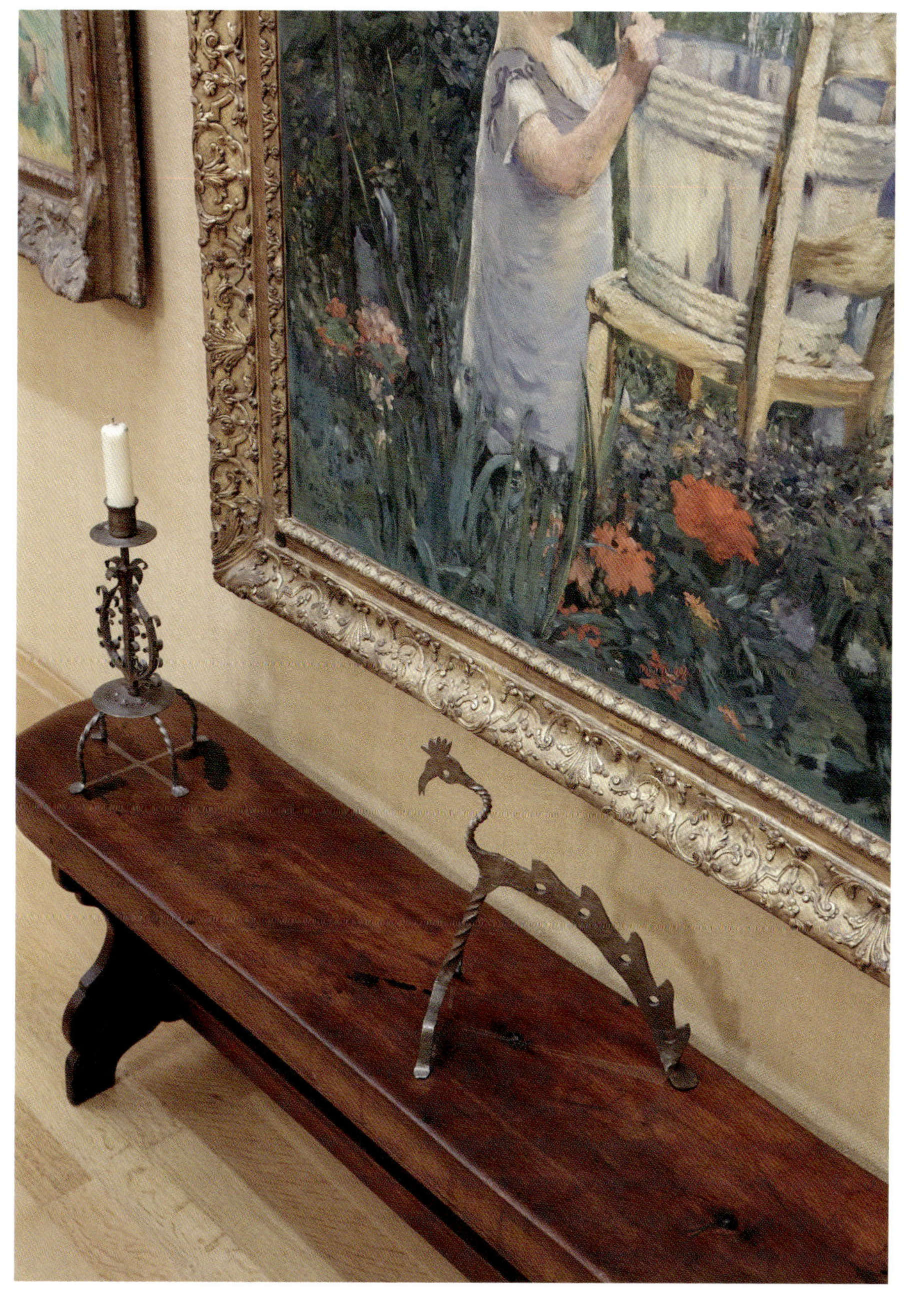

Andiron. Metal.

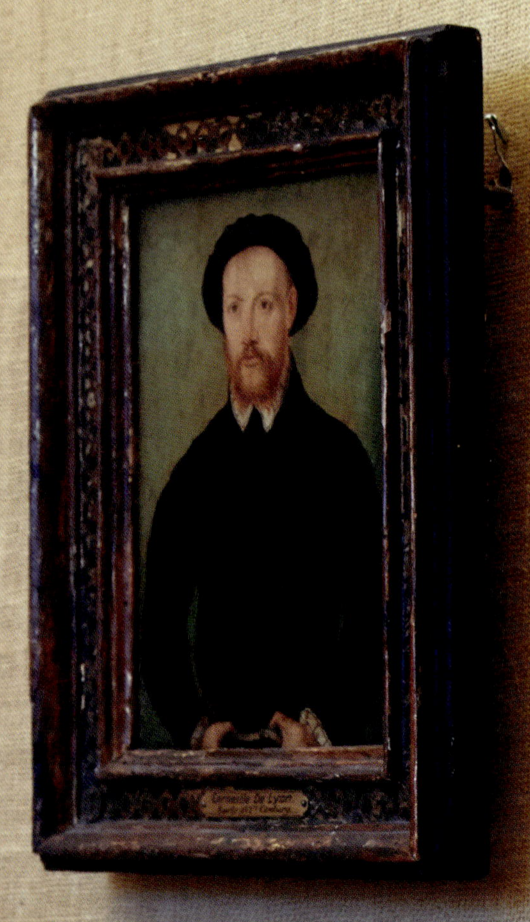

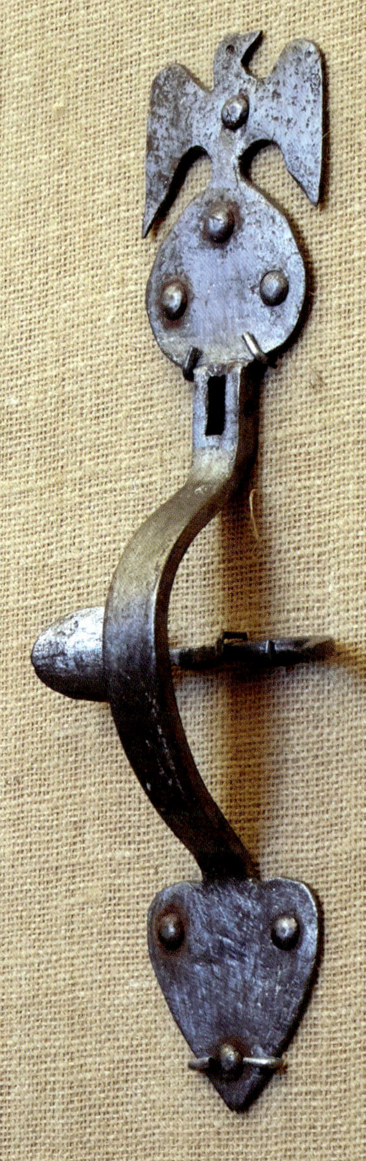

GALLERY 3

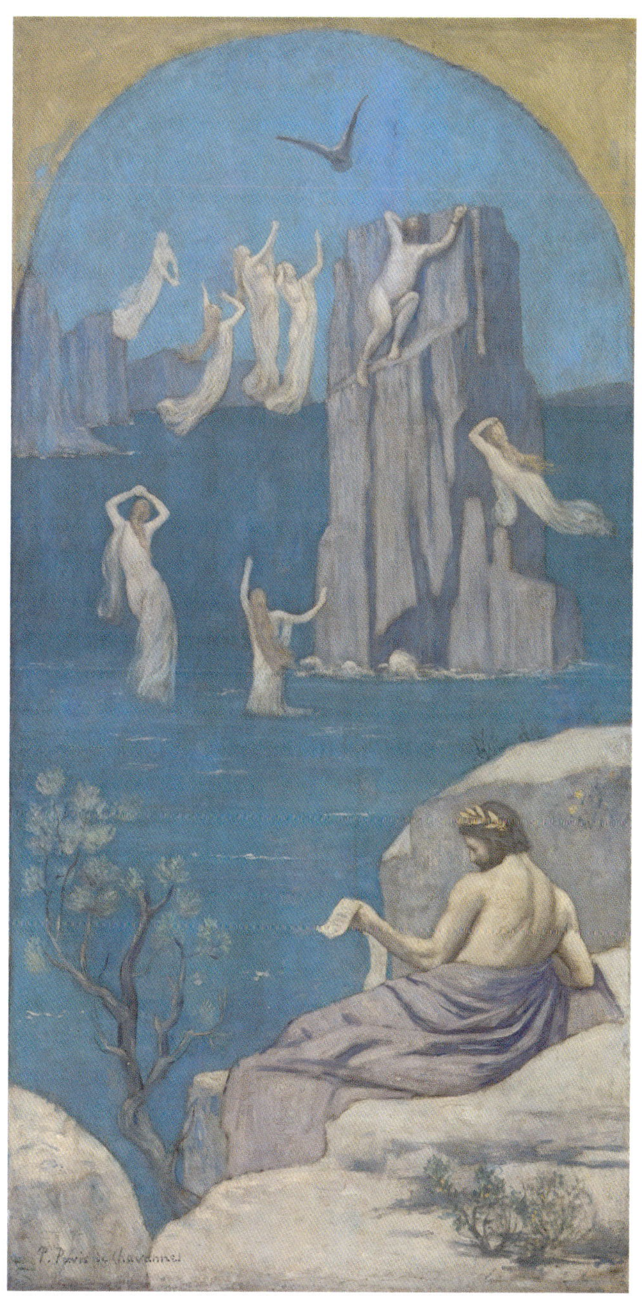

Hardware on the Walls

One of the birds in this gallery is a simple decorative flourish at the top of an iron hinge near a doorway. When asked by the American painter Stuart Davis why he had hung the many hinges, locks, tools, and antique iron objects among his paintings, Dr. Barnes wrote that the "arabesques, patterns, etc., discernible in a picture have their analogue, sometimes a very close one, in the iron work," and that he regarded "the creators of antique . . . iron just as authentic an artist as a Titian, Renoir, or Cézanne."

As if to punctuate this sentiment, the small bird on the hinge is diagonal in the room to another bird, an eagle, winging its way to the Greek hero Prometheus in a painting by Pierre Puvis de Chavannes. Puvis de Chavannes was an acclaimed Salon painter of the nineteenth century, whose classically inspired work obtained the highest recognitions from the French government and the Académie. To find his work in this room surrounded by humble hardware is quintessentially "Barnesian" in educational philosophy: mixing high and low, craftsman and painter together.

Handle, American. // Pierre Puvis de Chavannes. *Dramatic Poetry* (*Aeschylus*), c. 1896.

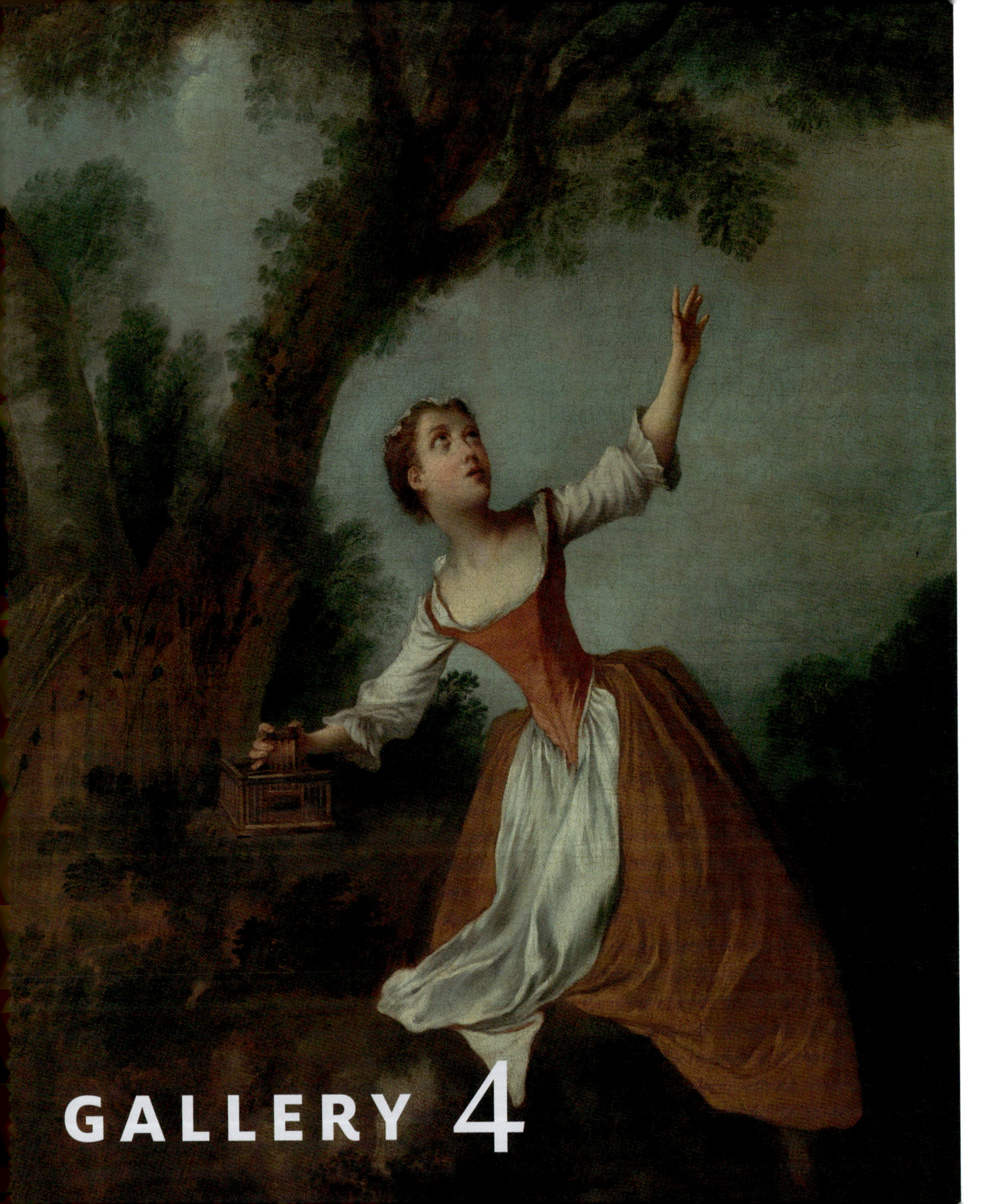
GALLERY 4

Storytelling without Words

Gallery 4 shows Dr. Barnes's deliberate hand in arranging his collection to embellish the paintings and create new stories in his installations. In the painting *Open Cage—Girl in Landscape*, attributed to the French rococo artist Nicolas Lancret, a girl holds an empty birdcage, posed in expressive alarm at the bird that has just fluttered away. Dr. Barnes responded to this dramatic painted narrative by filling in, on the wall above, a large metal bird to stand in for the one the artist had merely suggested in his painting.

Nicolas Lancret. *The Open Cage*, 18th century.

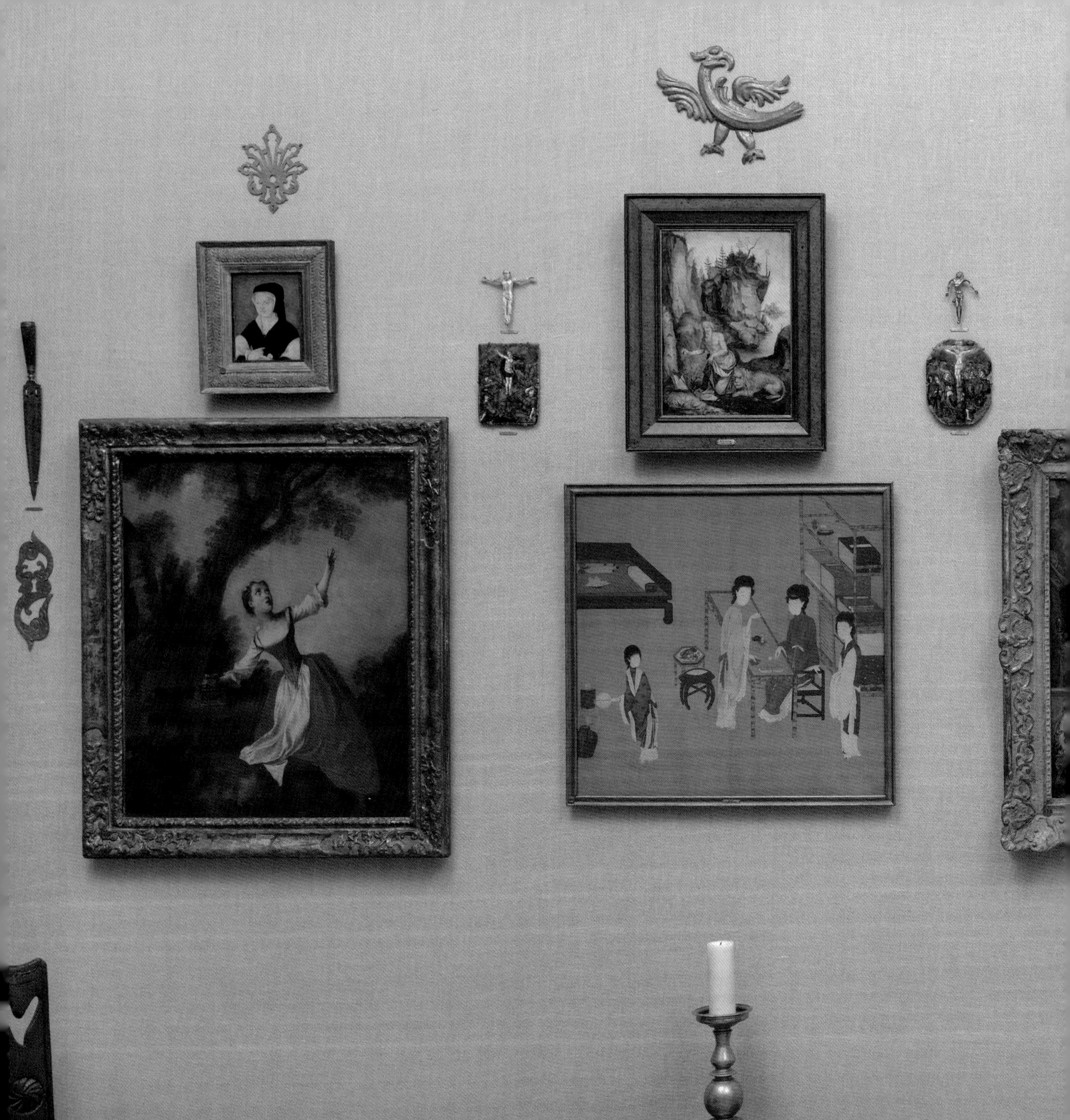

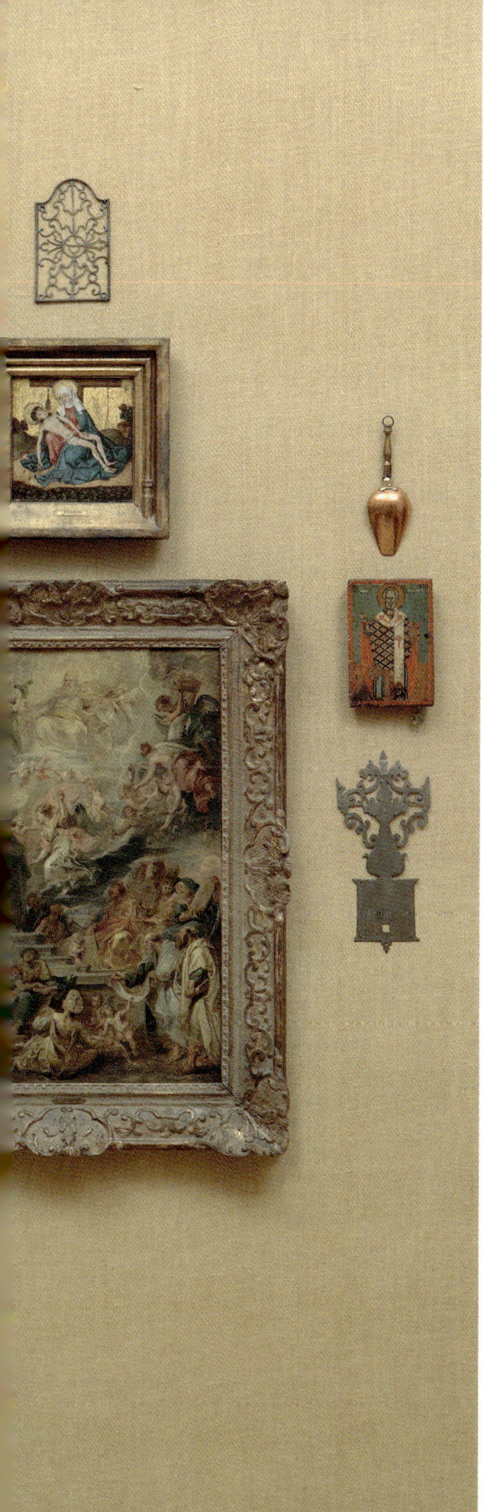

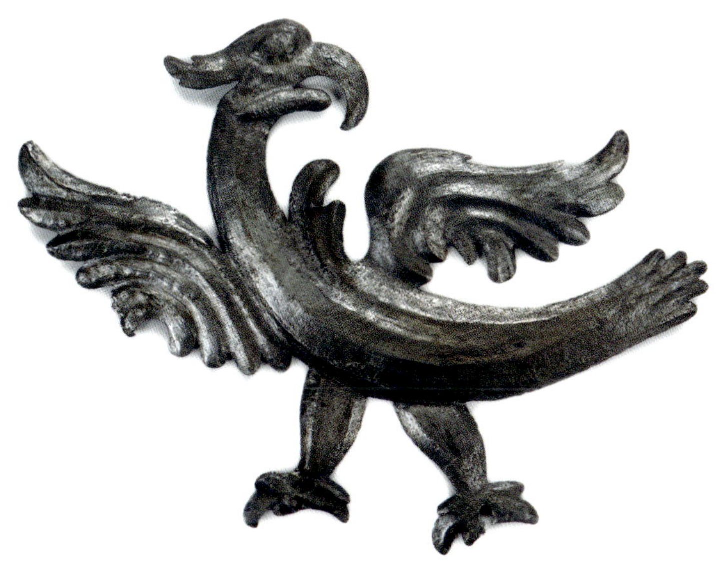

Ensemble view, Room 4, north wall. // Door Decoration, 18th century.

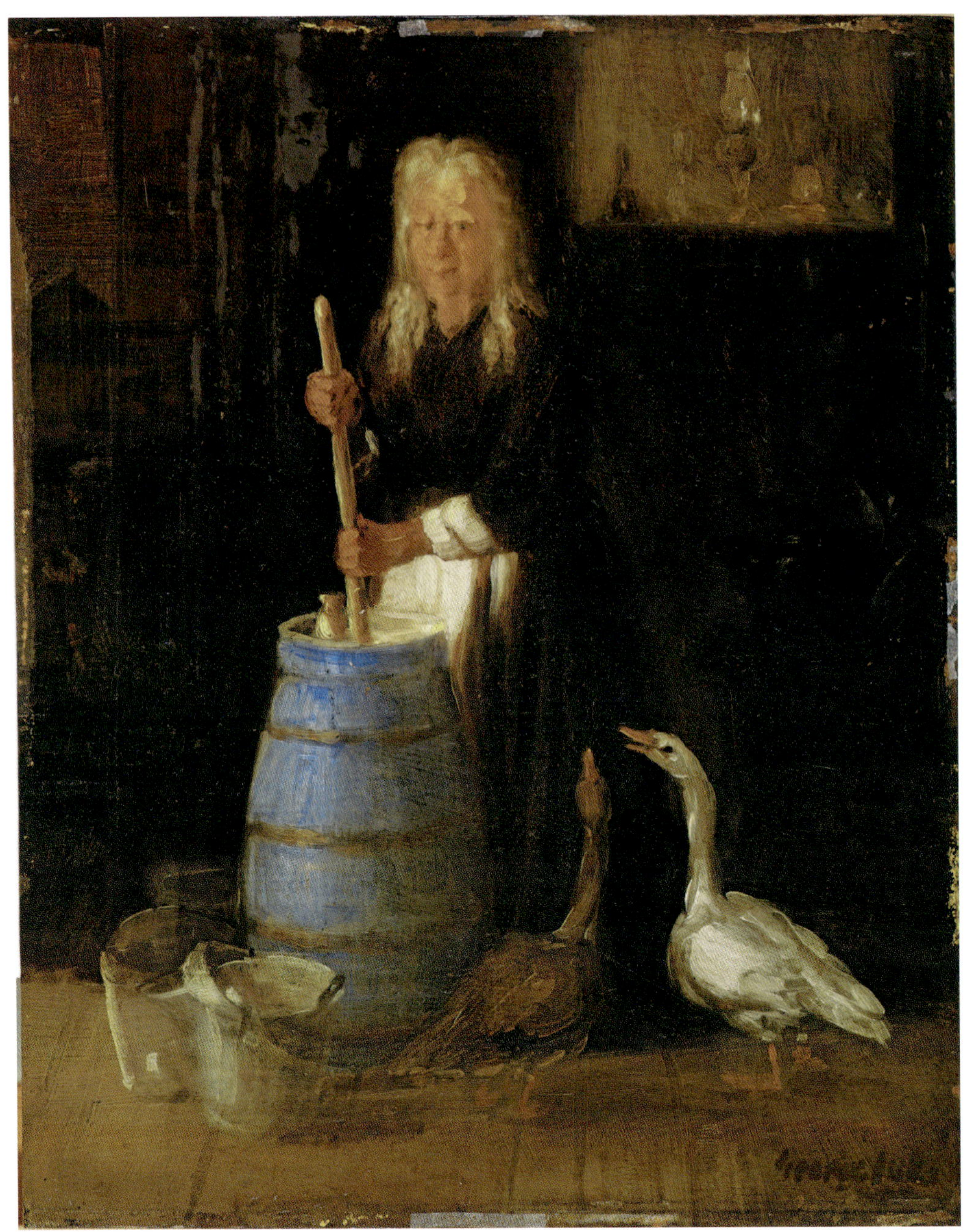

 George Benjamin Luks. *The Blue Churn*, c. 1908–1910.

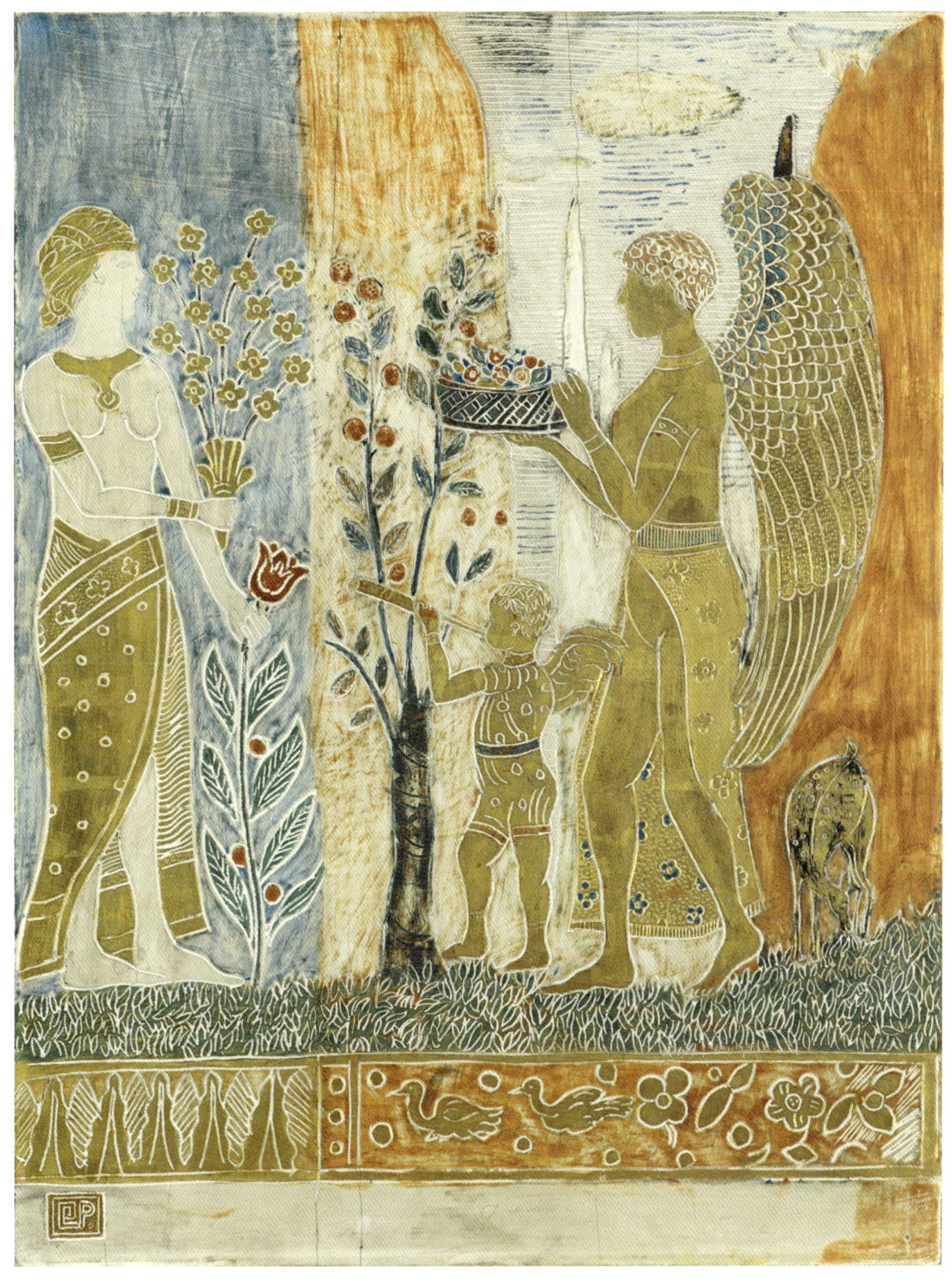

Charles Prendergast. *The Offering*, c. 1915–1917.

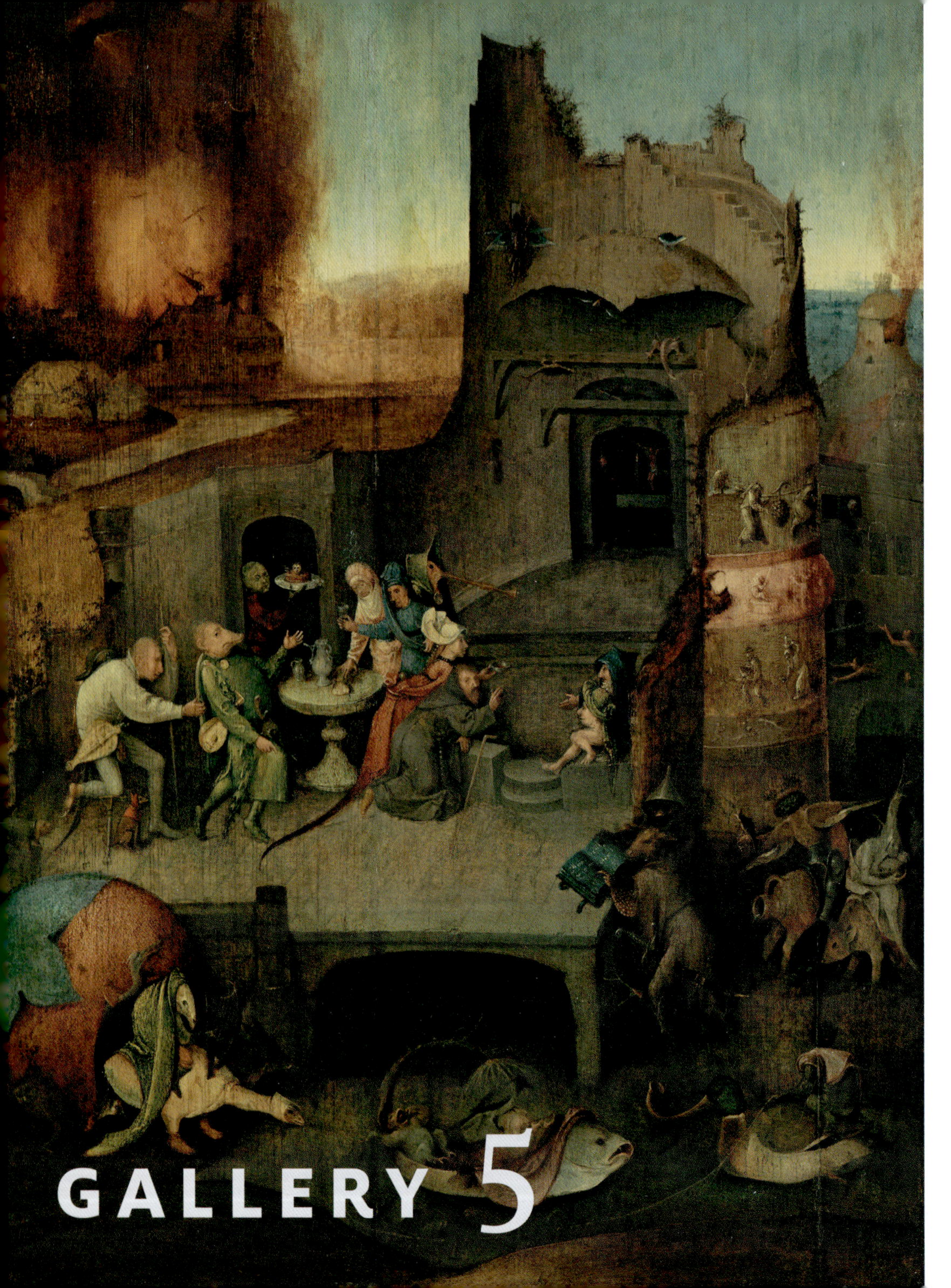
GALLERY 5

Dragons and Birds

Many of the anthropomorphic monsters and hybrid creatures in Hieronymus Bosch's works have birdlike parts, as is true in this small painting with a mallard duck, a goose-like creature, a long-billed hooded creature, and various dragons. The symbolism in Bosch's fantastical and sometimes gruesome paintings is widely debated, since he left no letters or journals to help us interpret them. One intriguing bird found here is a tiny owl, nearly obscured in the shadow of a persimmon along the left edge. The persimmon itself brims with birds, including a heron and a European goldfinch emerging from behind ghastly half-bird creatures. Owls are a frequent motif in Bosch paintings, peering out from niches, windows, and corners in a number of other notable compositions, including several in the well-known *The Garden of Earthly Delights*. They may symbolize attributes such as hidden wisdom or seeing in the dark.

Copy after Hieronymus Bosch. *Temptation of Saint Anthony*, mid-16th century.

This example is believed to be a copy after the Dutch artist, or a piece done in his style, rather than an original. It is based on the center panel of the *Temptation of Saint Anthony* triptych now in the Museu Nacional de Arte Antiga in Lisbon. In that version, the persimmon holds a goldfinch (among other lively characters), but the tiny owl tucked away in the shadowy corner is unique to the Barnes version.

The dragons and mythical creatures in this work are echoed by another piece in Gallery 5, a winged metal dragon on the opposite wall by the doorway, as if, as in the preceding room, a subject from within a painting has taken three-dimensional form and fluttered out into the gallery.

Copy after Bosch. *Temptation of Saint Anthony*, detail.

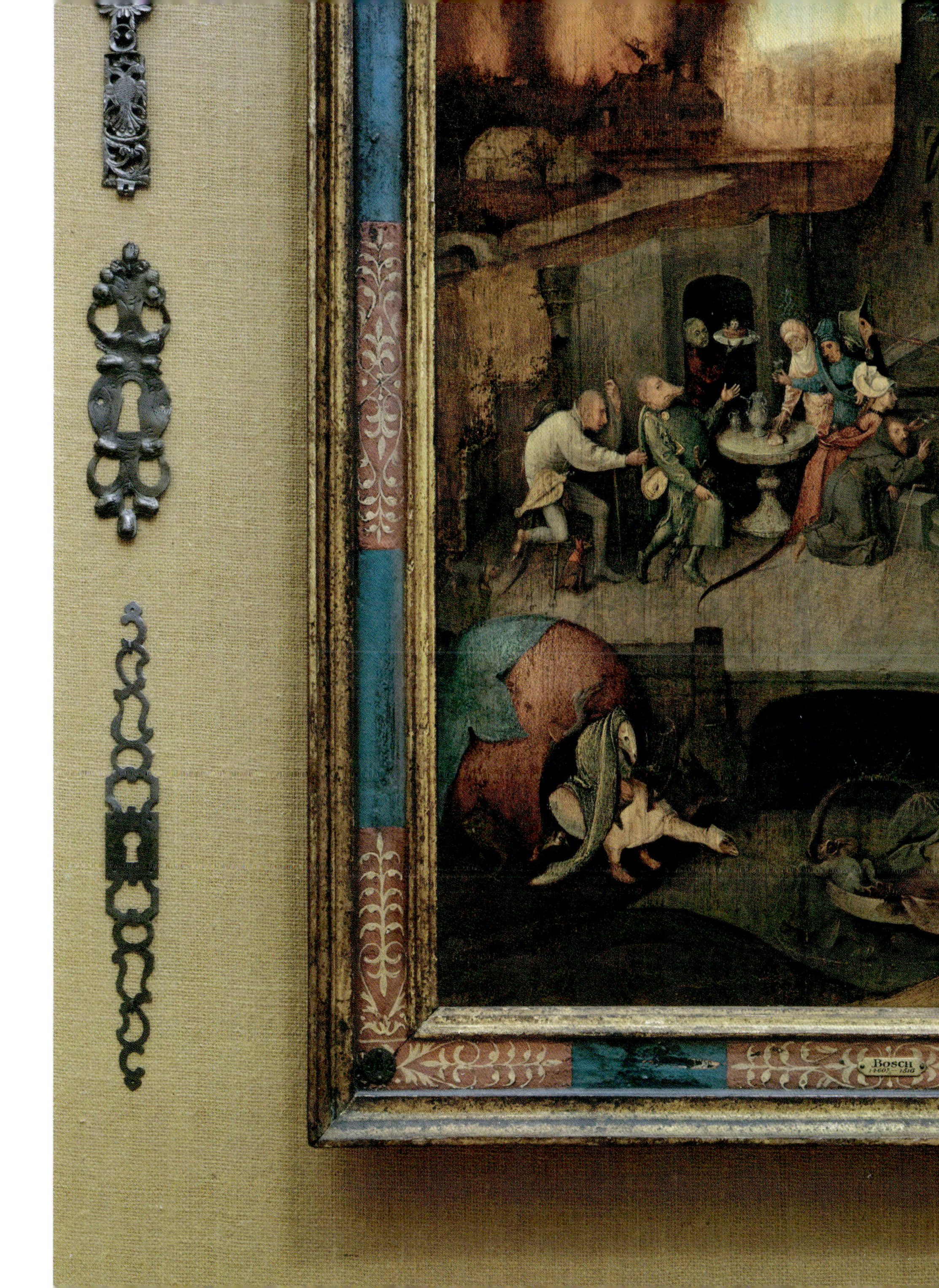
BOSCH
1460? – 1516

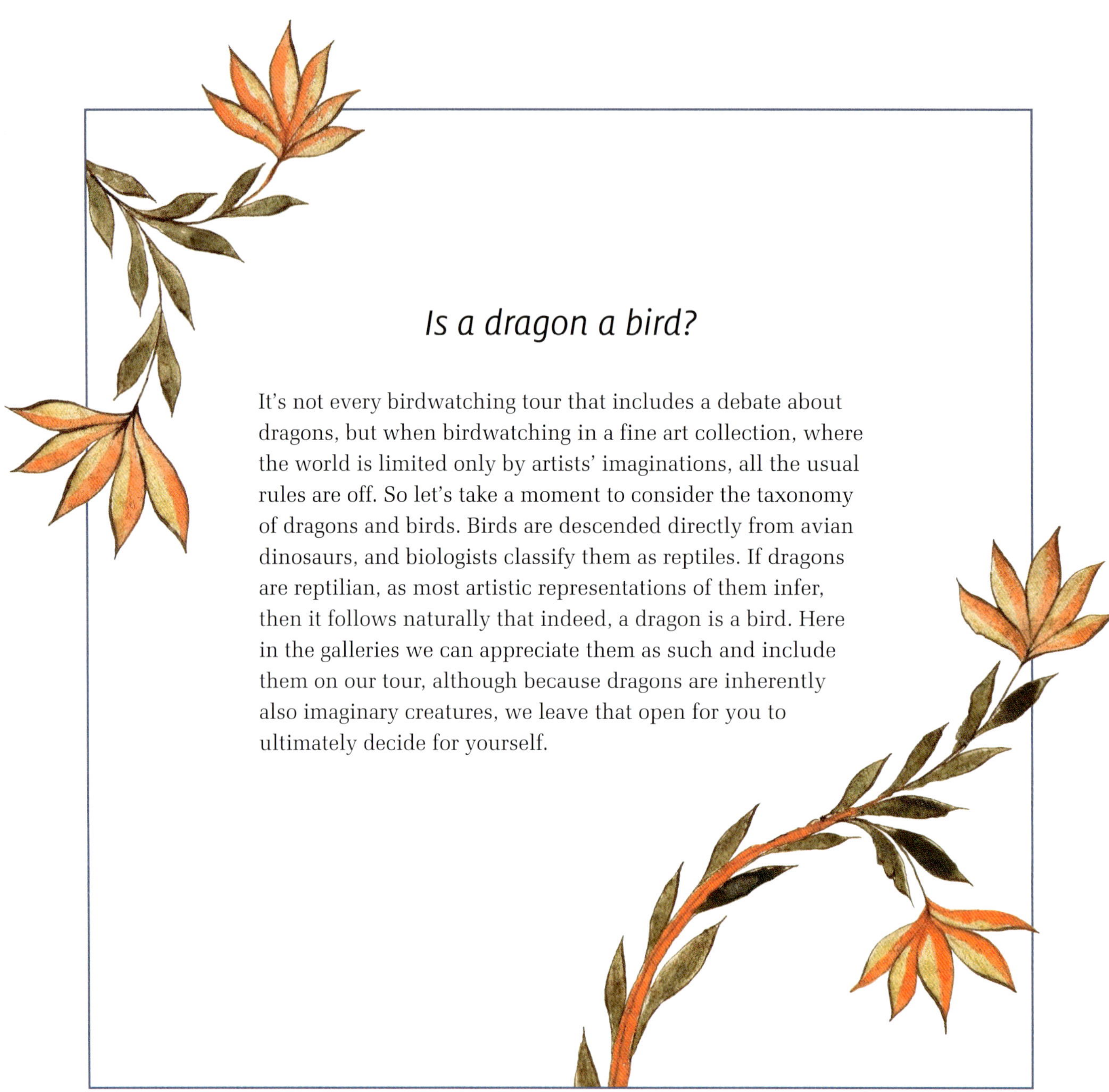

Is a dragon a bird?

It's not every birdwatching tour that includes a debate about dragons, but when birdwatching in a fine art collection, where the world is limited only by artists' imaginations, all the usual rules are off. So let's take a moment to consider the taxonomy of dragons and birds. Birds are descended directly from avian dinosaurs, and biologists classify them as reptiles. If dragons are reptilian, as most artistic representations of them infer, then it follows naturally that indeed, a dragon is a bird. Here in the galleries we can appreciate them as such and include them on our tour, although because dragons are inherently also imaginary creatures, we leave that open for you to ultimately decide for yourself.

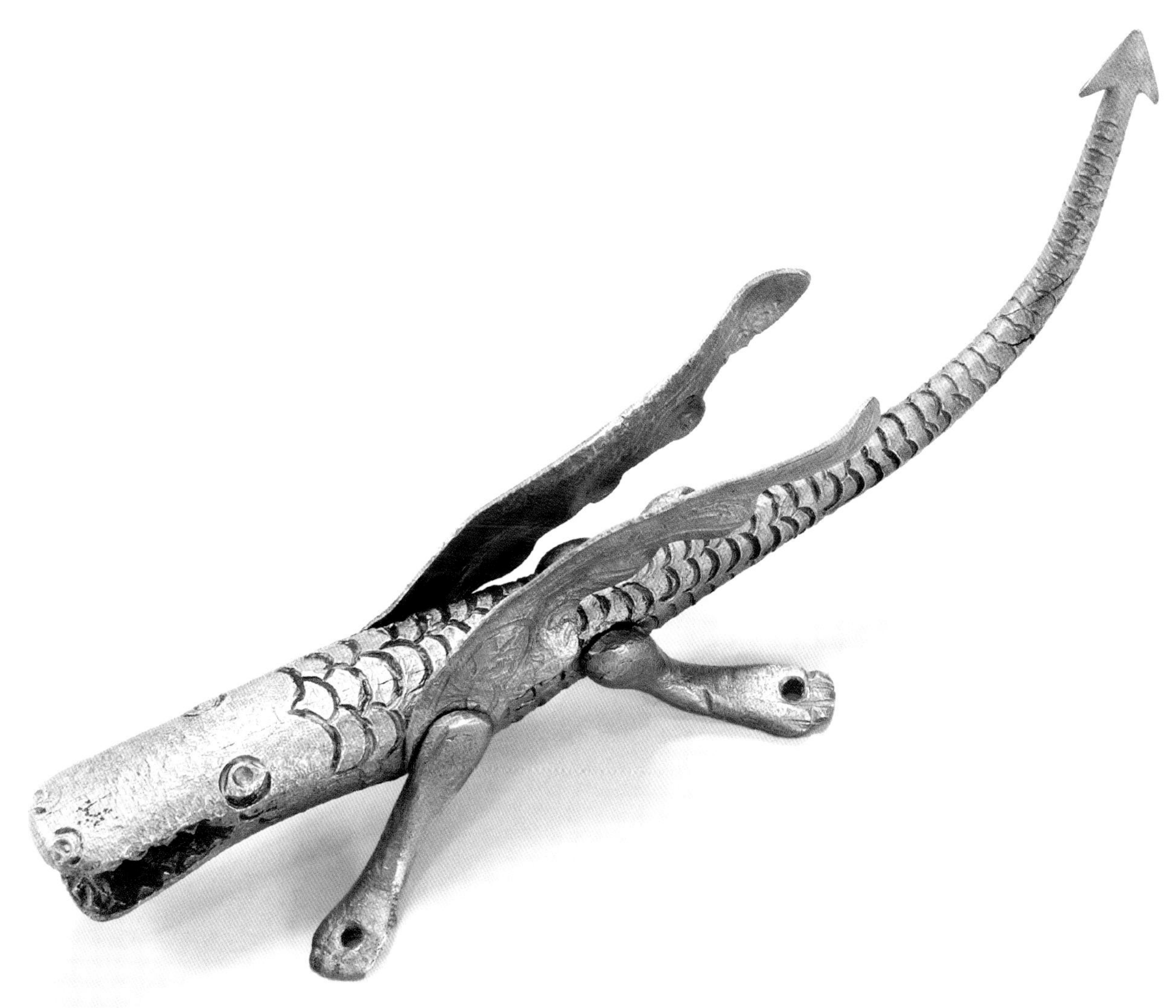

Decorative Element, 16th–17th century, Spanish.

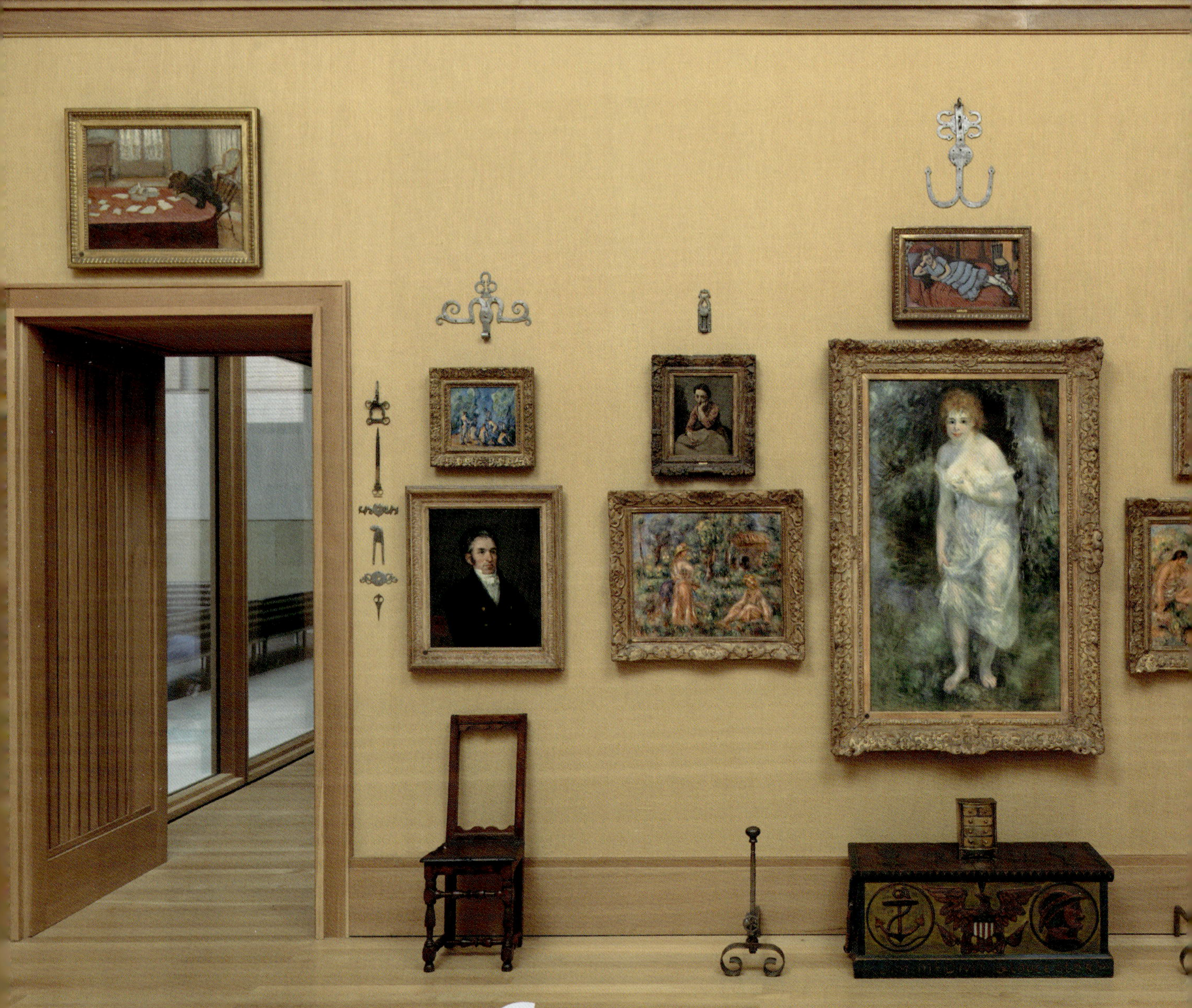

GALLERY 6

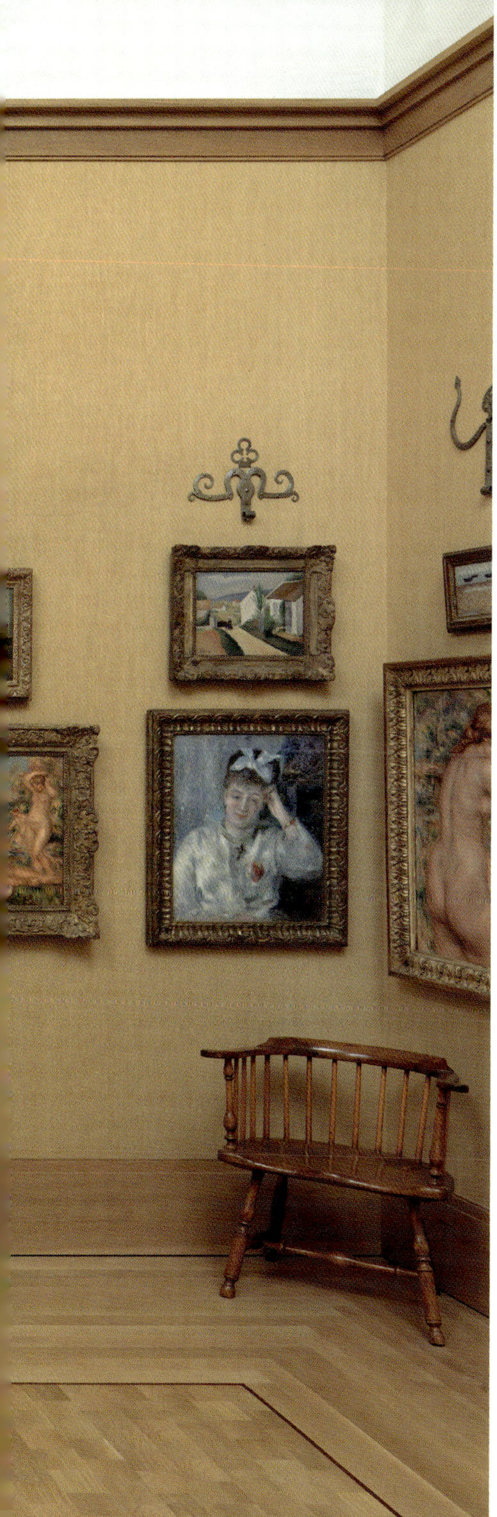

A Distinctly American Collection

The nautical designs (sailor's silhouette, anchor, and ship's wheel) carved into this blanket chest were common on painted trunks of English sailors of this time, and the bird (an eagle with wings outstretched, and shield with stars and stripes, adapted from the Great Seal of the United States) adds an American flourish to the British tradition.

This eagle, an overt patriotic symbol, is particularly interesting in the context of this gallery because of the way Dr. Barnes used this room to situate American painters as equals to their European counterparts. In the early twentieth century, Paris was still the center of the art world, and American painters were considered secondary in the art market—but Dr. Barnes made a decisive statement in this room, placing Maurice Prendergast alongside French painters Gauguin, Renoir, and Seurat on one wall, and directly comparing Pennsylvania native Charles Demuth to Renoir on another wall. In this context, this simple blanket chest with its proud eagle shouts a triumphant announcement of equivalency between the American artists and their European forebears.

Ensemble view, Room 6, east wall.

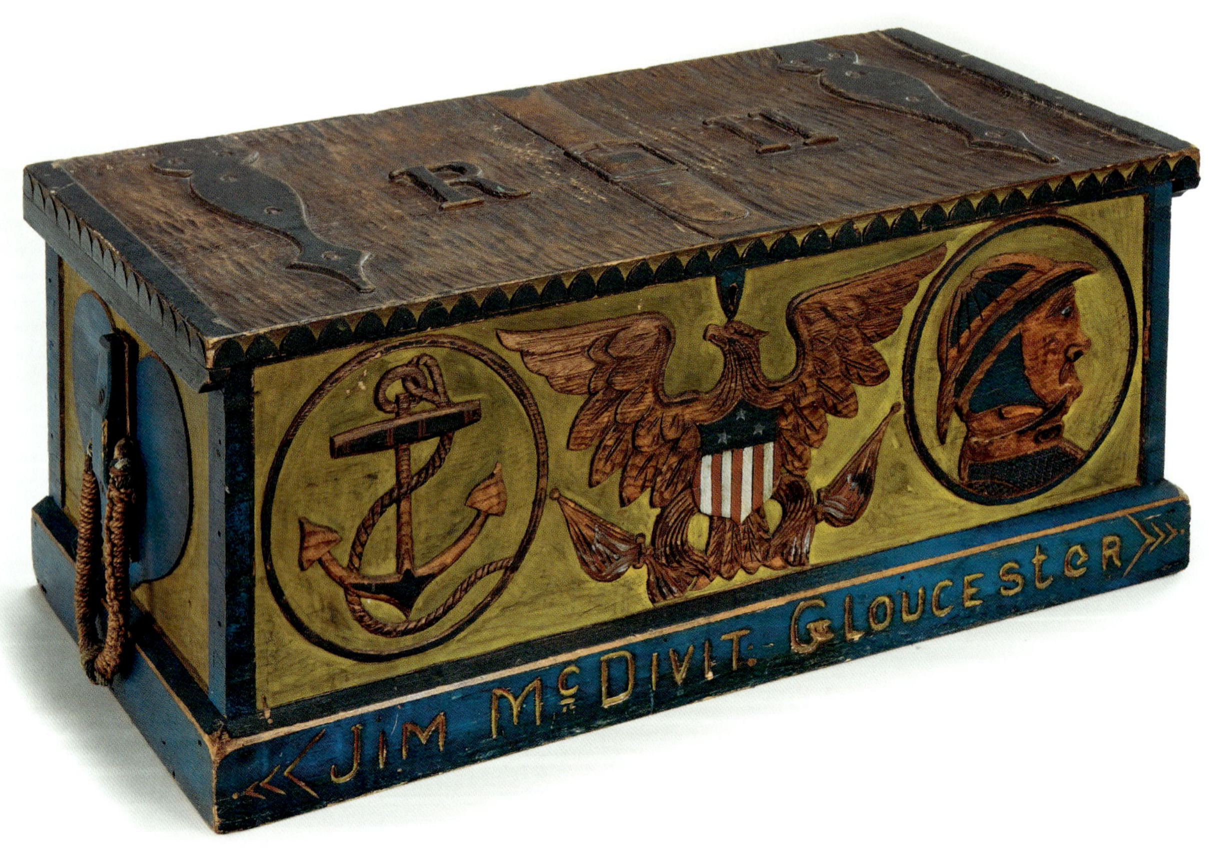

 Sea Chest, c. 1840.

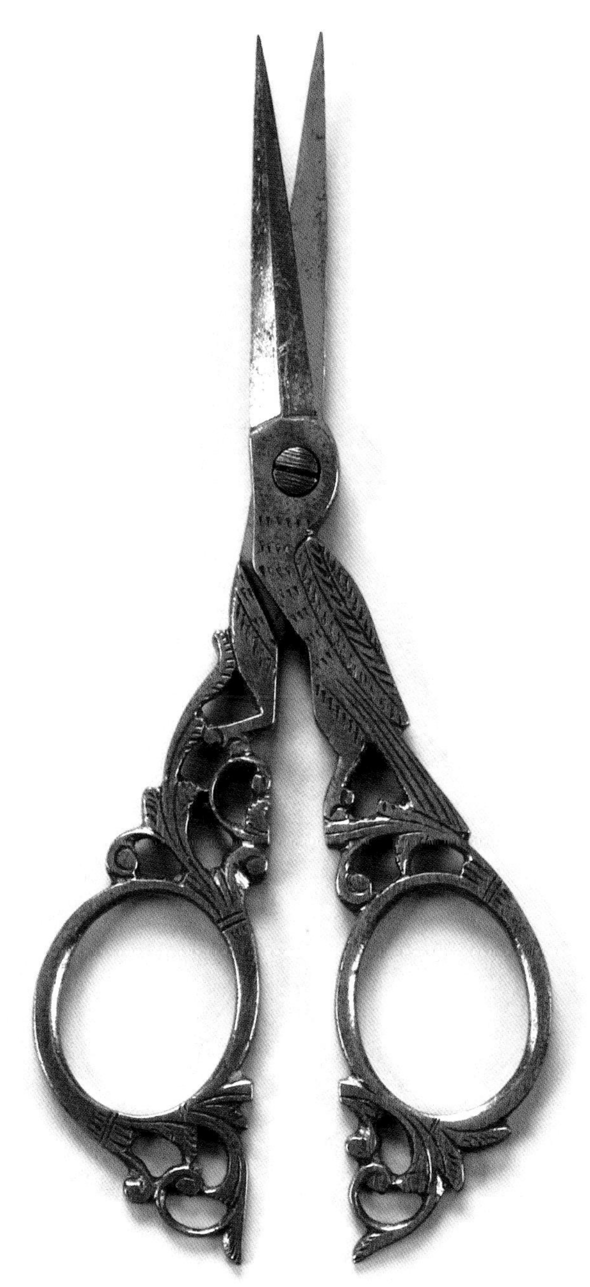

Embroidery Scissors, 18th century.

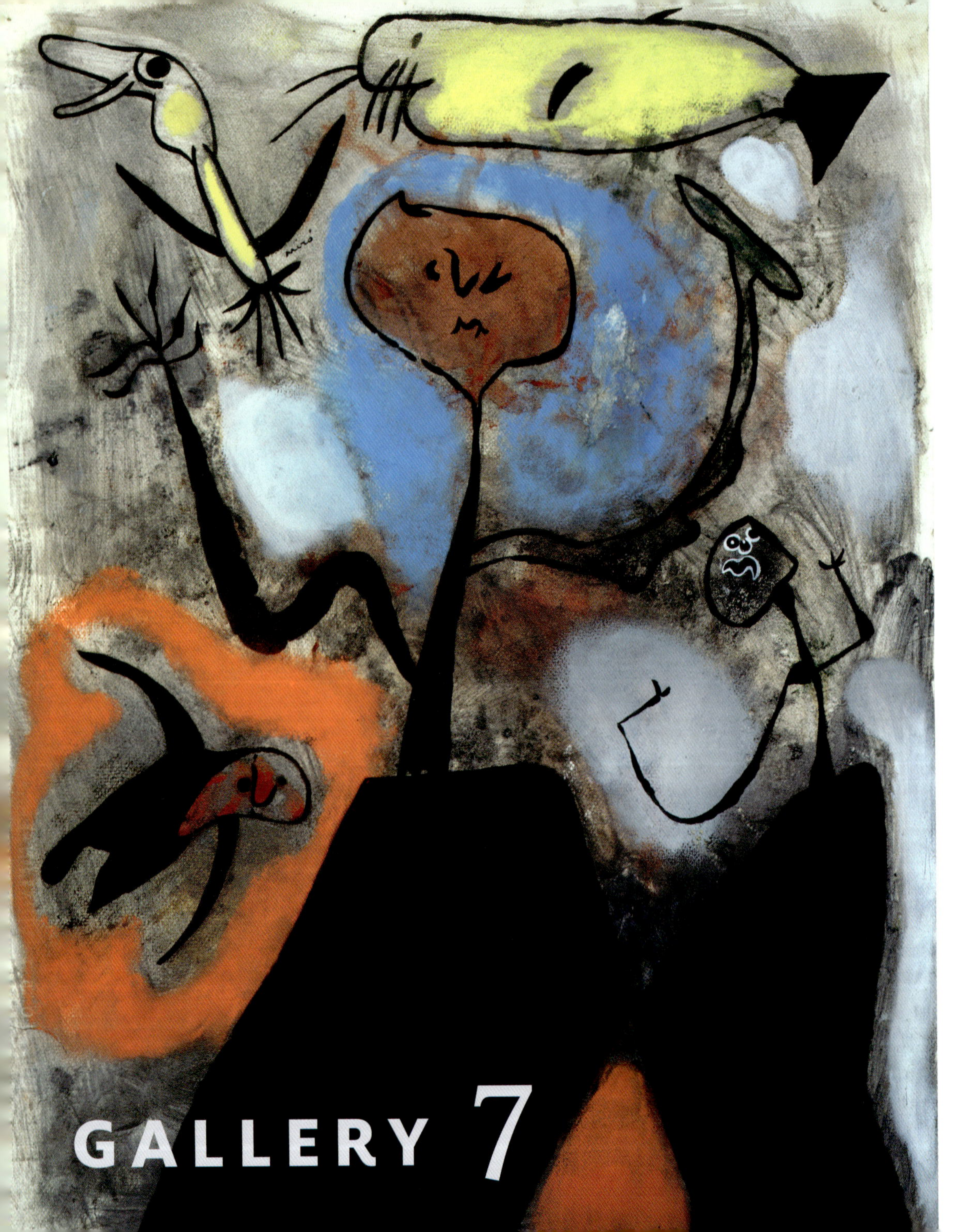
GALLERY 7

Form over Function

This composition, *Two Women Surrounded by Birds*, by Joan Miró, is the centerpiece to another installation in ironwork arranged by Dr. Barnes. Just to the left of the Miró painting hangs a standing figure composed of a metal hoe head, a hinge for the body, and a handle from a wooden bucket making up shoulders and arms. Barnes often repeated compositions from paintings in ironwork arrangements nearby, and, in this corner, the Miró figure (with long arms extended) is balanced by the ironwork to the left, and the bird from the painting is repeated in the cookie cutter overhead. Even the metal cistern and basin in the corner stands like a human figure with head, shoulders, belly, and legs, echoing the paintings around it.

Joan Miró. *Two Women Surrounded by Birds*, 1937.

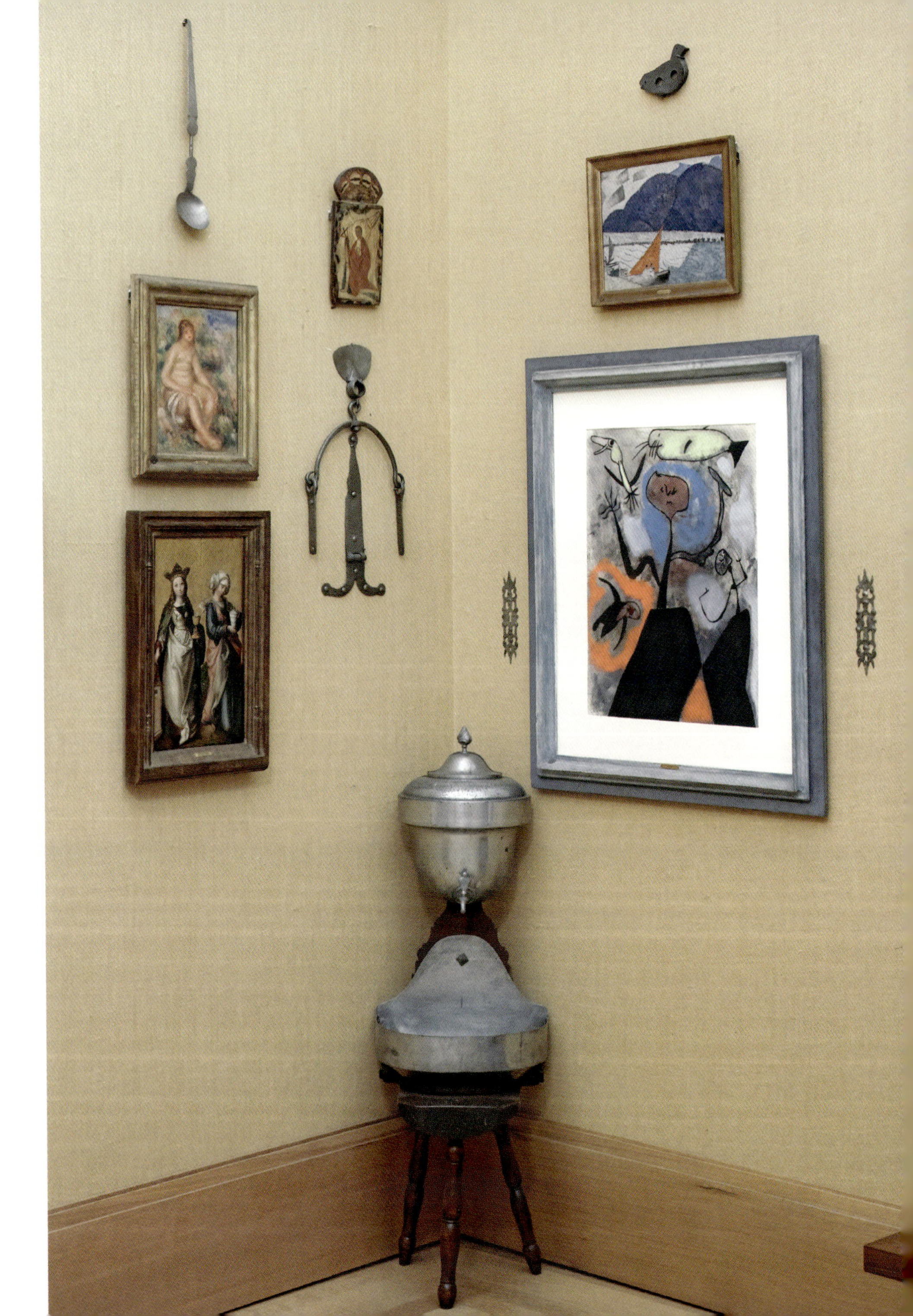

The wingless bird cookie cutter flying overhead in this wall composition originally would have had a handle. Dr. Barnes often disassembled objects to hang on the wall, concerned with aesthetic form over practical function. Elsewhere in the collection are other cookie cutters: a rabbit and a horse, found in Gallery 9.

Ensemble view, Room 7, west and north walls.

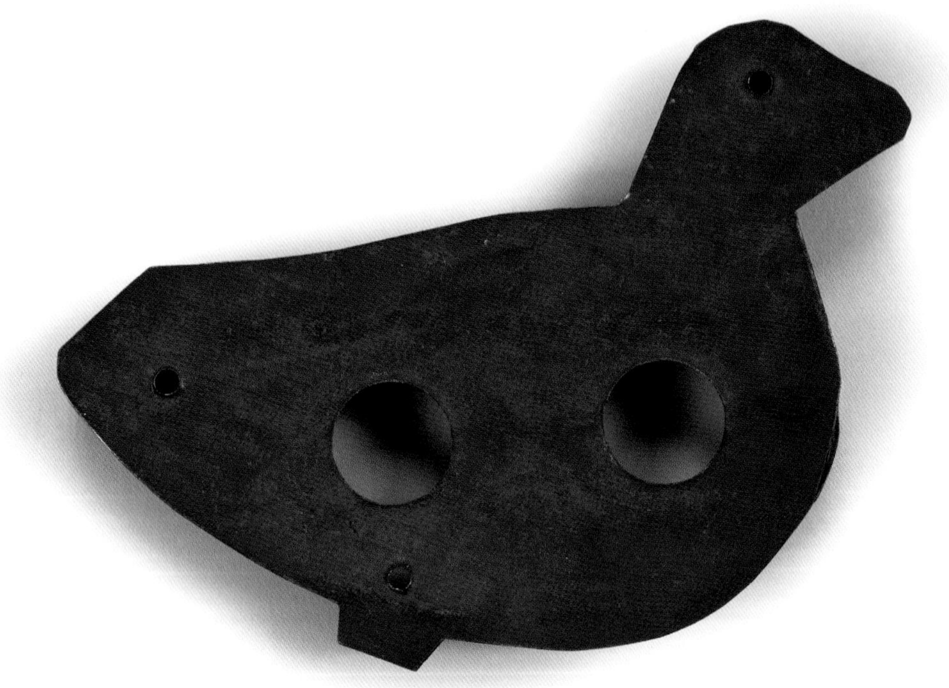

 Cookie Cutter, 19th century.

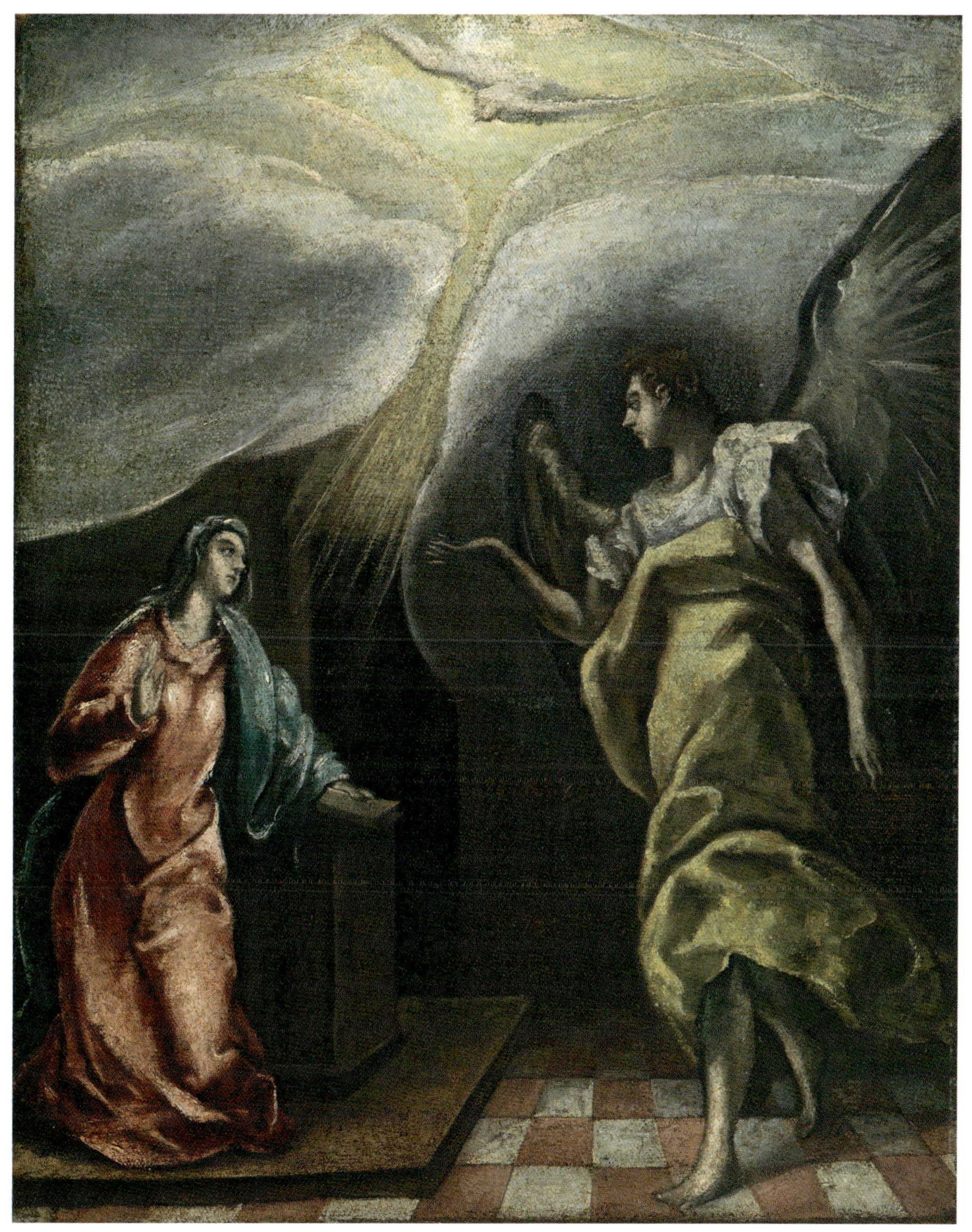

After El Greco (Domenikos Theotokopoulos). *Annunciation*, Possibly 17th century.

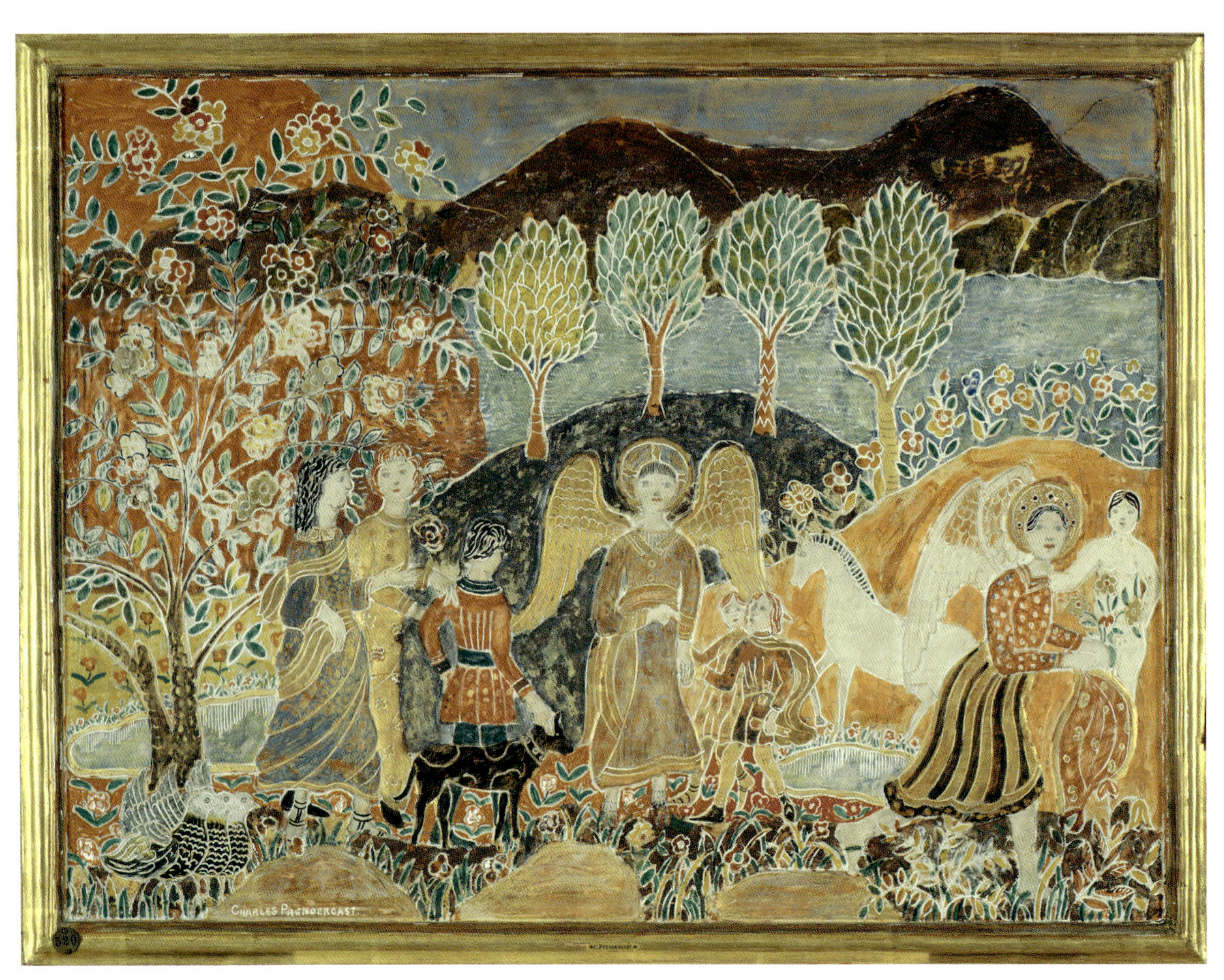

GALLERY 8

Close Connections

Dr. Barnes's choices in art were highly personal and idiosyncratic. His collecting practices differed from other art collectors of his time, who aspired to encyclopedic collections that would inform on the whole of art history. Barnes's collection instead focused on his favorite artists, making no apologies for the unevenness of his preferences ("I am convinced I cannot get too many Renoirs," he once said, and this room shows a strong assortment of those), and on artists whom he knew personally, often buying work from friends or from his students.

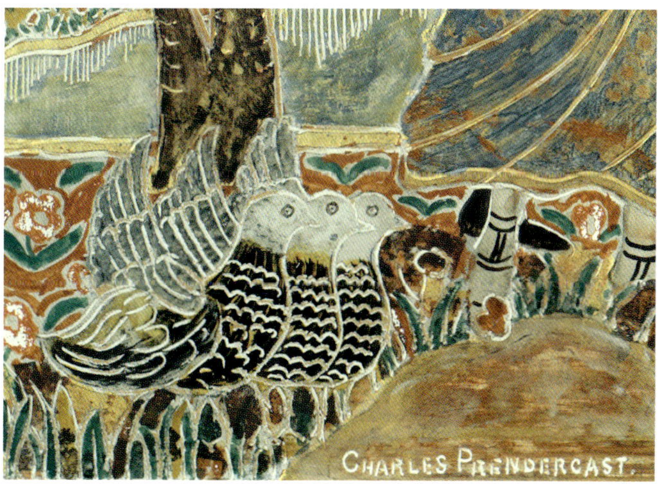

Charles Prendergast. *Angels*, c. 1917.

The American painter Charles Prendergast was one such personal friend. Dr. Barnes first met Prendergast when buying frames for paintings in his collection. Prendergast was a painter as well as a frame maker. Charles and his brother Maurice (a painter as well, whose work Dr. Barnes also collected) often used the materials and techniques of their trade as painting techniques. The bodies of these ground fowl show off these techniques, such as a thick layer of gesso with decorative lines incised in the surface, and gold leaf applied as another color alongside the oil paint.

This painting hangs high over a doorway of this room, and just to the side of the same doorway is a funny little nutcracker bird, turning the same direction as Prendergast's birds, as if running to catch up with the pheasant flock just above.

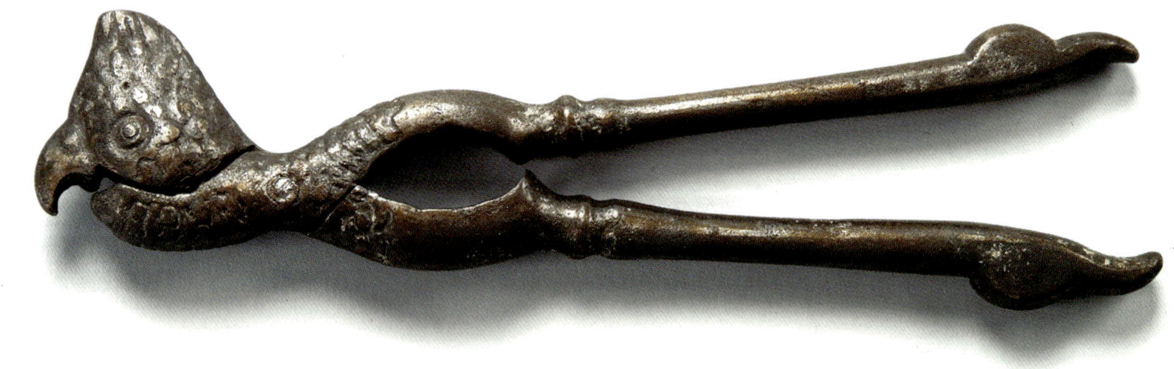

 Nutcracker, 19th century. // Ensemble view, Room 8, west wall.

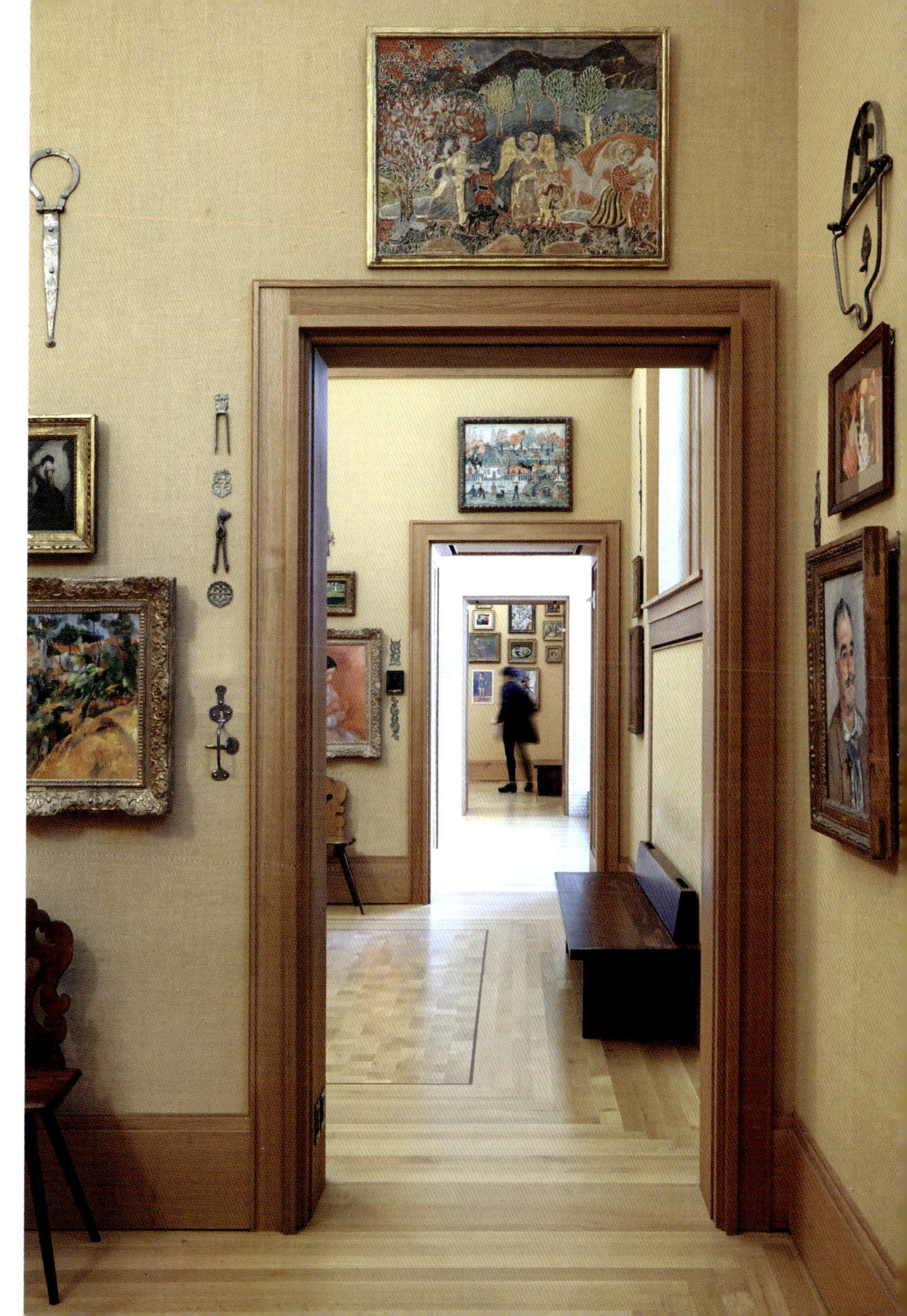

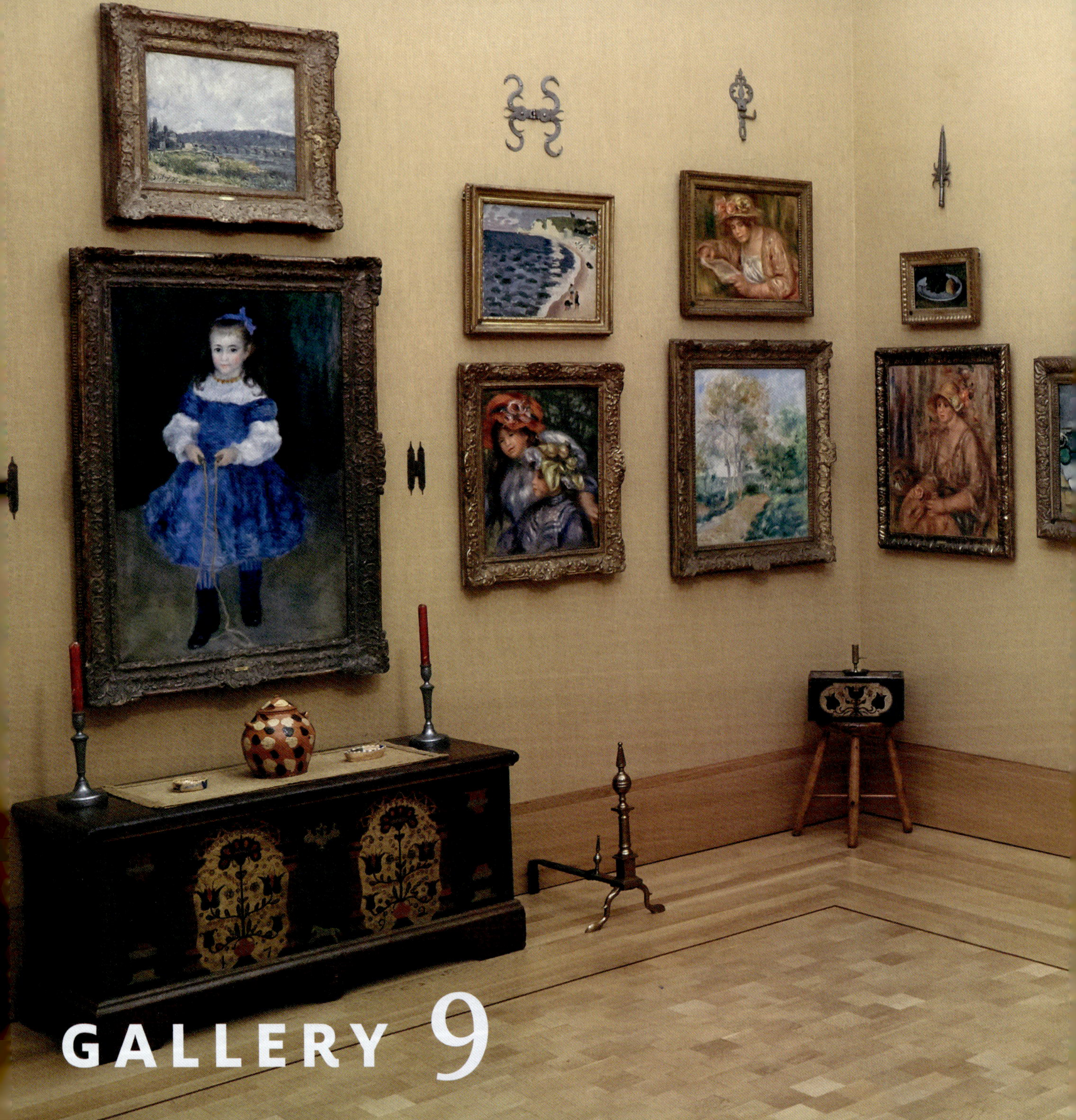

GALLERY 9

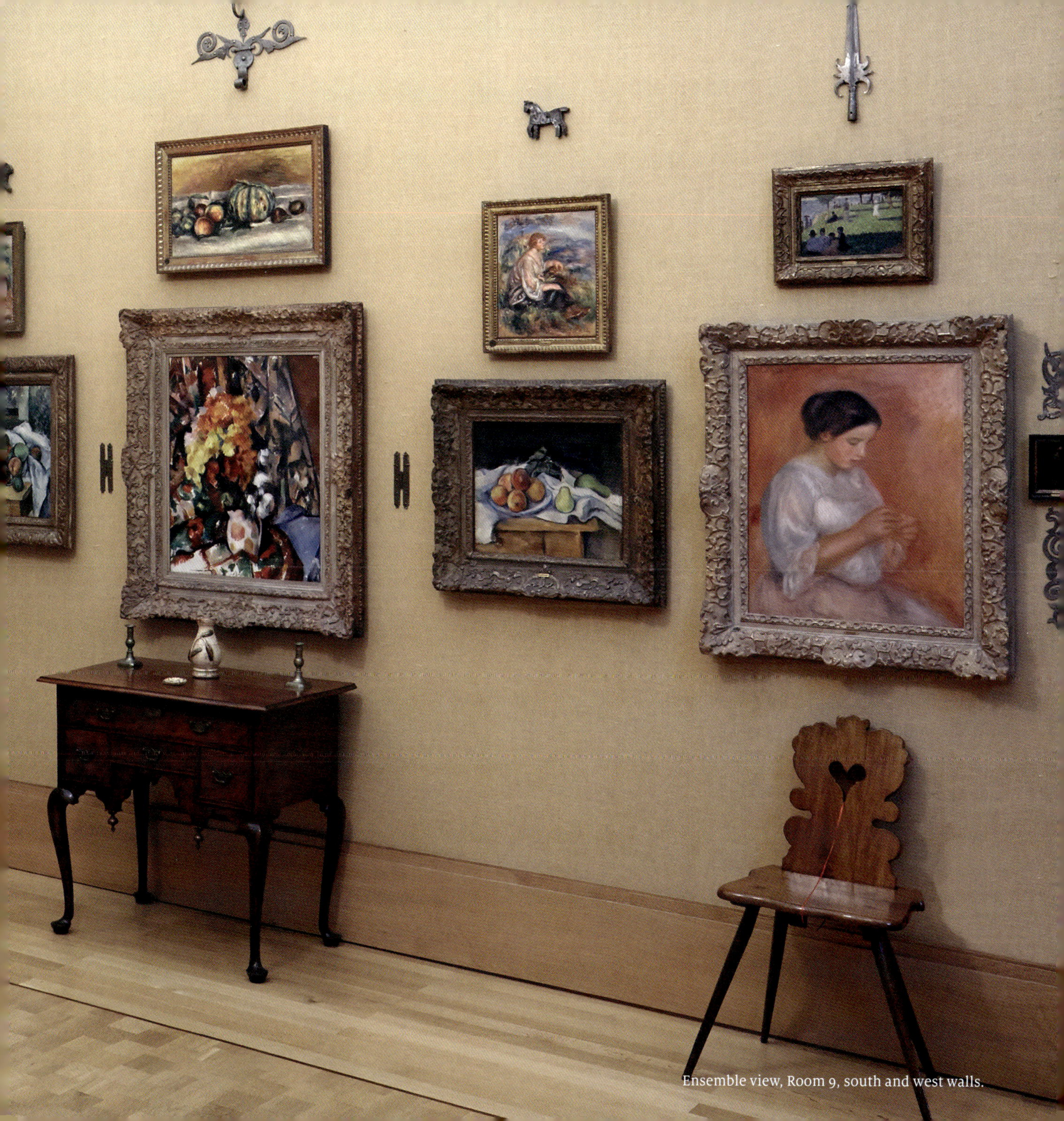

Ensemble view, Room 9, south and west walls.

The Mystery Deepens

Here we find the first gallery in which a vigilant birdwatcher may come up shorthanded: Can it be, a room without a bird? Yet, here, in one painting, a young girl by French painter Henri Rousseau proffers the viewer an entire basket of eggs. If the intention was to leave a bird in every room, is Dr. Barnes offering us an existential question or a winking joke, “Which comes first?”

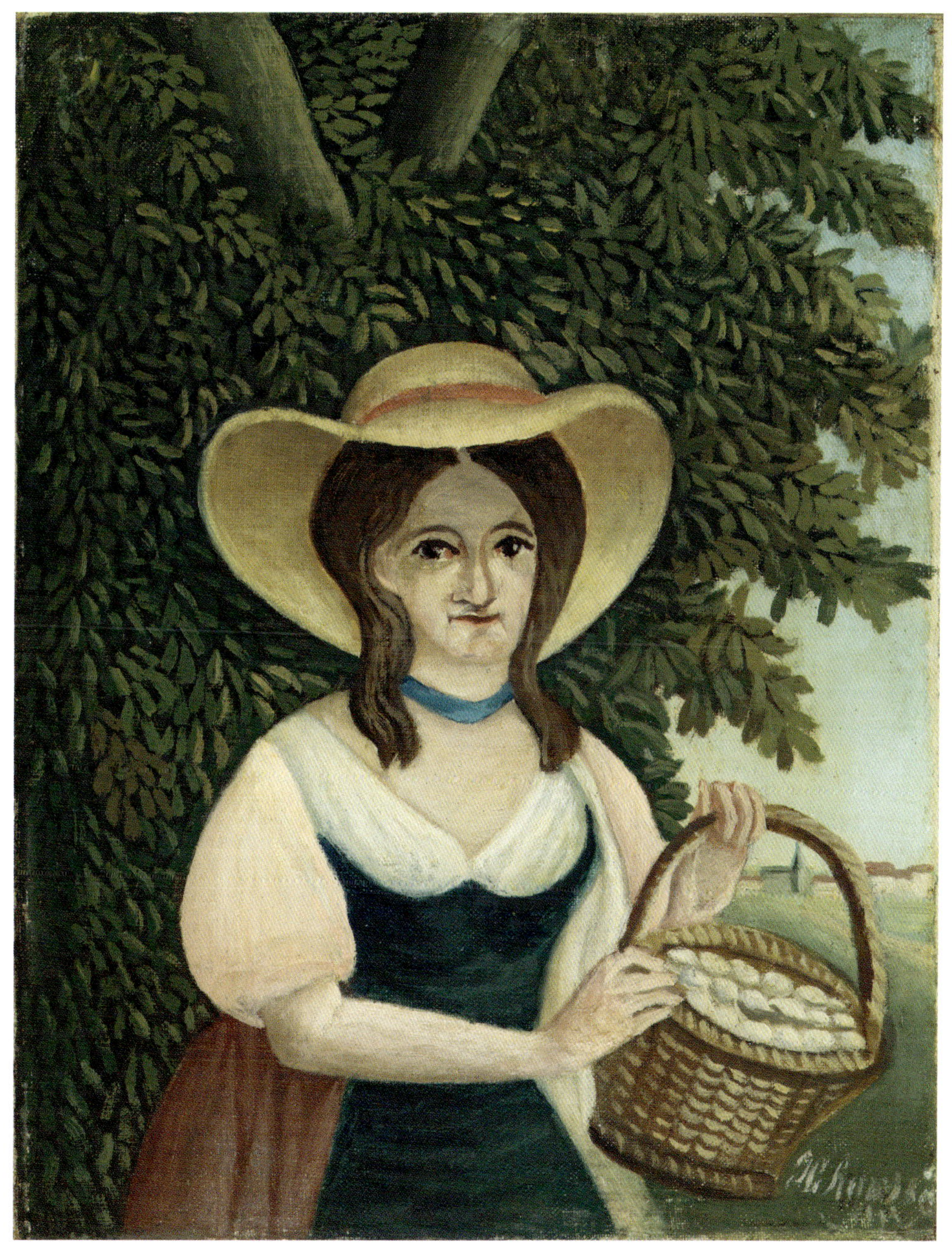

Henri Rousseau. *Woman with Basket of Eggs (La Femme au panier d'oeufs)*, probably 1905–1910.

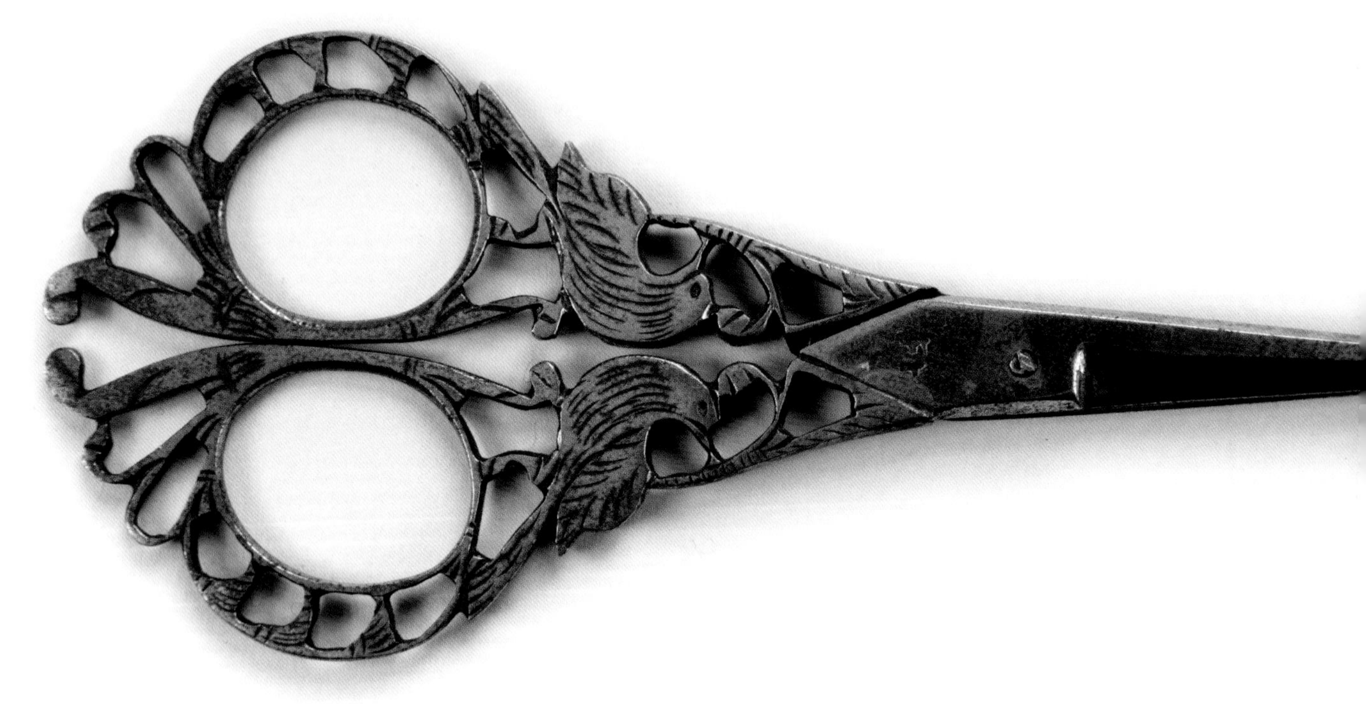

GALLERY 10

The Art in Everyday Life

The tiny sewing scissors in Gallery 10 is familiar to contemporary crafters. Sewing scissors with decorative birds have been popular for fine needlework for a long time, and even those who don't sew may have nostalgic personal connections to similar bird scissors stored in familial sewing baskets.

Scissors, 18th–19th century.

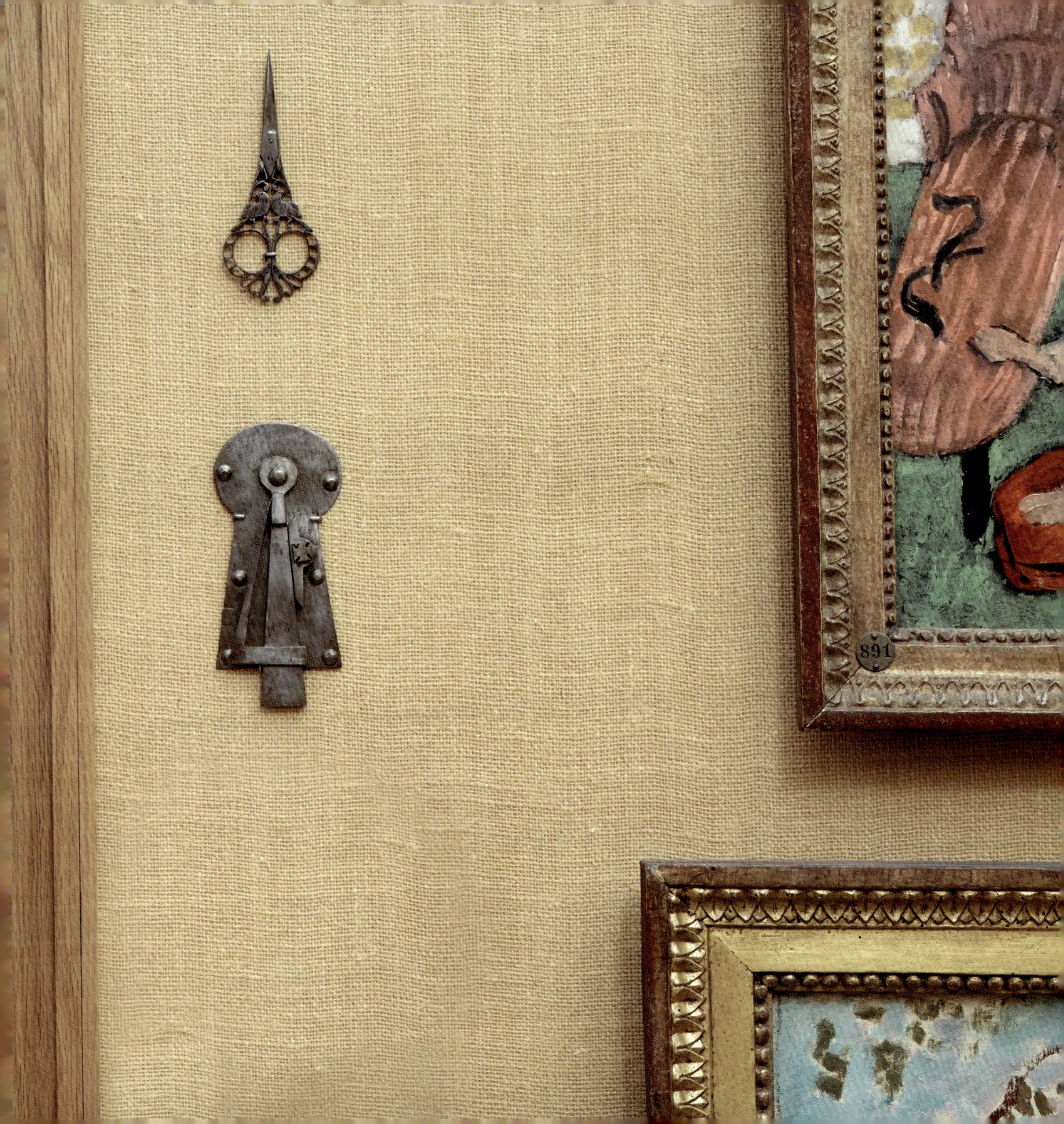
891

The inclusion of such commonplace objects next to the great modern masters in painting such as Modigliani, Picasso, and Matisse, whose work dominates this room, or, as this is, next to a composition by Chaim Soutine is part of what makes the Barnes ensembles often perplexing to those expecting traditional museum displays. The challenge of analyzing "high art" (and, for its time, very provocative art) interspersed with small, mundane household items creates a wealth of small surprises for the viewer.

Ensemble view, Room 10, east wall.

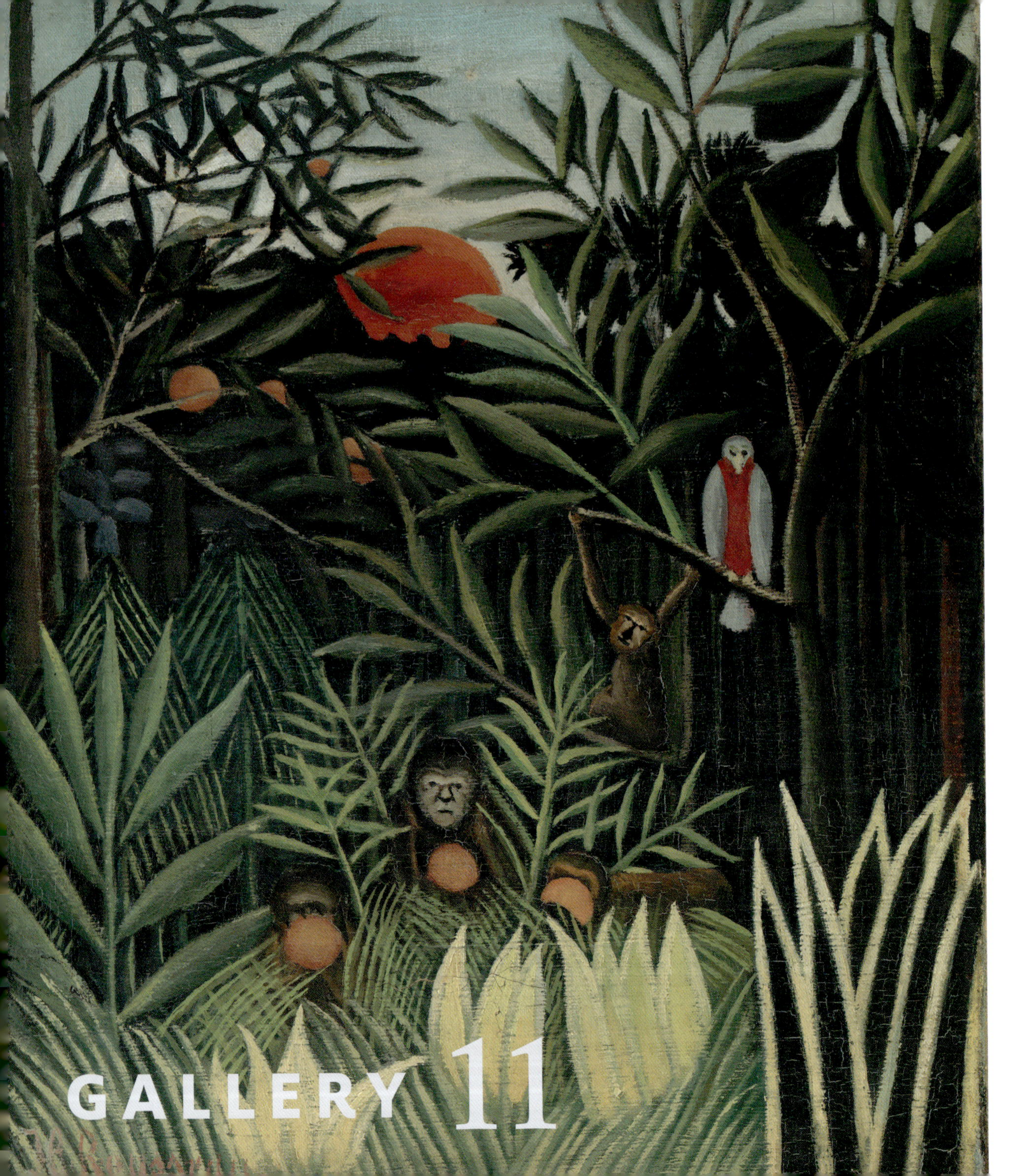
GALLERY 11

Motion and Stillness

One bird here features prominently as if posed as the subject of a portrait: *Monkeys and Parrot in the Virgin Forest* by Henri Rousseau. Rousseau was a Parisian tax collector who came to the attention of the art world when the painter Pablo Picasso befriended him and began to share his "naïve" paintings with his artist and collector friends. A native of France, Rousseau painted many exotic landscapes and lush tropical jungles, but his personal experience with such habitats came only from visits to the Jardin des Plants in Paris. His resulting scenes often have a strong component of fantasy or dreams. This quizzical parrot in its botanical jungle has anthropomorphic qualities common of Rousseau's animals.

Henri Rousseau. *Monkeys and Parrot in the Virgin Forest (Singes et perroquet dans la forêt vierge)*, c. 1905–1906.

All around this room, Dr. Barnes juxtaposed painters whose work contains fine, precise details, flattened spaces, and a sense of stillness (such as Rousseau, an unnamed German master, and Jean Hugo) with painters such as Matisse, Picasso, Miró, and Soutine, whose works are painted loosely with broad expressive gestures and lots of movement. The room offers other indications of motion: in the spread wings of angels to two "windmills" created in ironwork over storm-tossed trees by Soutine. Incongruously, the birds, which we might expect to symbolize activity or to take flight in the works full of motion and weather, appear instead as examples of stillness and constraint, perched with wings folded demurely, in the hands of those painters whose works fall on the detailed and precise end of this room's spectrum.

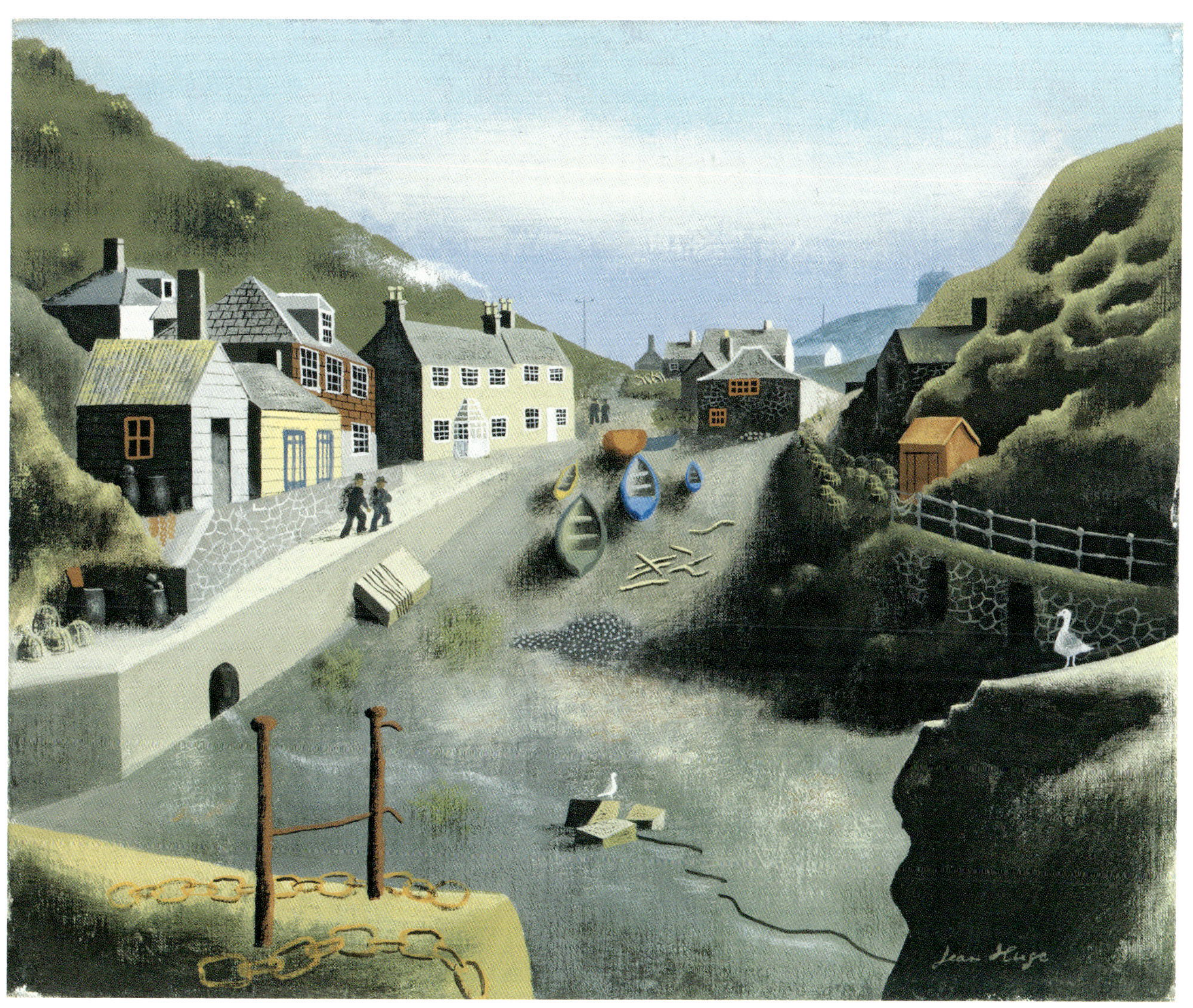

Jean Hugo. *Mullion Cove*, April 1933.

Friends and Family

This little composition was made by Albert Nulty, who worked for Dr. Barnes as his "curator of collections." This role encompassed many jobs, from framing and caring for the paintings to assisting with the installation of the large Matisse mural in the center gallery. Nulty was such a close friend and confidante of Dr. Barnes that in their travels together, they were dubbed "The two Alberts." He even named his son Albert Barnes Nulty. The inclusion of informal pieces from friends and family like this one shows a more casual, familial side of the collector.

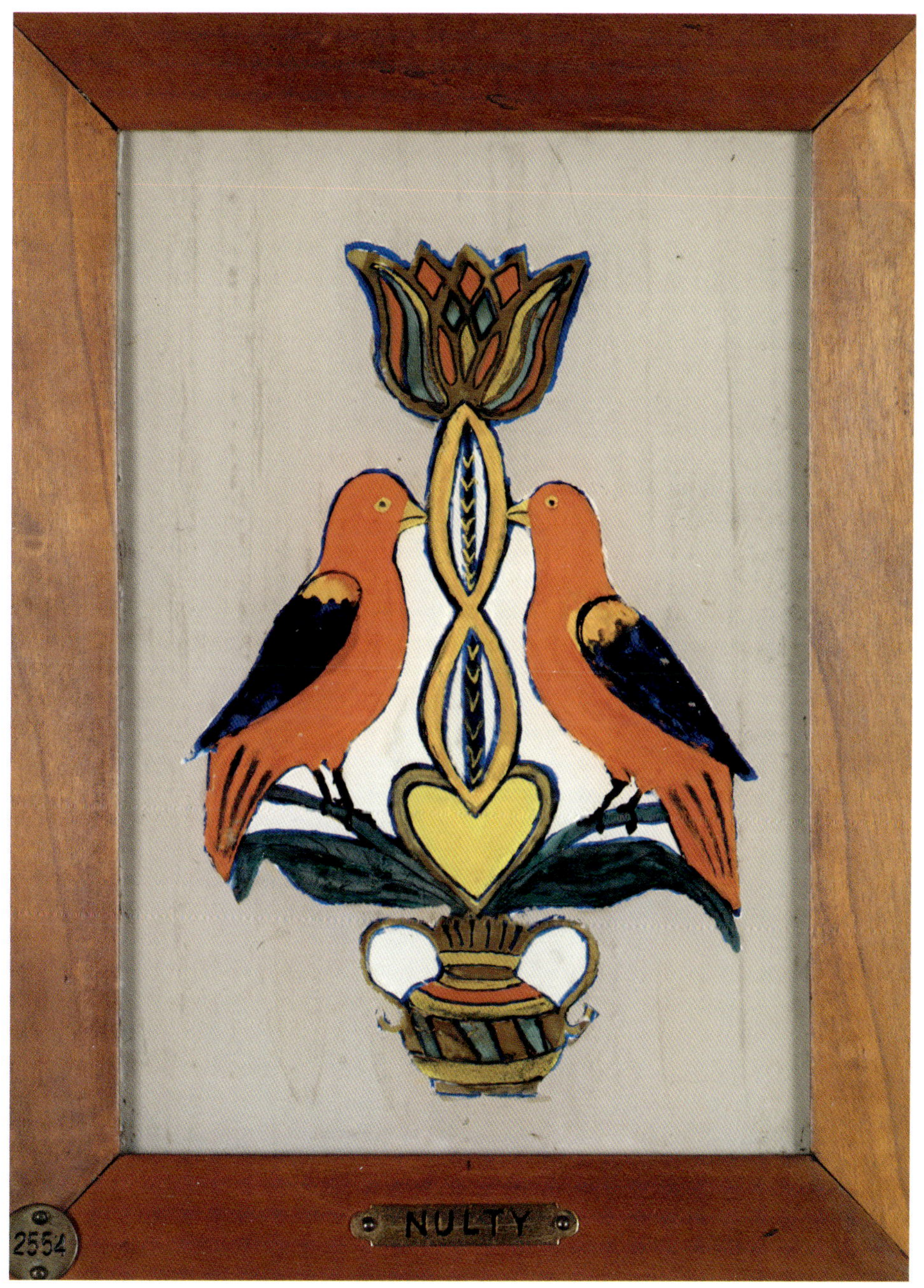

Albert H. Nulty. *Pennsylvania Dutch Motif*, 1940s.

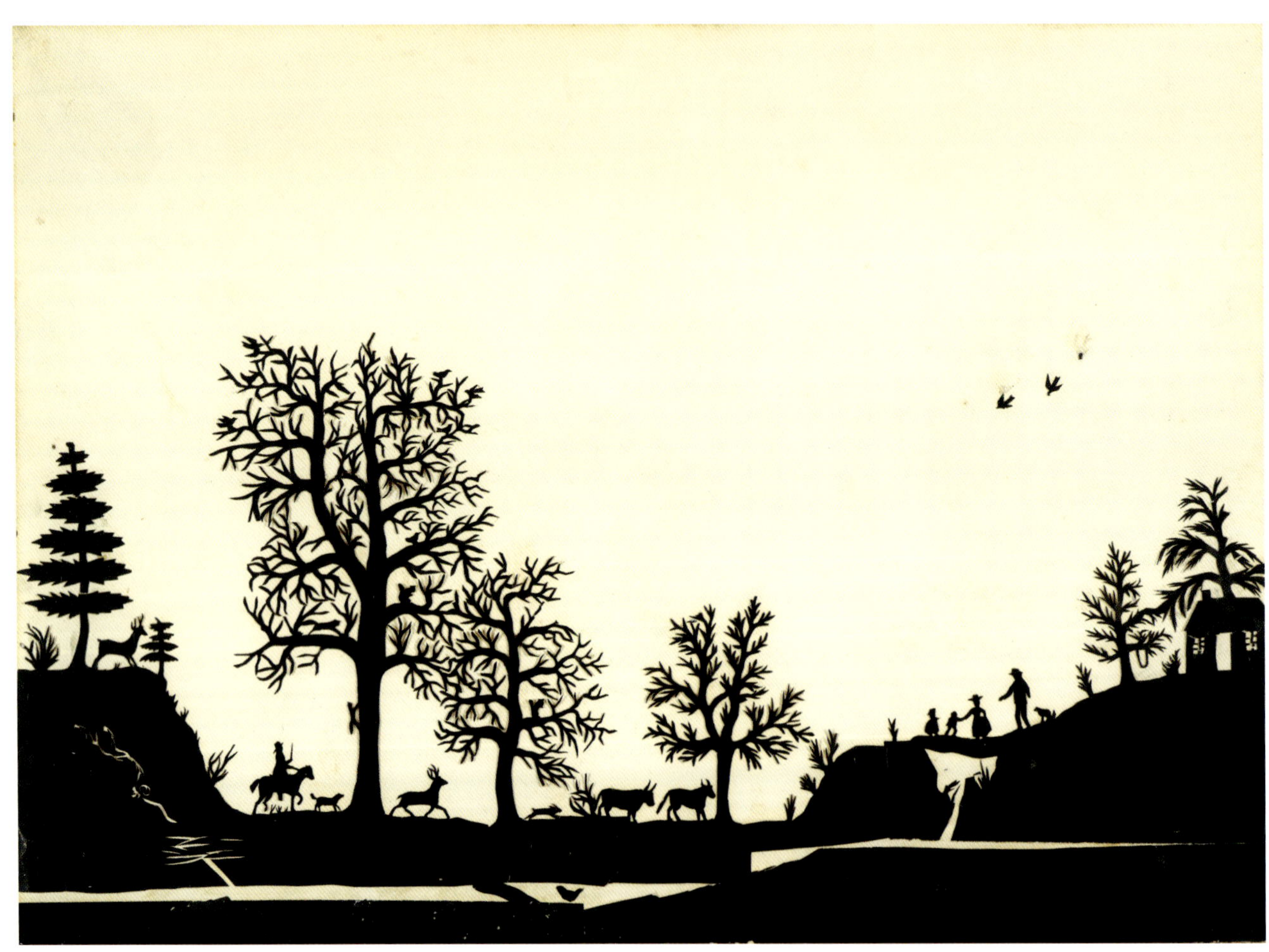

 Susan Cray. *New Jersey Cut-Out*, 1843.

The cut-paper silhouette composition in this room also comes from close to home. Susan Cray is one of more than thirty women artists represented in the Barnes collection. This style of Swiss German black-paper *Scherenschnitte* paper cutting was brought to the United States by Pennsylvania Germans. Dr. Barnes purchased many Pennsylvania German works of art, and a large amount of ironwork and furniture in the collection, from local antiques dealers.

Luigi Settani, who made this farm scene with a turkey and chickens or ducks, was also a student of Dr. Barnes's and a personal friend.

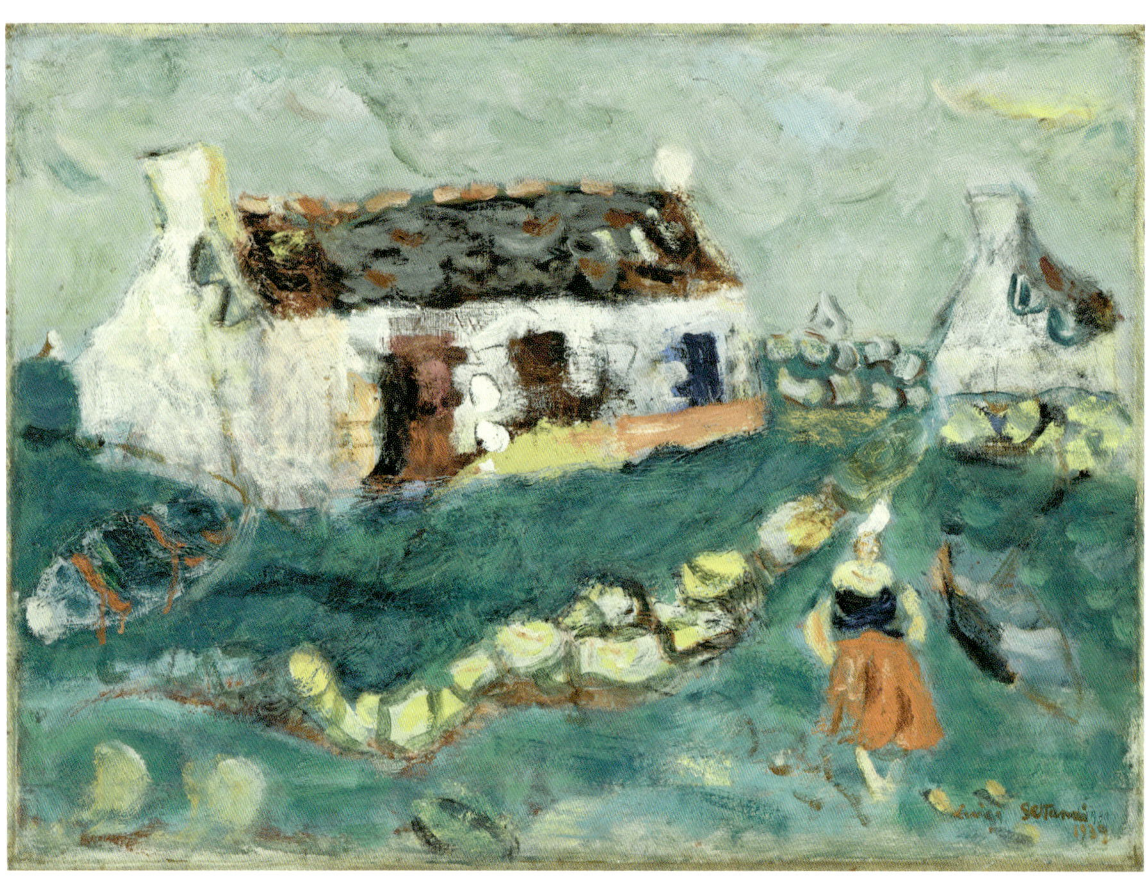

 Luigi Settanni. *Landscape in Brittany* (*Pont l'Abbé Figure*), 1939.

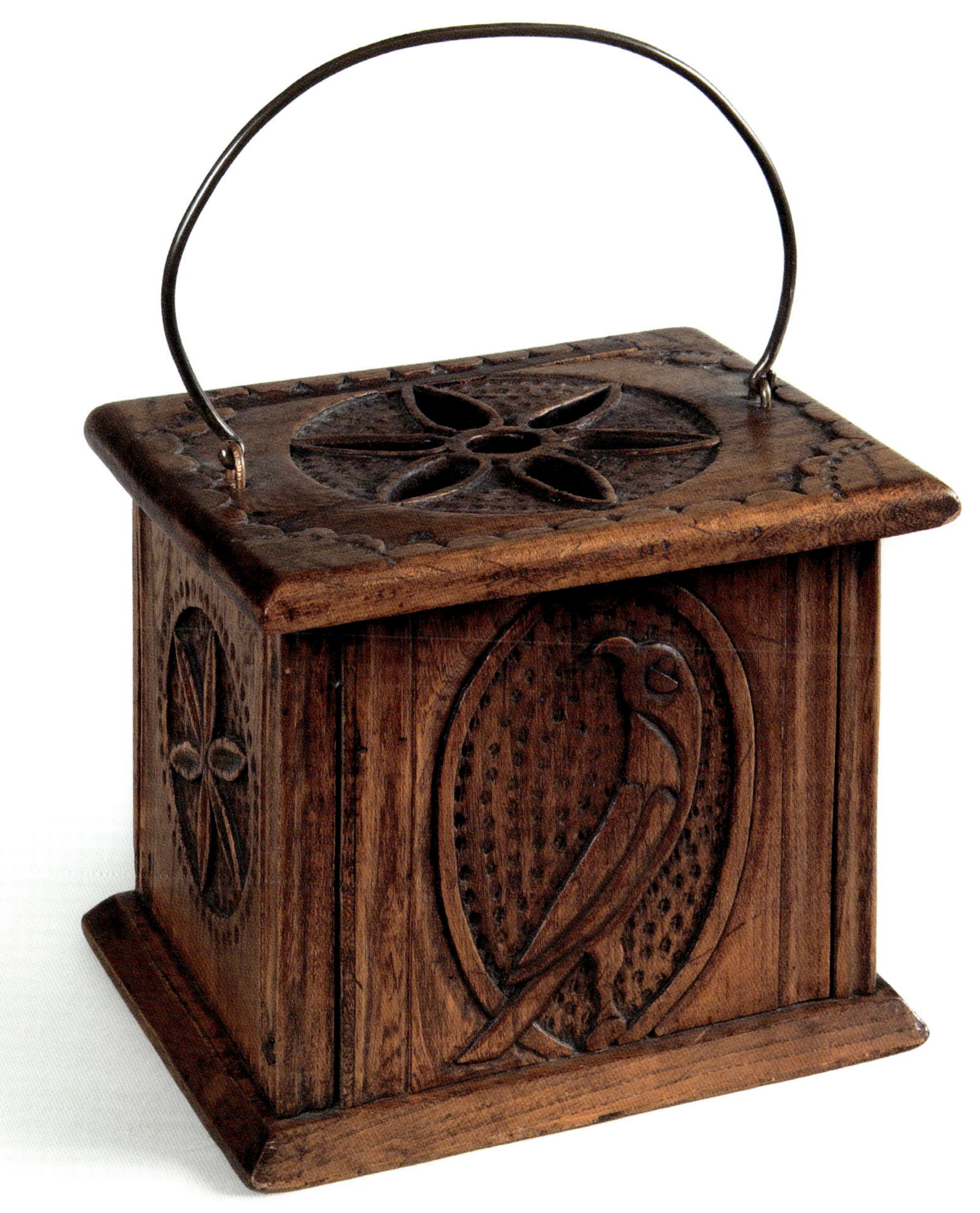

Box. Wood.

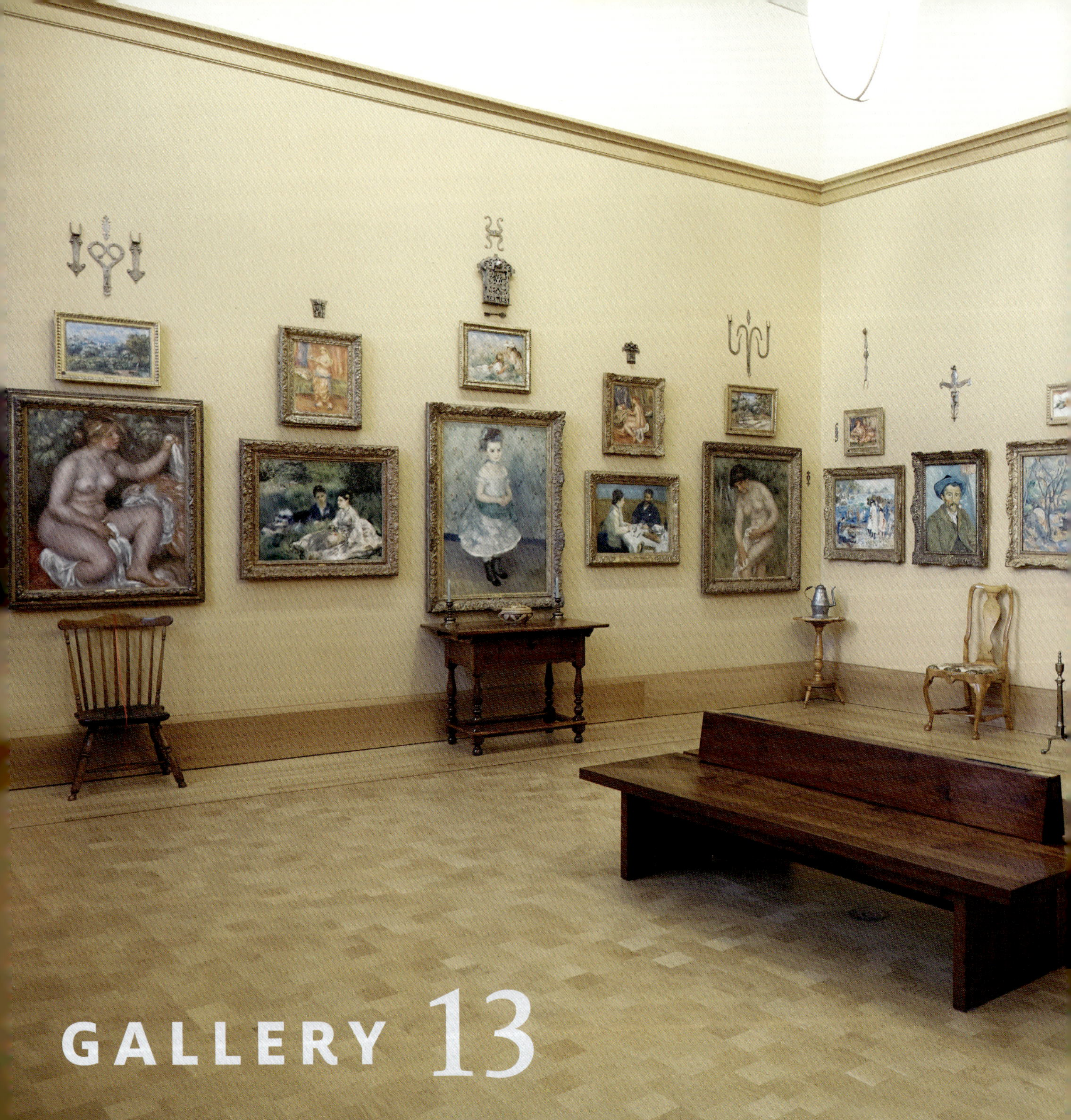

GALLERY 13

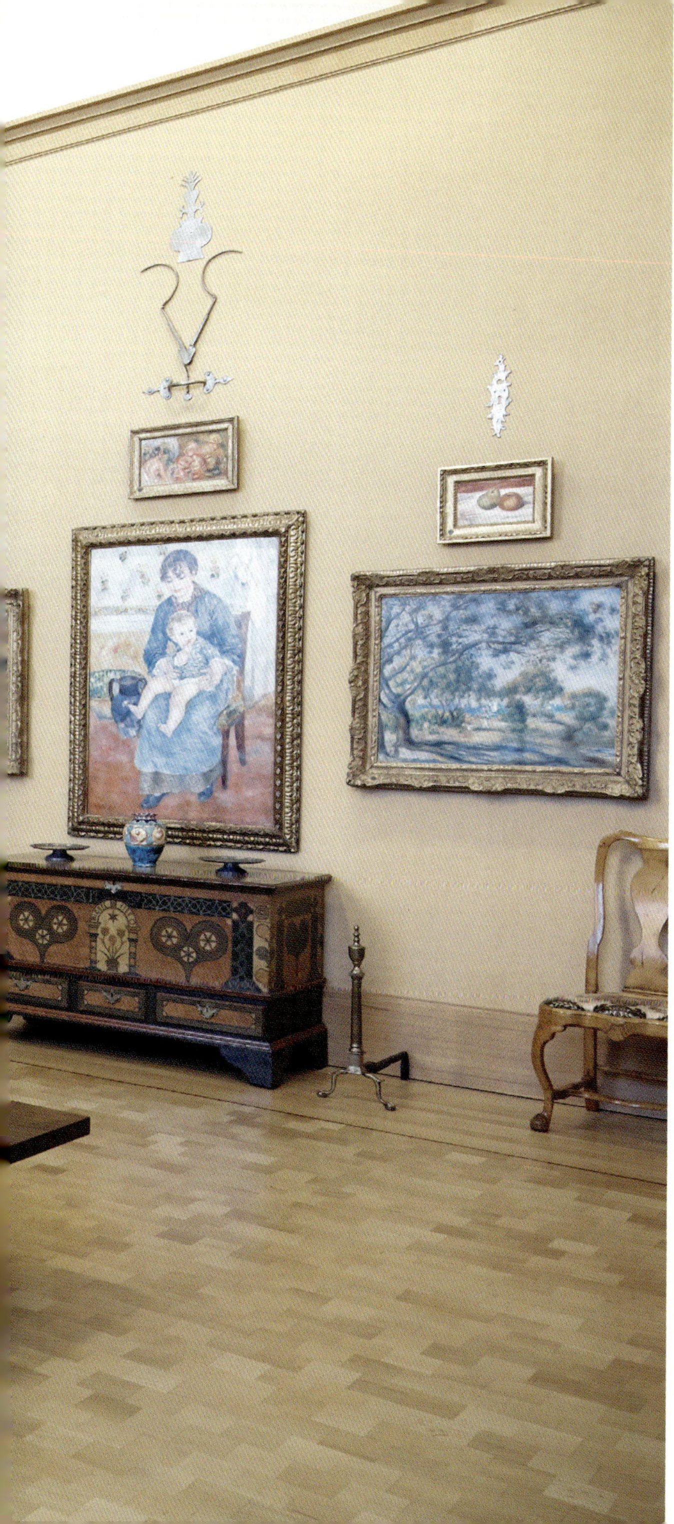

Lush Green Landscapes

Gallery 13 offers a variety of objects decorated with birds, from a salt-glazed jug to punched-tin lidded coffeepot. Perhaps the most curious of these is a bird-shaped metal clamp. Secured to a wooden end table, with a round top standing on four flared legs, the clamp serves no functional purpose here and, in fact, inhibits the use of the table's built-in drawer. The metal clamp simply perches, like a lively bird let loose in the room.

Ensemble view, Room 13, west and north walls.

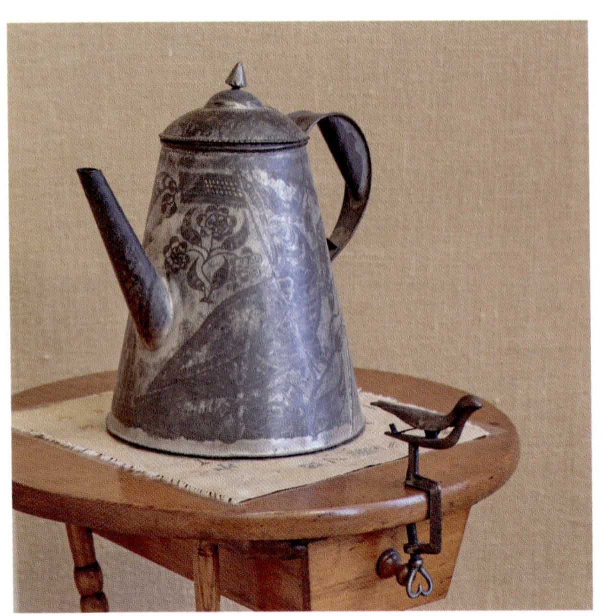

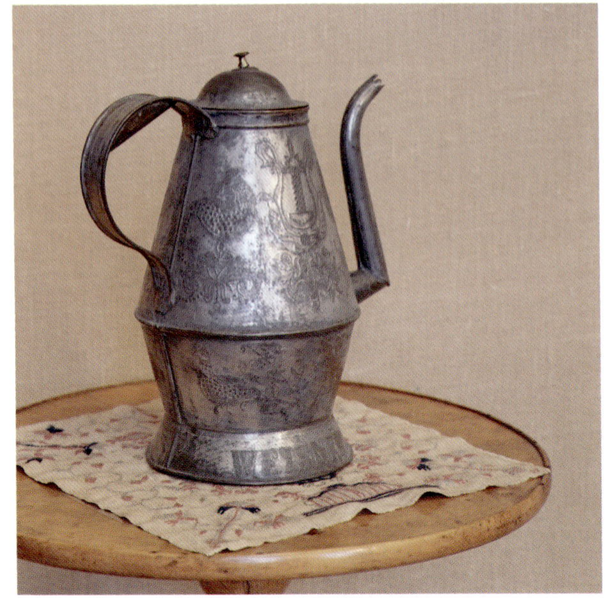

None of the birds, however, come from paintings, which is unusual since a large number of the works in this room depict lush green landscapes and forest scenes. Greenery even infuses many of the portraits and figure paintings in this room. You can imagine the sounds of the birds in the fields, forests, landscapes, and waterways all around the walls of this gallery. By inserting these decorative objects, Dr. Barnes once again uses his installations to enrich the paintings in his ensembles with extra life and movement.

Vise. // Willoughby Shade. Coffeepot, 1840s.

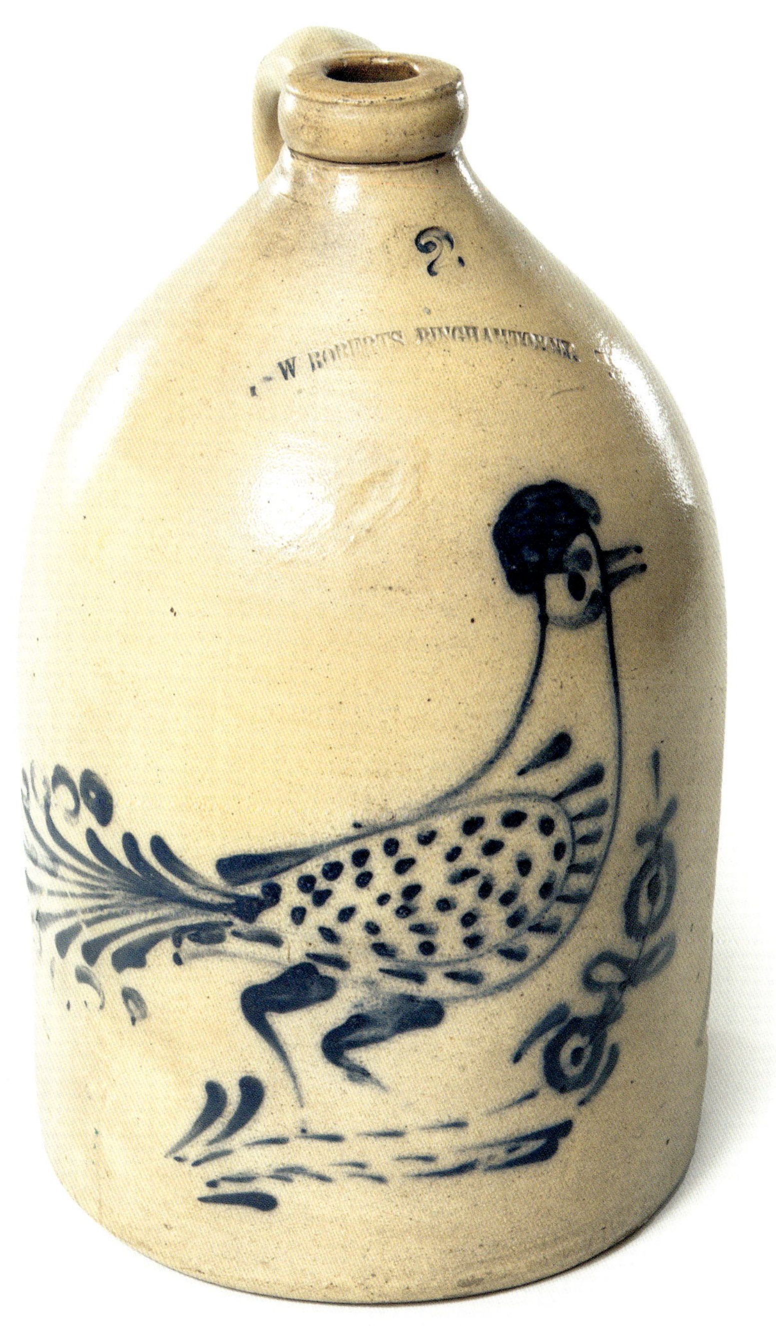

William Roberts. Jug, 1869–1880.

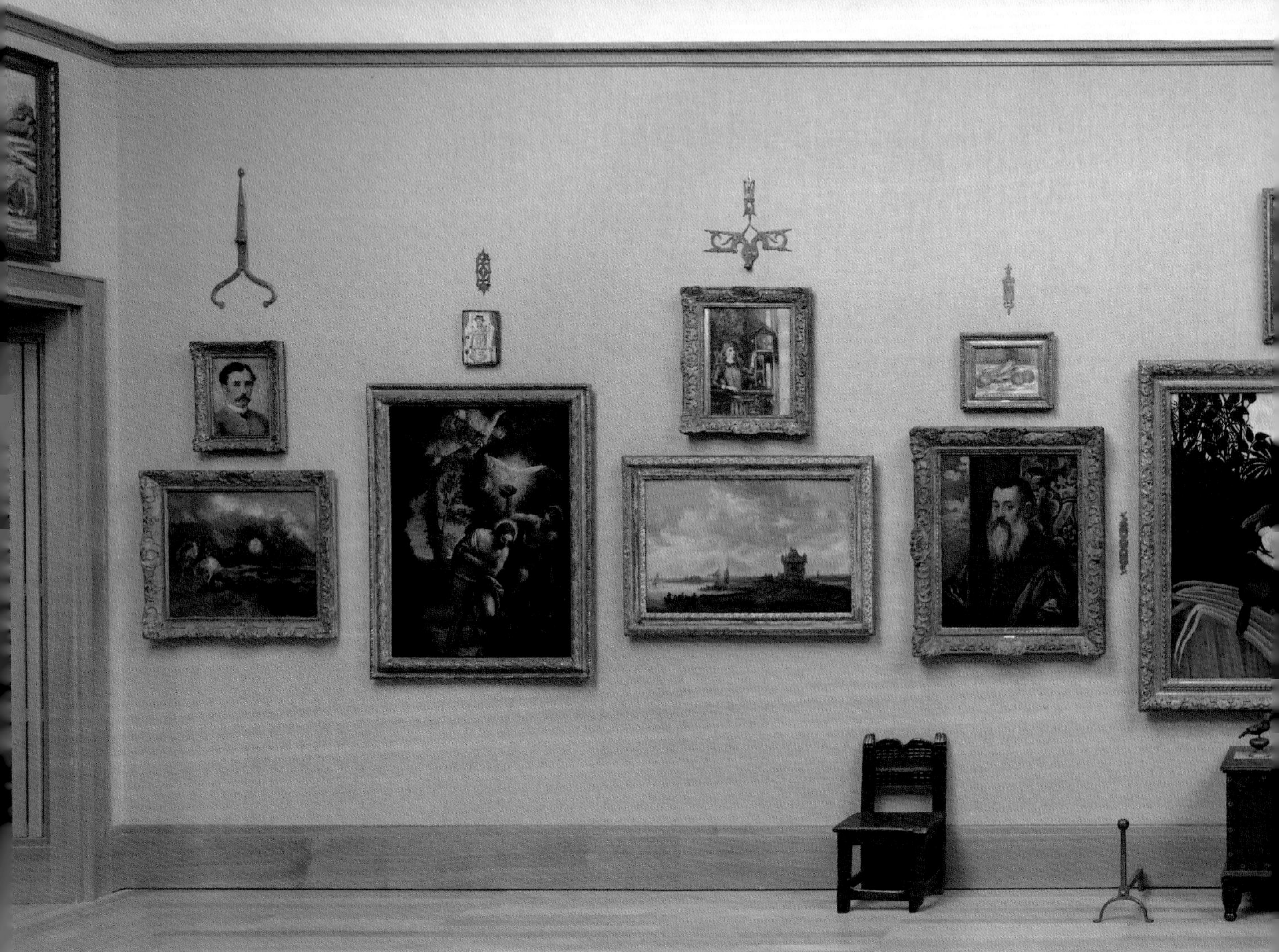

GALLERY 14

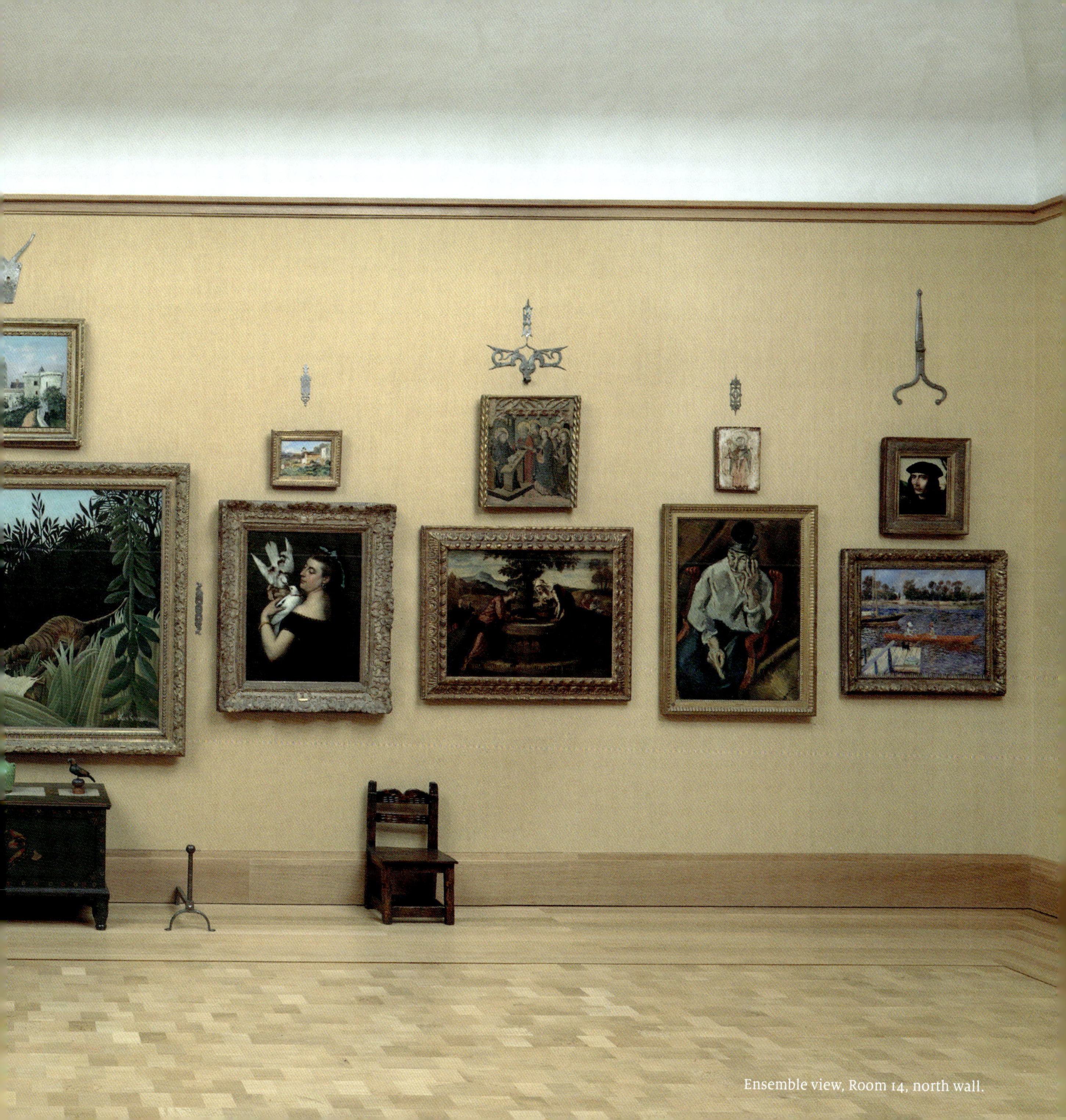

Ensemble view, Room 14, north wall.

Art History Flyby

The north wall of Gallery 14 offers a mini lesson on the turning points of art in the late nineteenth century, enacted entirely in birds. Dr. Barnes believed that modern art was best understood in the context of artistic traditions, so let's take a look. In this ensemble, the long-standing painting tradition of old masters is represented in the Veronese painting, second from the left. Once, the most-revered paintings focused on grand subjects from history, literature, and the Bible. Here, the bird is the Holy Spirit descending on Christ at the time of his baptism in the form of a dove—a common motif of Christian iconography in Western art. Gustave Courbet, however, represented farther along the same wall, spurned those traditions, and that symbolism. Courbet believed in a new theory of "Realism" in which a painter focused on the reality of everyday life rather than on allegory, myth, or literary subjects. He said, "I have never seen either angels or goddesses, so I am not interested in painting them." Courbet's birds in *Woman with Pigeons* are just birds. Contrasting Courbet's pigeons across from the Old Master Veronese highlights this debate and the transition in subject matter that greatly occupied the art world in the late nineteenth century. While his subject matter reached forward, Courbet still adhered to traditional painting techniques. He painted in exacting detail and built up thin layers of color over a dark ground, creating a luminous surface.

Veronese (Paolo Caliari). *Baptism of Christ*, mid-16th century.

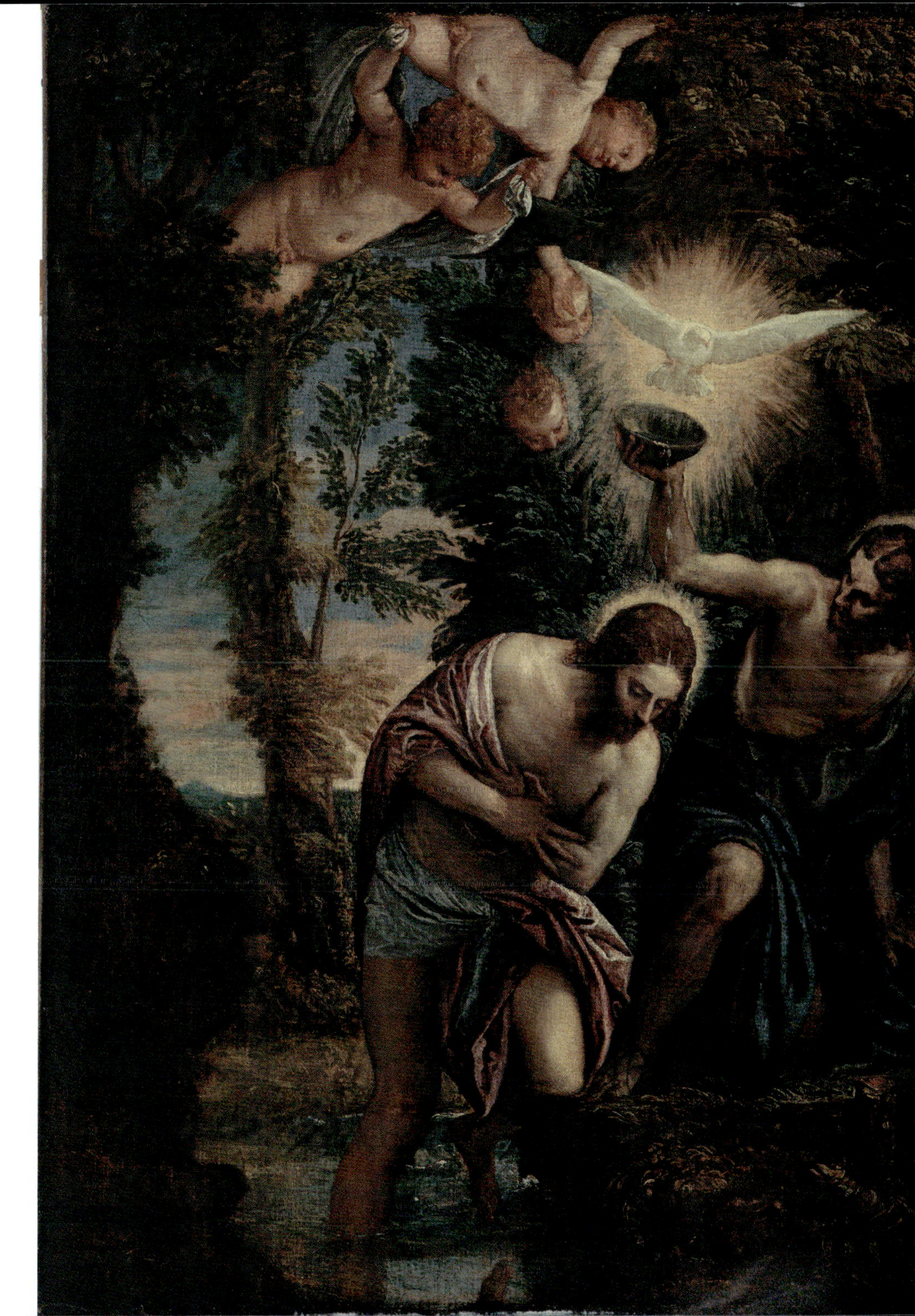

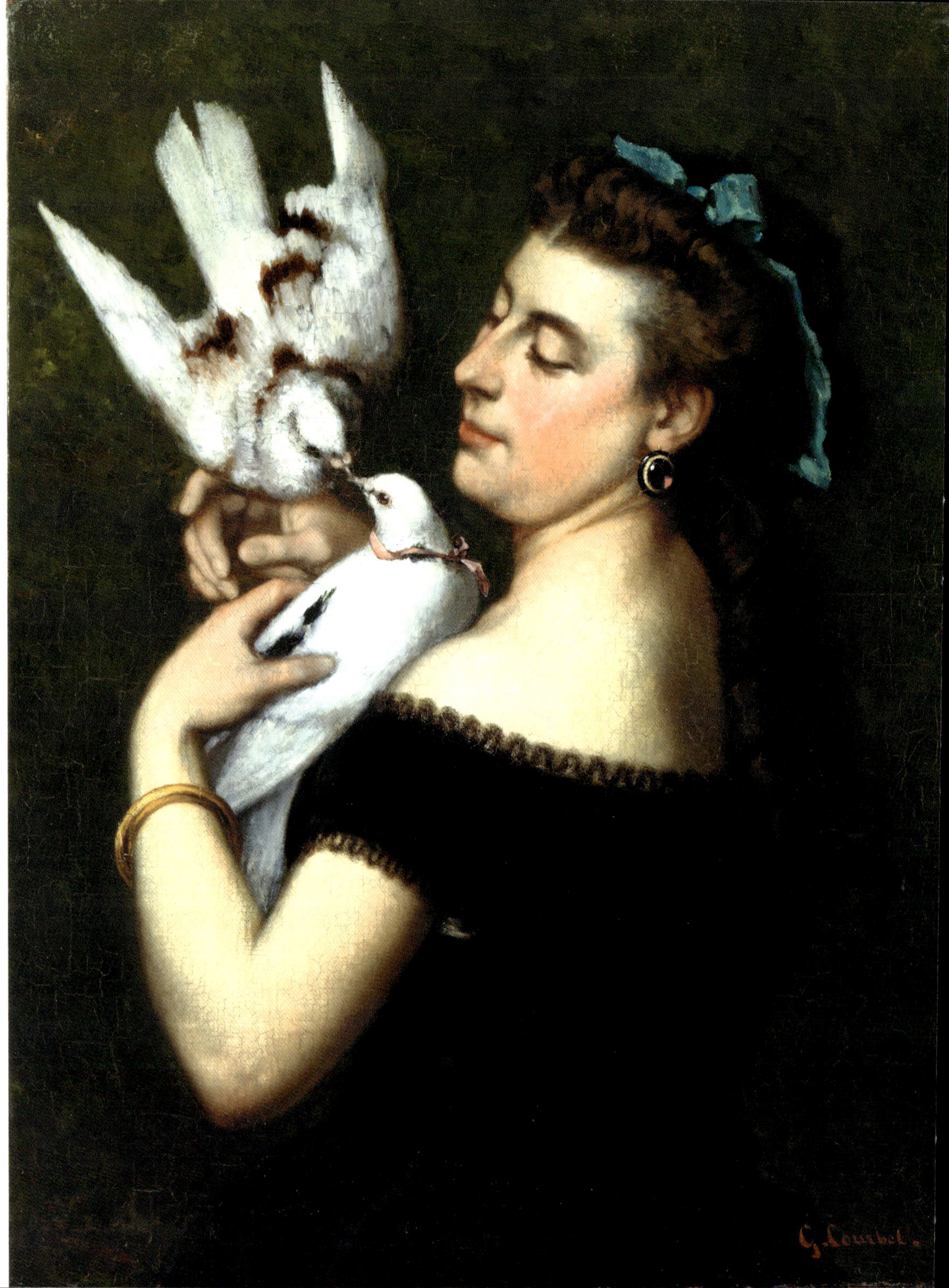
G. Courbet.

The advent of impressionism, however, subverted both subject matter and painting style. The impressionists, represented here by Paul Cézanne's *Woman with a Birdcage*, no longer followed the same traditional painting techniques that Courbet did. Instead of building the surface of their canvases with thin glazes, they painted with thicker paint, which by the mid-nineteenth century was increasingly available ready-mixed for purchase and no longer required the artist to mix each color individually from pigments ground by hand. Now painters applied paint quickly, focusing less on any careful illusion of reality and more on the expressive qualities of a passing moment. Following the birds in this installation, we find that Dr. Barnes crafted a timeline of art history, showing a step-by-step progression from the traditions of painting to the advent of modernism both in subject and style.

To tie this progression all together, a small flock of birds center this wall's composition, both painted on the front of the wooden trunk and in the sculptural folk art pieces placed on top of it.

Gustave Courbet. *Woman with Pigeons*, mid-1860s.

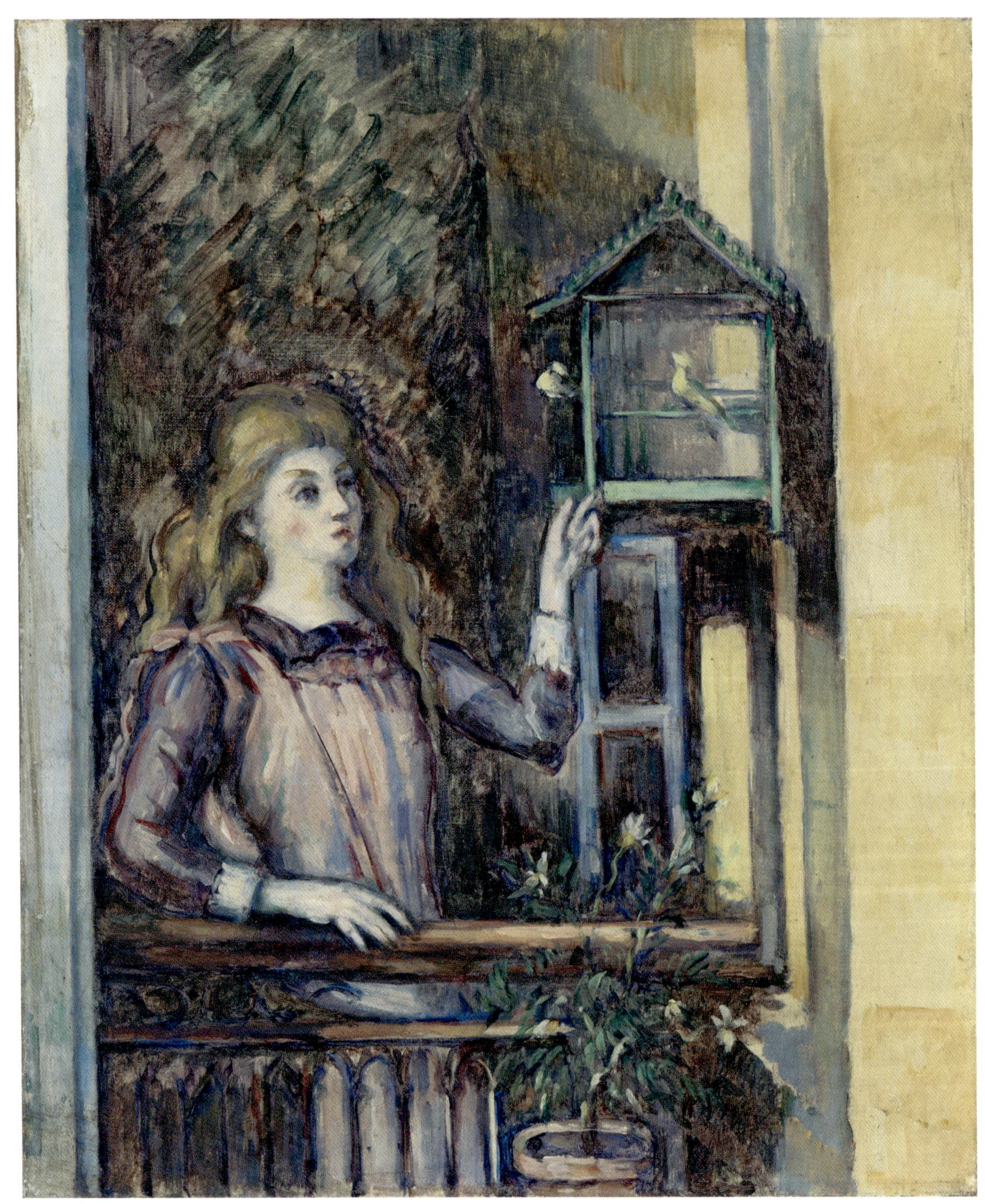

 Paul Cézanne. *Girl with Birdcage* (*Jeune fille à la volière*), c. 1888, or possibly later.

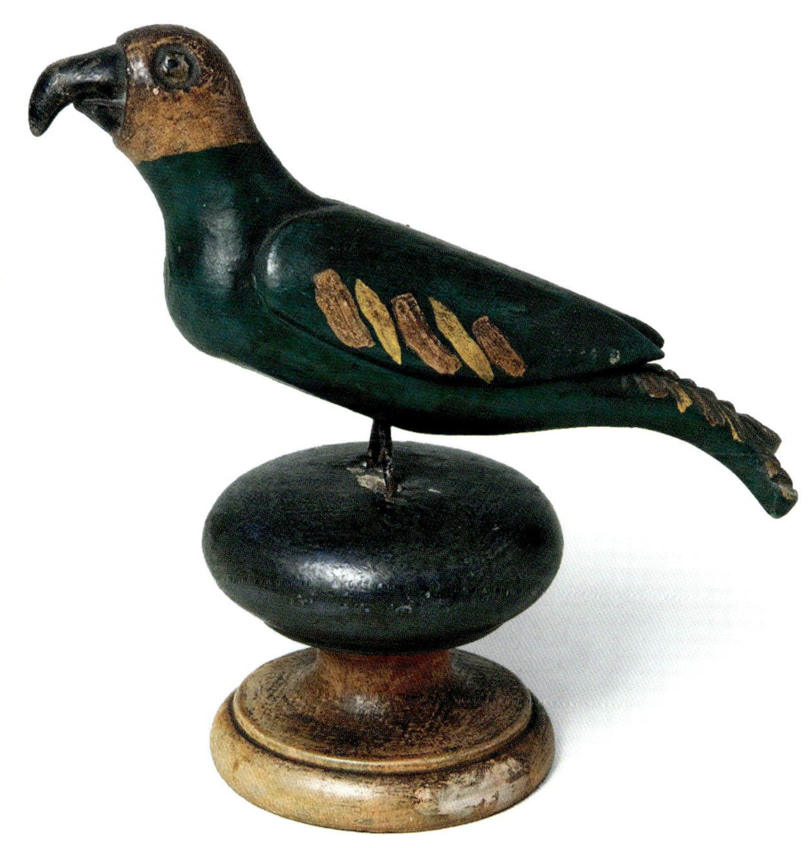

Parrot. Carved and painted wood.

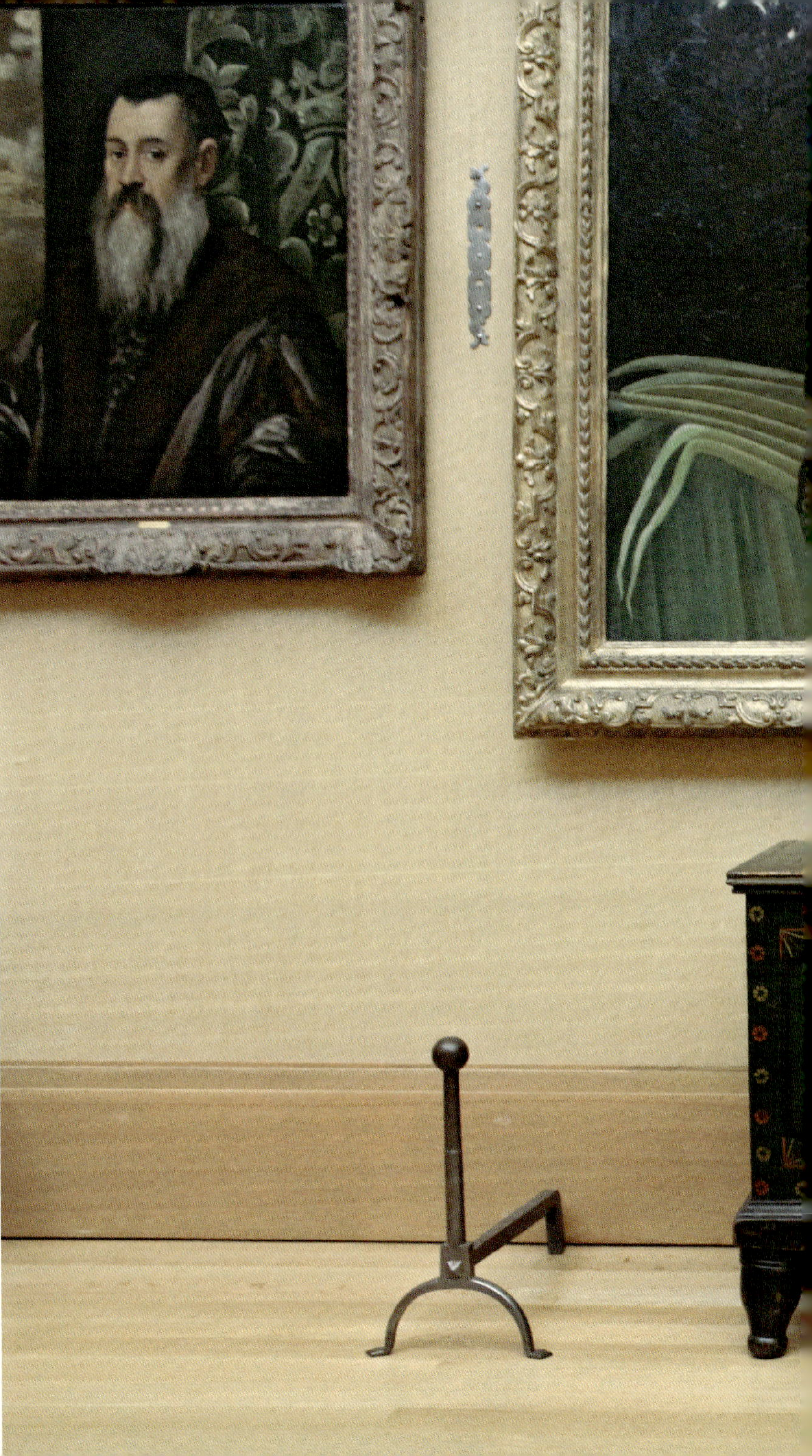

 Chest, c. 1840.

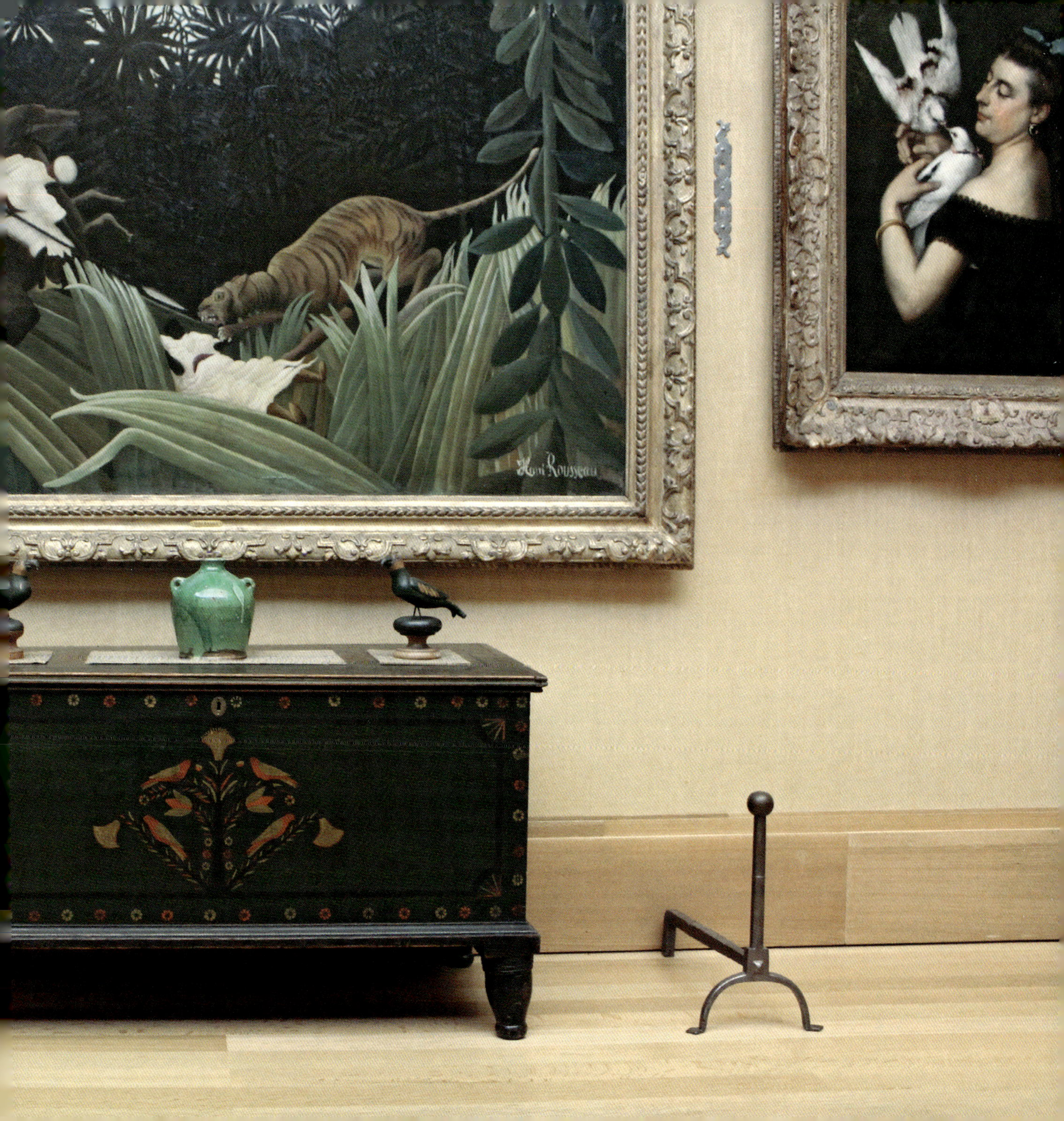
Henri Rousseau

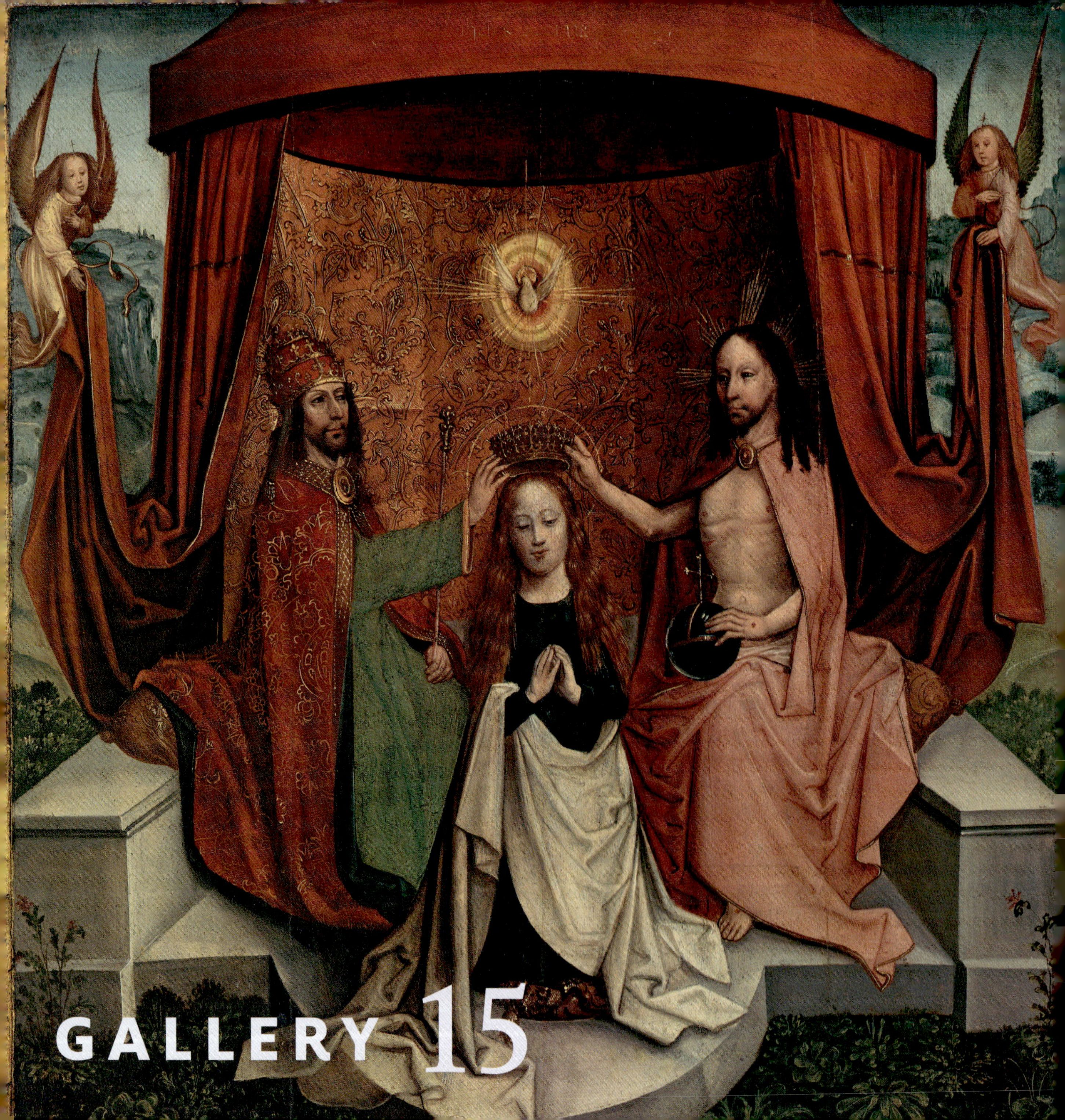
GALLERY 15

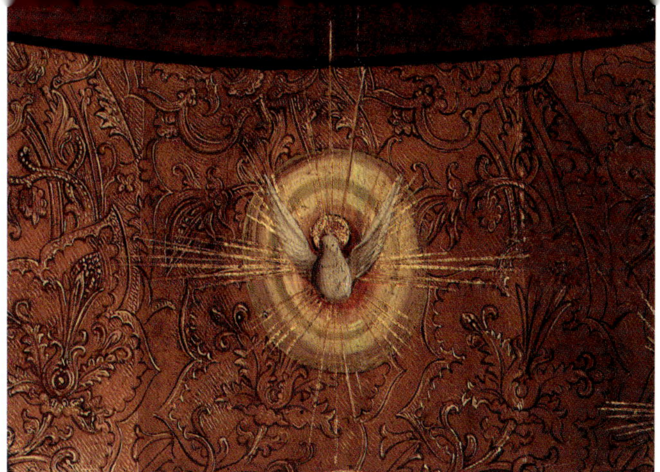

Flying around the World

Birds in Gallery 15 highlight iconography from different cultures of the world. The first bird is another allegorical symbol of the Holy Spirit from the Christian tradition. This time, the dove descends on the Virgin Mary at the point of Annunciation (the moment when the angel Gabriel informs her she will bear the incarnated Son of God).

Coronation of the Virgin, second half of the 15th century, Flemish.

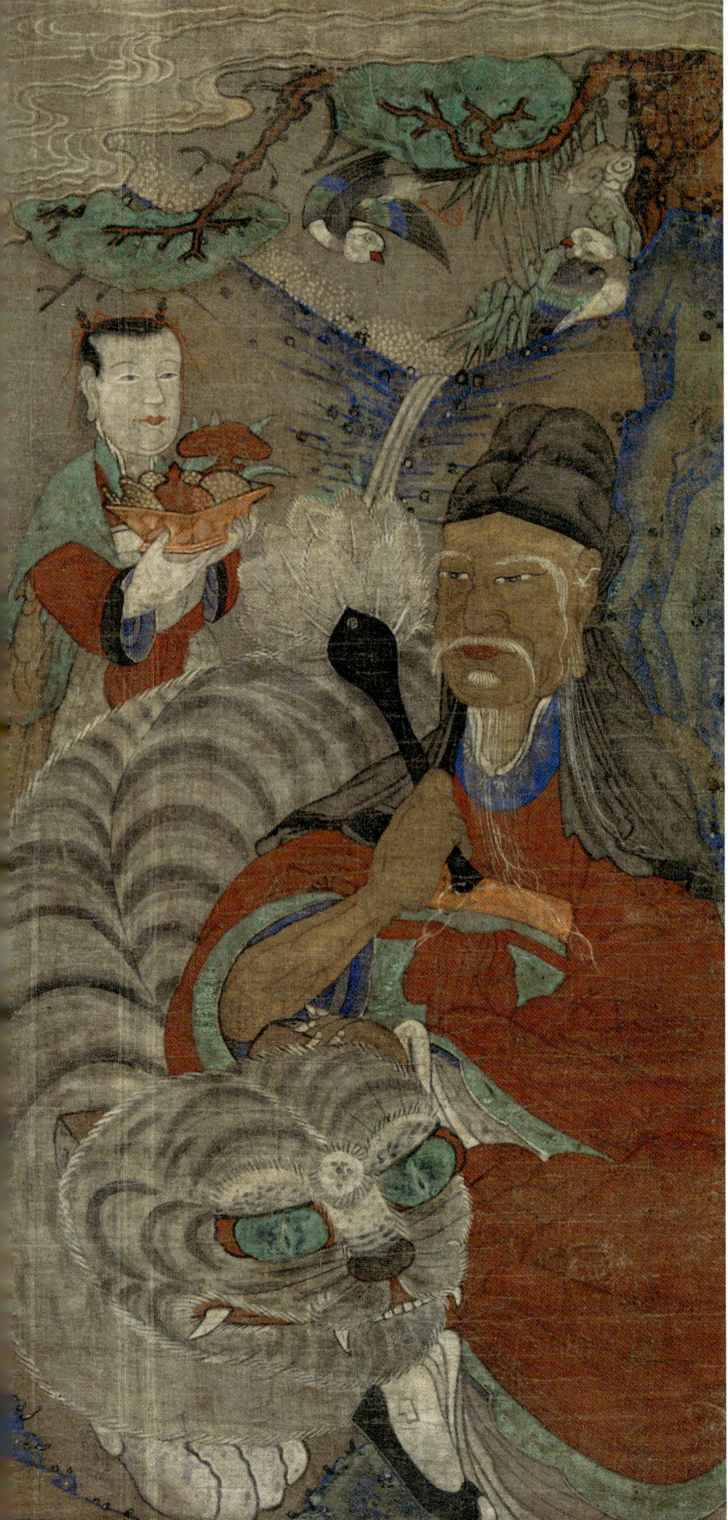

Balancing this dove on the opposite side of the ensemble, small birds flit in a pine tree at the top of a Korean composition from the sixteenth century, depicting a tiger and mountain god (*sanshin*). The mountain god, with his long eyebrows and a trailing beard, holding a fan, and the accompanying tiger are common and auspicious subjects in Korean painting, frequently displayed in Buddhist shrines. This imagery combines folklore and Buddhist tradition and was as familiar to viewers in its context as the Annunciation painting would have been to its European Christian congregants.

These two artworks with their small birds bracket another bird in the center of the glass display case: an Etruscan red-figure, bird-shaped clay pitcher from the fourth century, called an *askos*. The *askos* is shaped naturalistically, with a curved neck and columbine form, exquisitely detailed, with individually painted feathers. Along each side of the bird, a woman reclines with dark hair and a pair of unfurled wings—a *Lasa*, a minor Etruscan goddess figure. The pitcher may have been used to hold and pour scented oil.

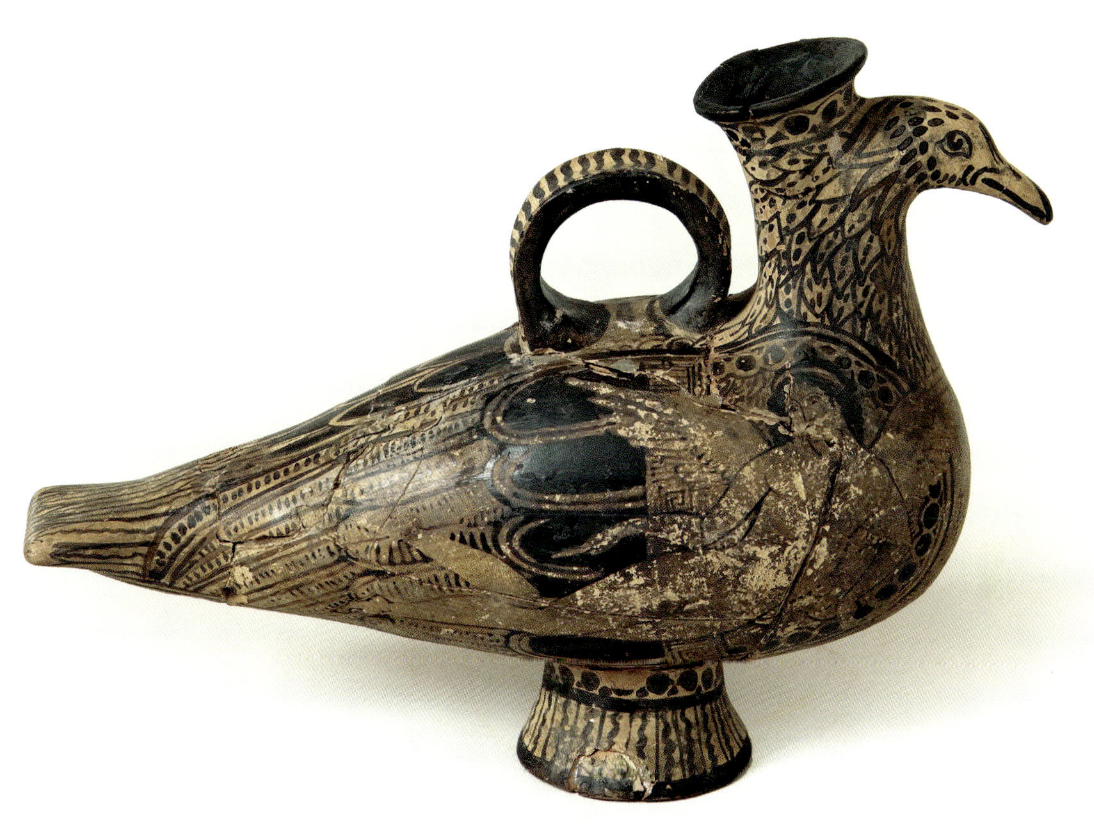

Sage with Tiger, 16th century, Korean. // Red-Figure Bird *Askos*, end of the 4th century BCE.

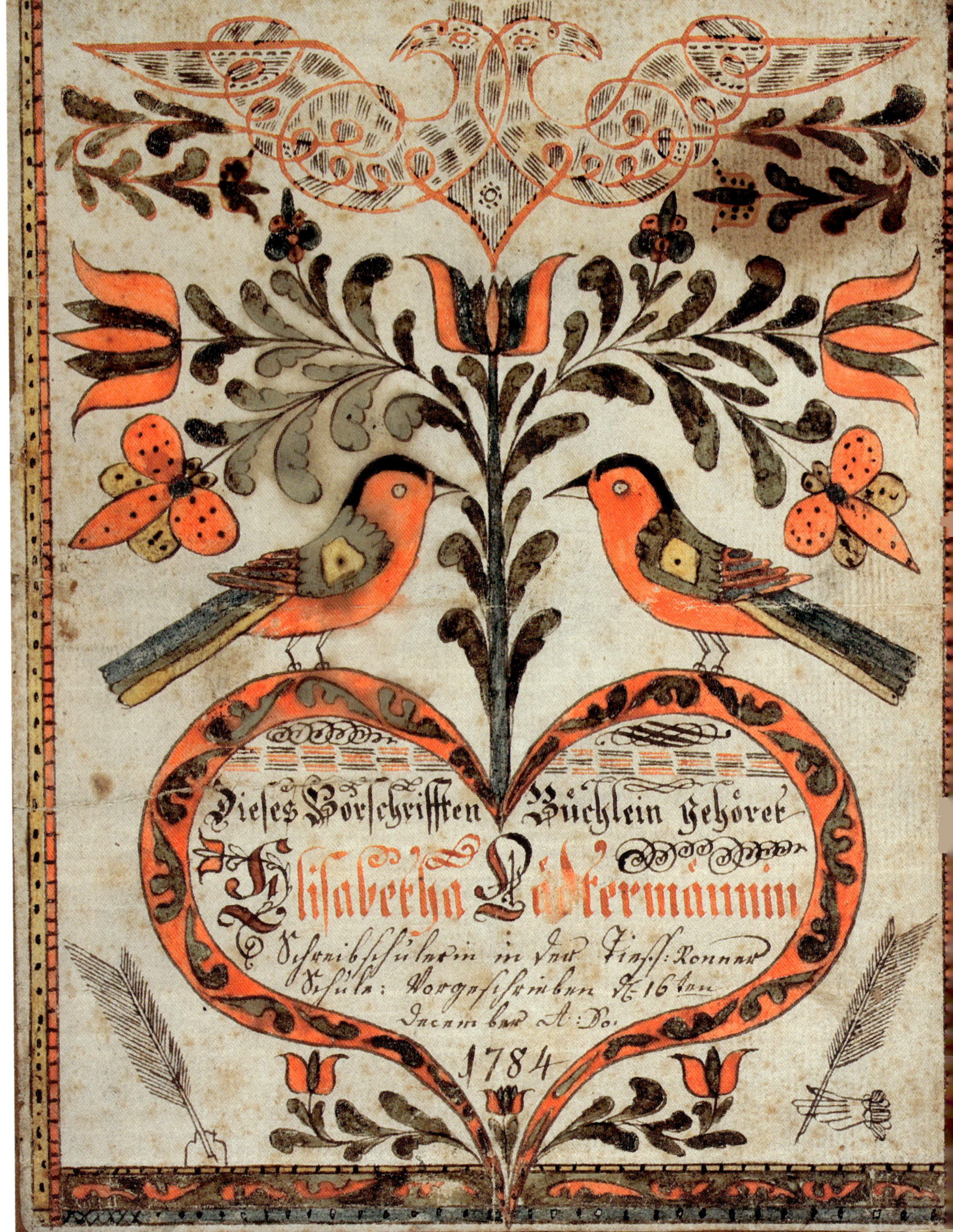

Dieses Vorschrifften Büchlein gehöret
1784

Across the room, near the doorway, hangs a Pennsylvania German Fraktur. Fraktur is a folk art tradition of the American Amish, Mennonite, and other religious separatist communities, named for its use of the German script by the same name. Fraktur pieces are often embellished family records such as certificates of marriage, birth, and baptism.

At first glance the birds in this room play a very minor role in the room's composition, secondary to significant works by Matisse, Renoir, and Cézanne. Yet, following the birds from one doorway to the next leads us in a migration across four cultures, four centuries, and four religious faiths, all in the space of one small gallery.

Johann Adam Eyer. *Cover for a Book of Copy Models* (*Vorschriften-Büchlein*), 1784.

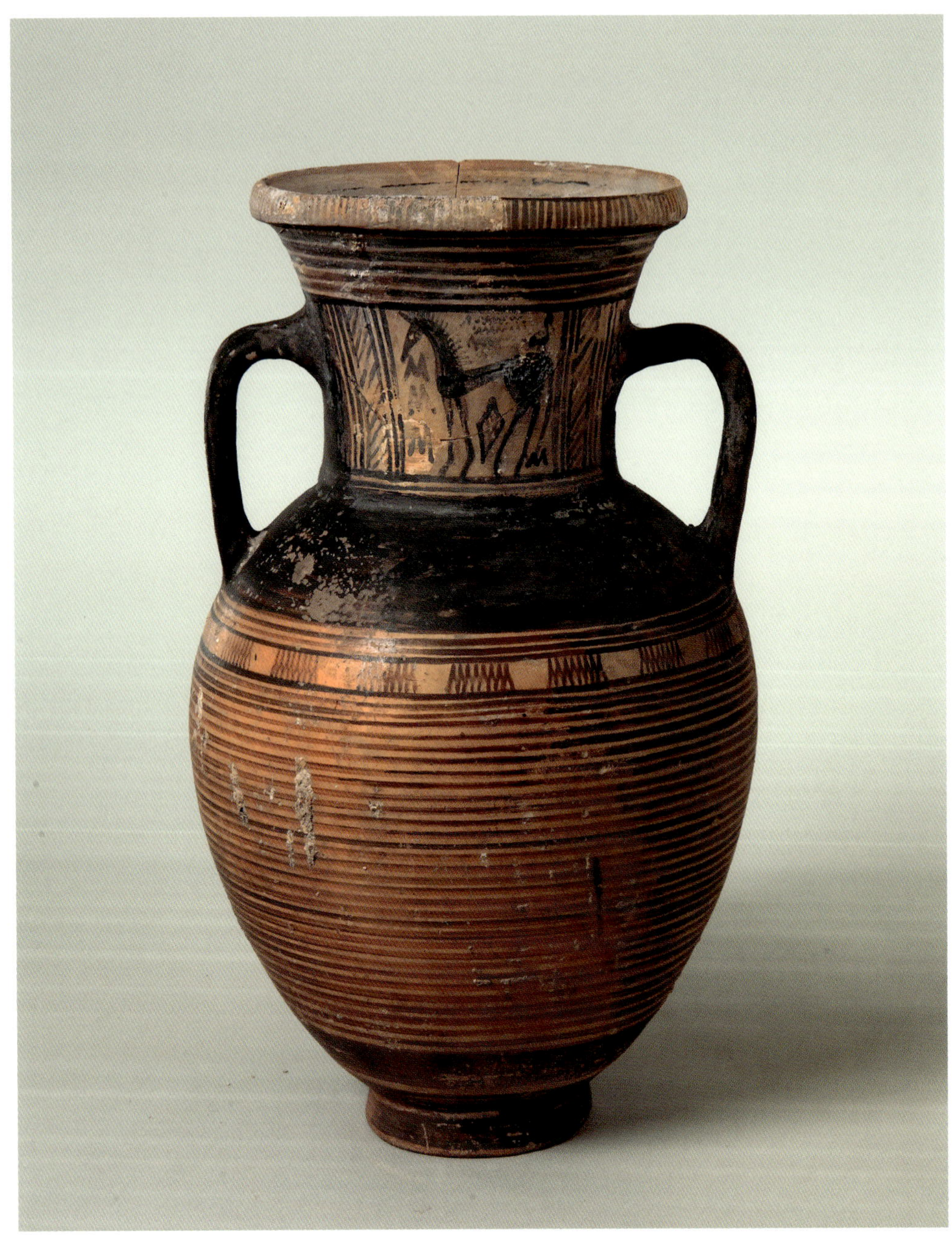

 Geometric Amphora, c. 770–750 BCE, Greek.

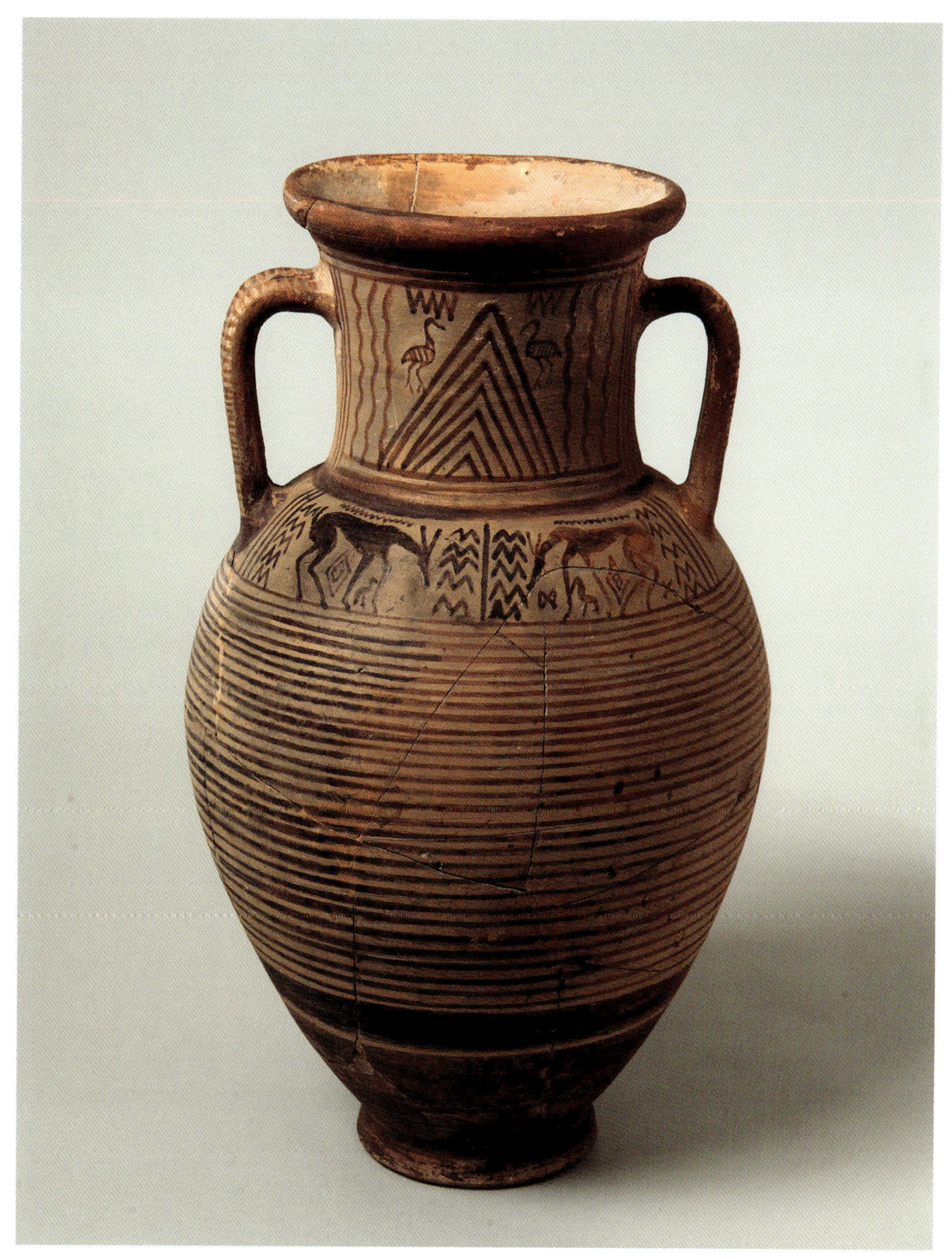

Geometric Amphora, possibly 8th century BCE, or possibly modern, Greek.

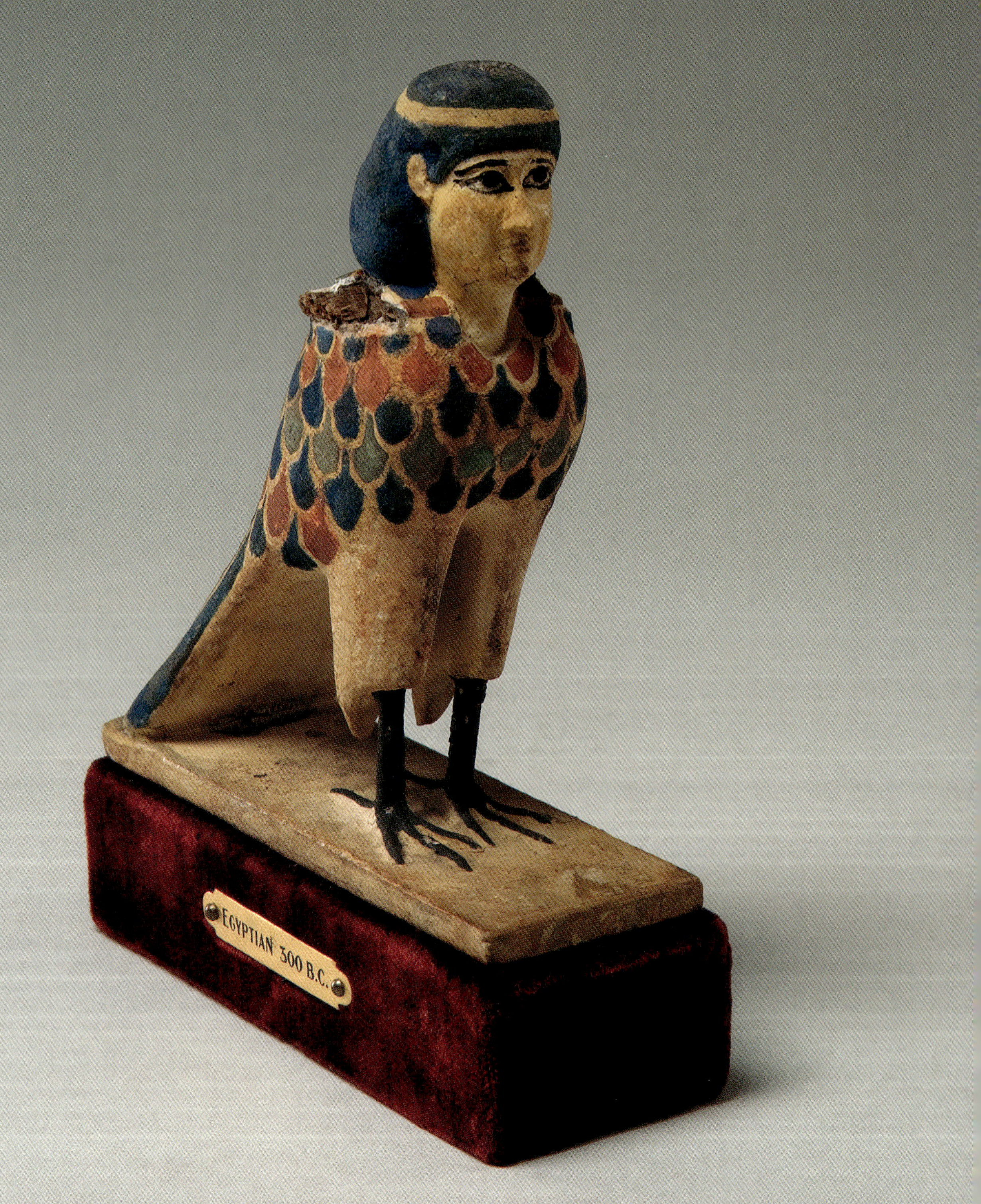
EGYPTIAN 300 B.C.

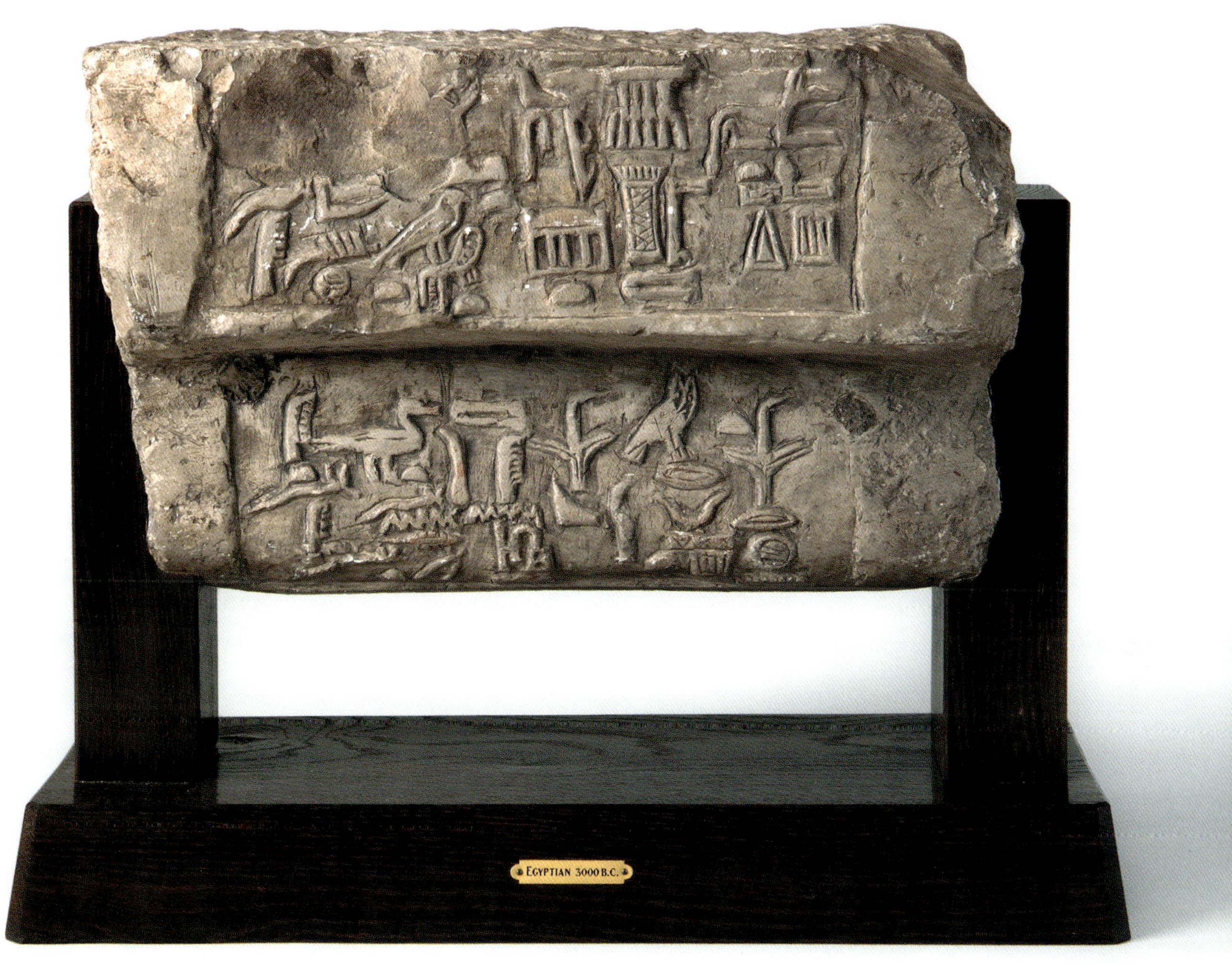

Statuette of a Human-Headed Ba-Bird, c. 300 BCE. // Relief, 2350–2130 BCE, Egyptian.

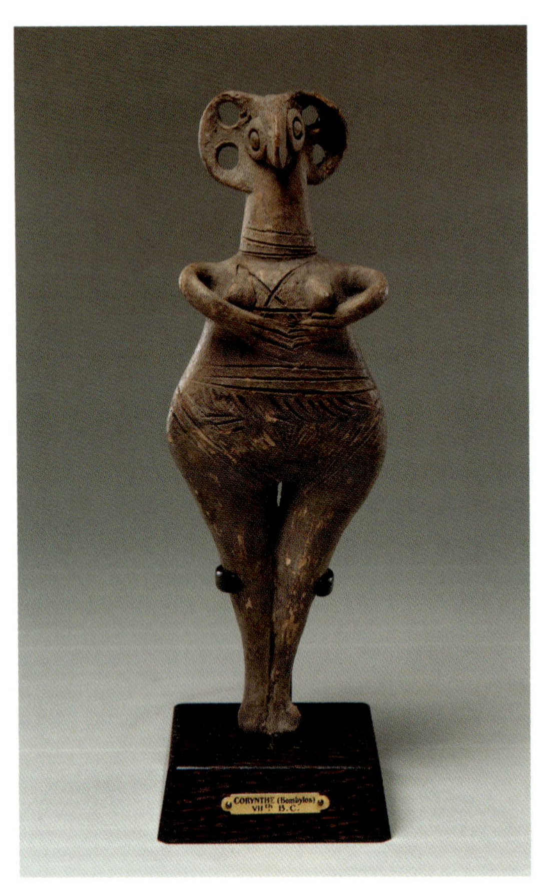

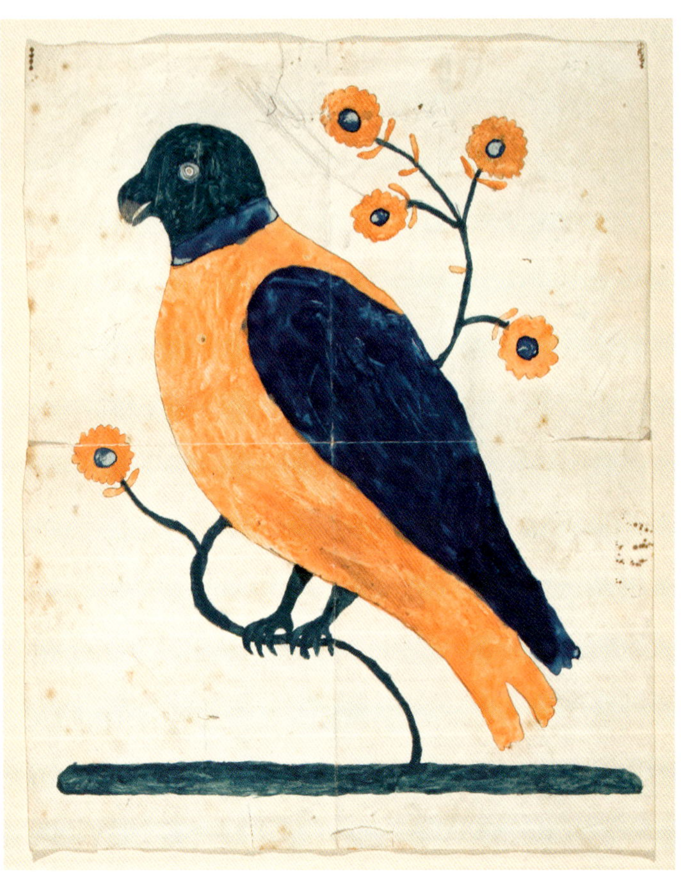

GALLERY 16

Home and Away

An assortment of antiquities—Greek, Roman, and Egyptian sculptures and artifacts—balance pieces from closer to home, such as Charles Prendergast's work, redware pitchers, and a Pennsylvania German *Distelfink* bird. The *Distelfink* is a stylized bird common in Fraktur art and is based on the European goldfinch (see Gallery 22).

Dr. Barnes bought most of his most ancient artifacts, such as the Greek and Egyptian pieces in his collection, through his Parisian art dealers. He did not personally travel outside Europe and North America. Antiquities were much in demand on the European art market, and while he obtained some lovely specimens of ancient Greek ceramics and sculpture, other pieces that make up this part of the collection have since been determined to be more modern in origin.

"Bird-Face" Goddess, c. 1450–1200 BCE // *Bird on Twig*, 19th century.

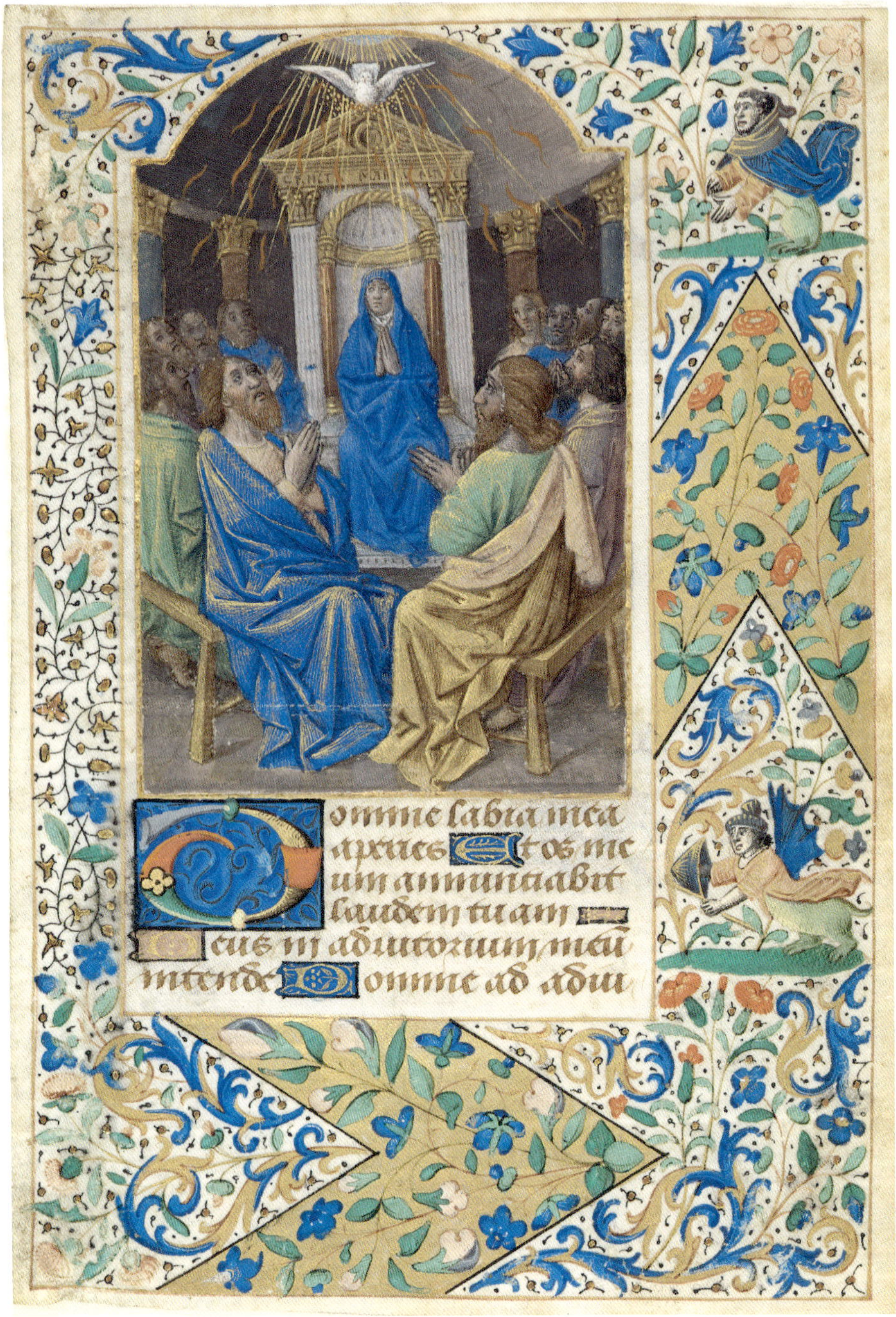

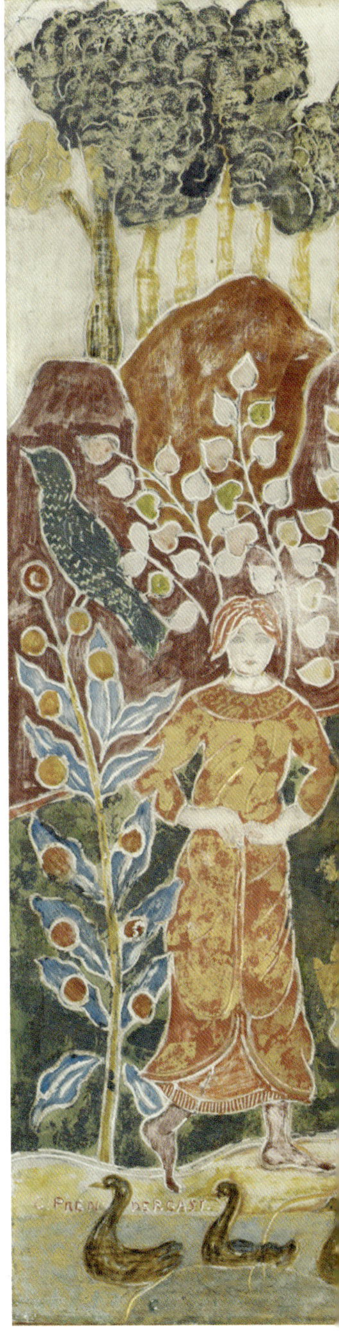

Jean Bourdichon. *The Pentecost* or *Descent of the Holy Spirit*, from a Book of Hours, 1470–1480.

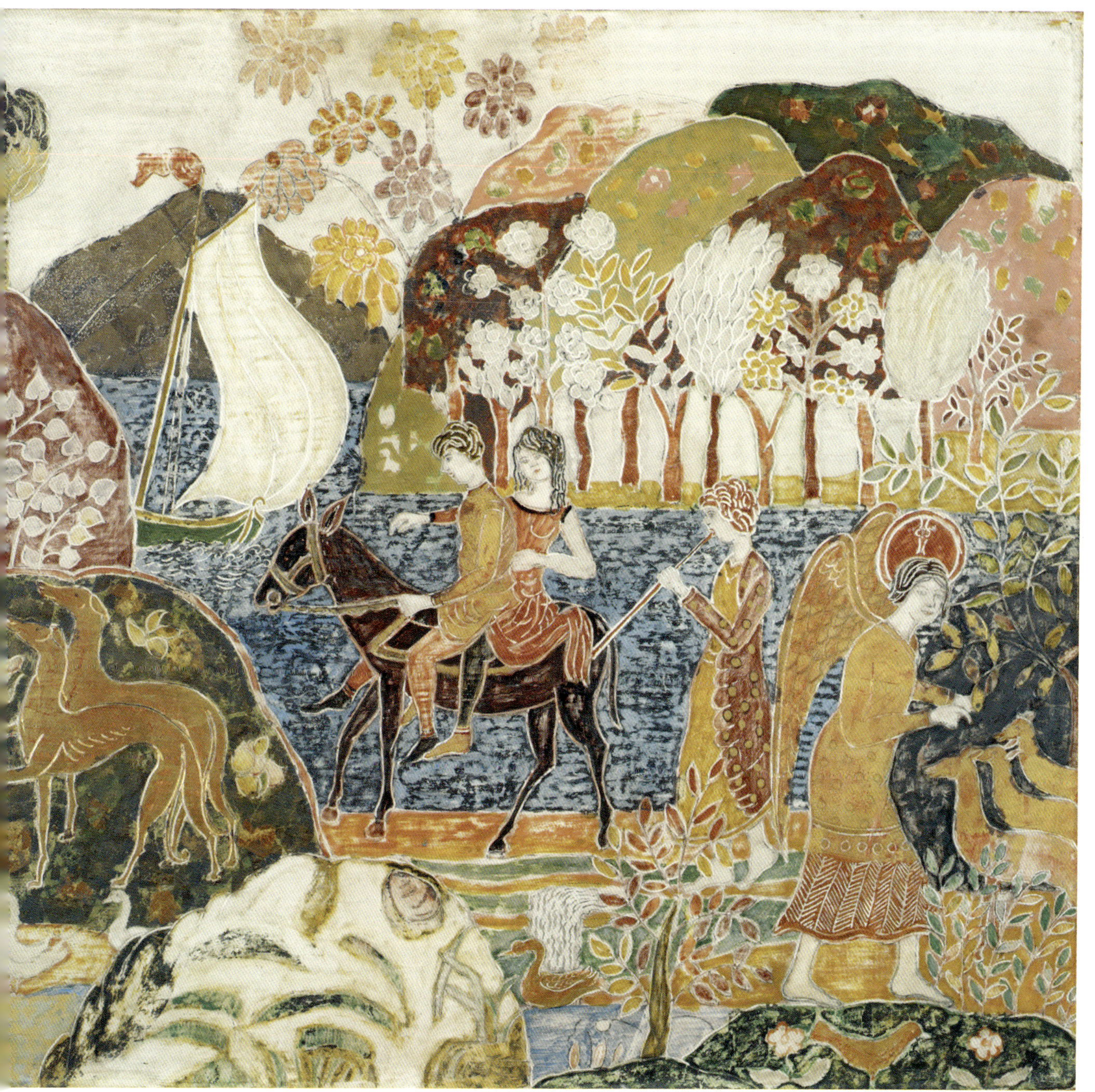

Charles Prendergast. *Two Figures on a Mule*, c. 1917–1920.

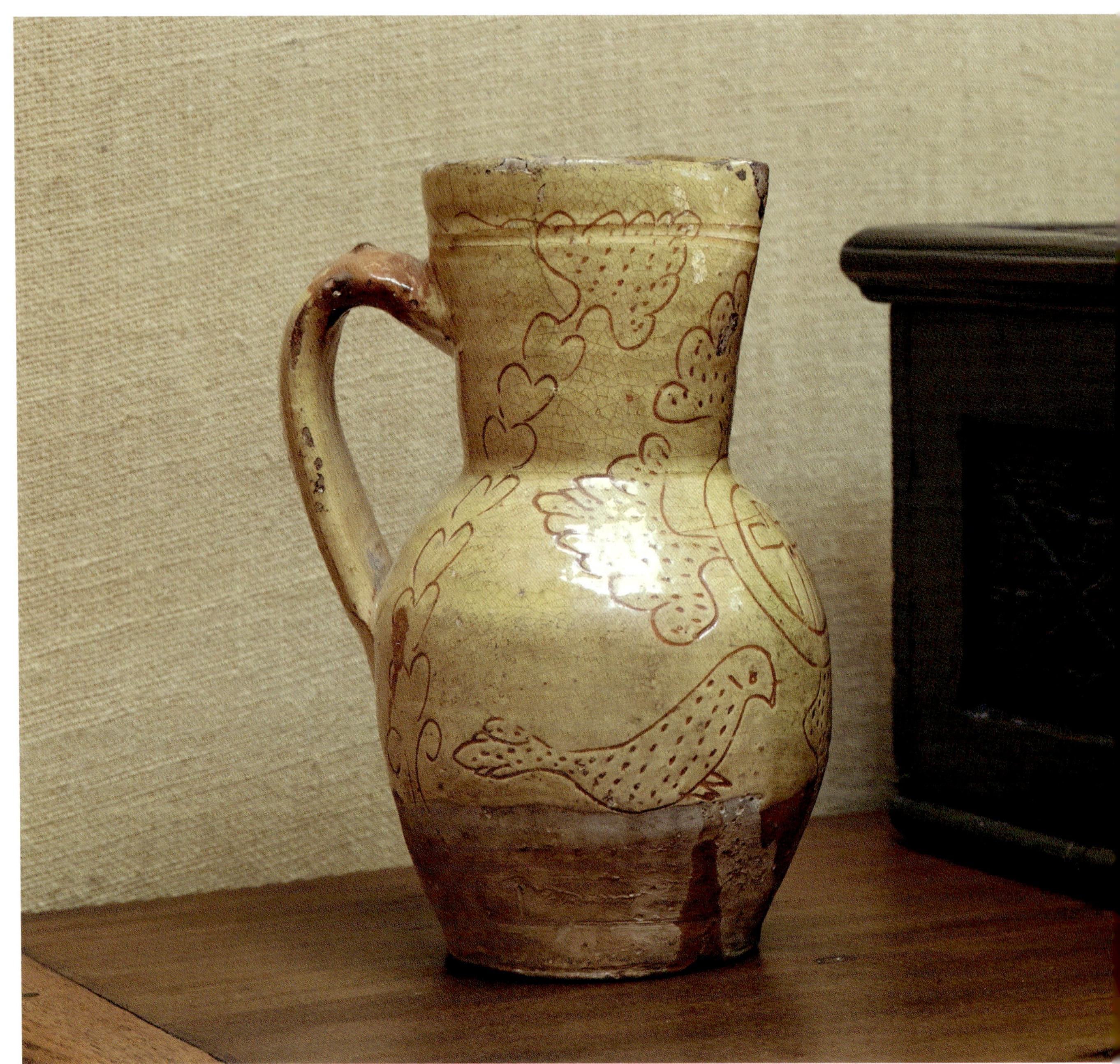

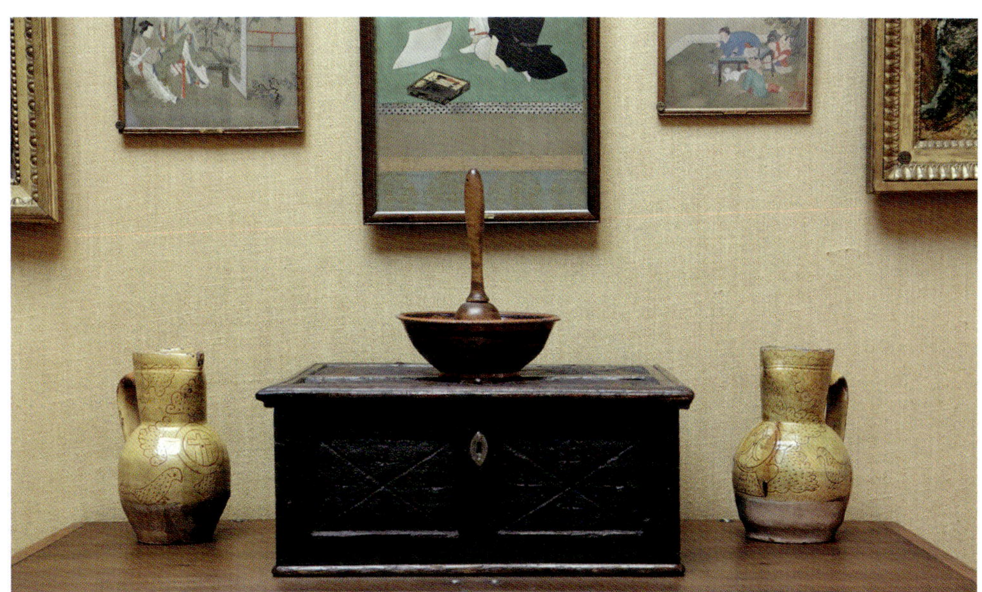

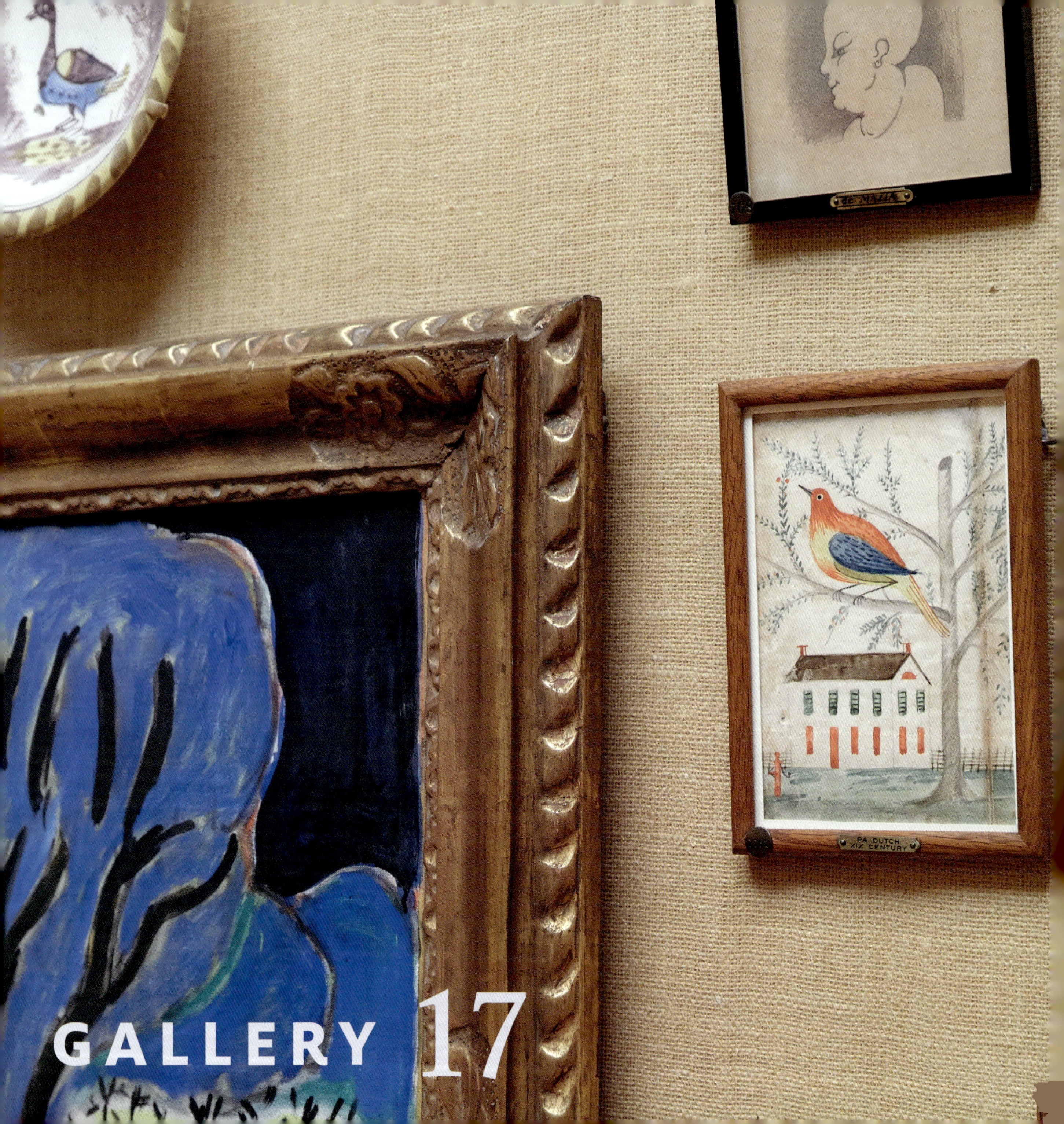

GALLERY 17

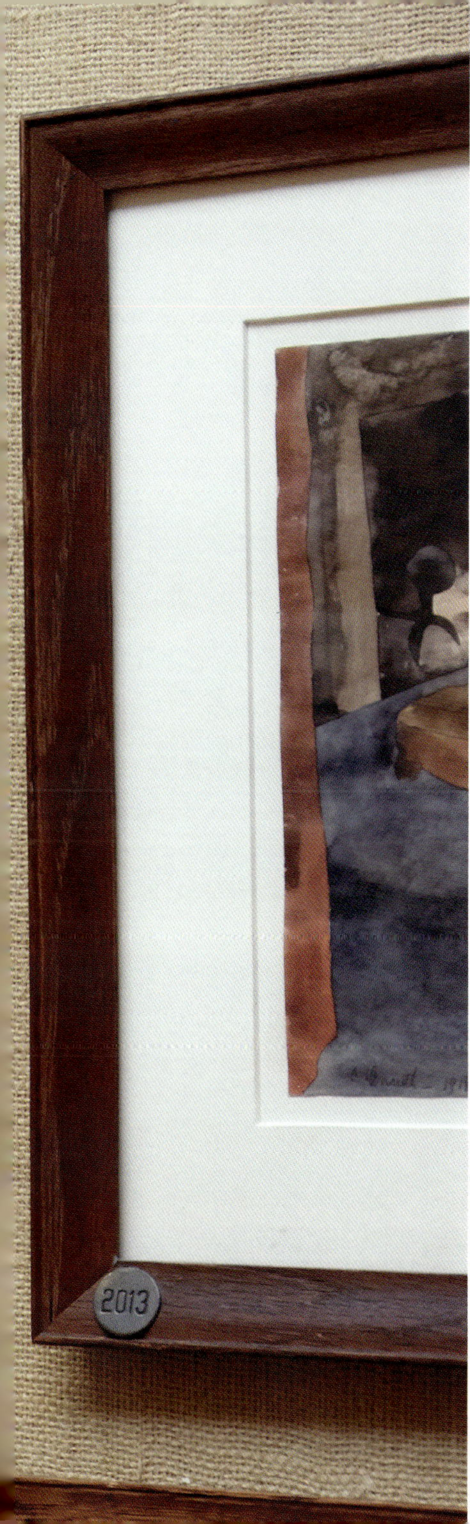

Pennsylvania Roots

A native Pennsylvanian, Dr. Barnes had a strong interest in early-nineteenth-century Pennsylvania German painting. He wrote that it was "perhaps the only painting done in America that might claim to have an identity of its own," since "practically all other painting in America has followed so closely the European traditions that a distinctively American form of painting does not exist" (Barnes 1925). It may well have seemed that way from a vantage point so early in the twentieth century, but no matter how his assertion holds up today, his collection holds a large assortment of decorative designs of Pennsylvania German birds and flowers, many of which gather in Gallery 17. A few of these may also be the work of Dr. Barnes's friend and assistant, Albert Nulty.

House and Bird on a Tree, 19th century.

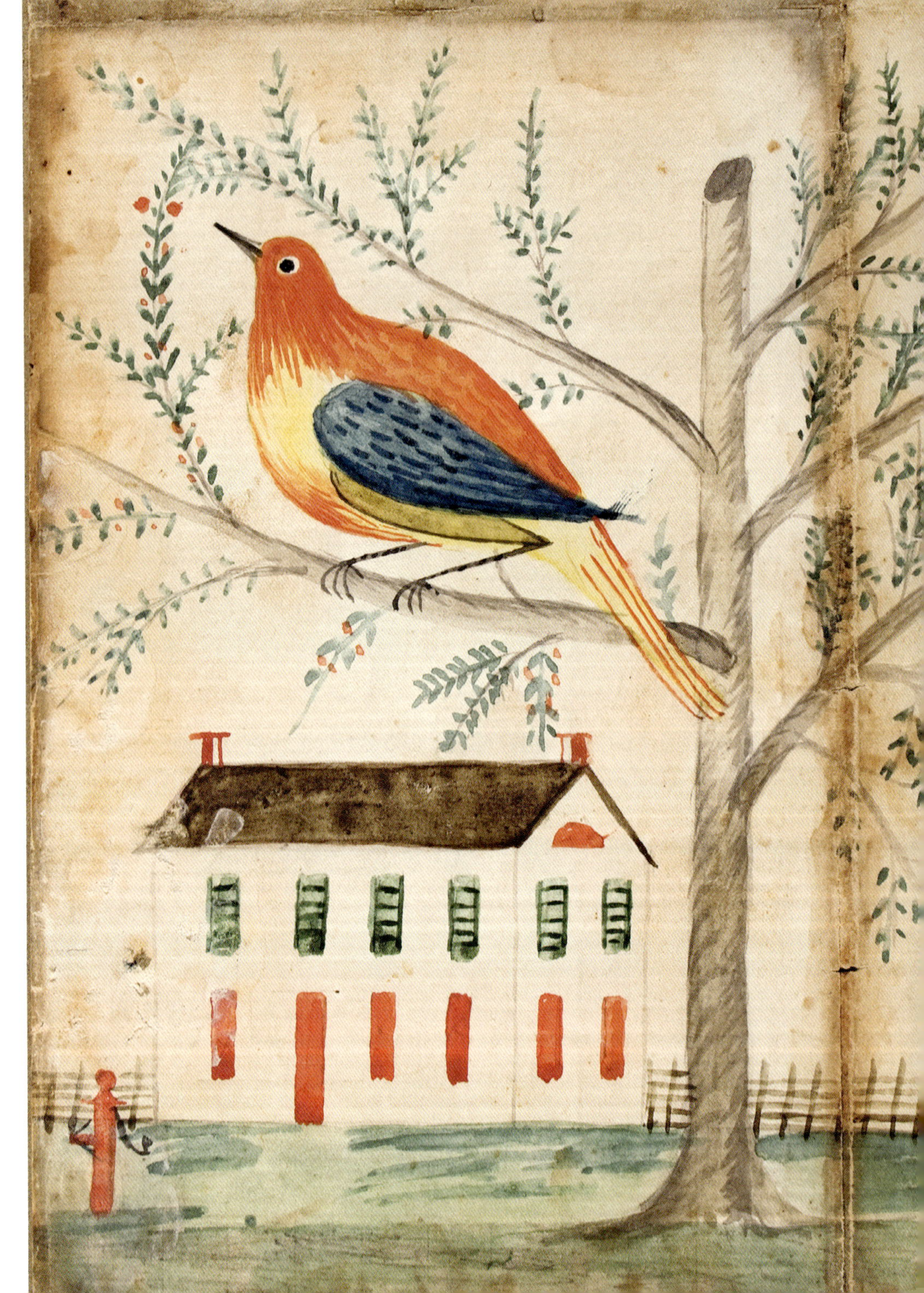

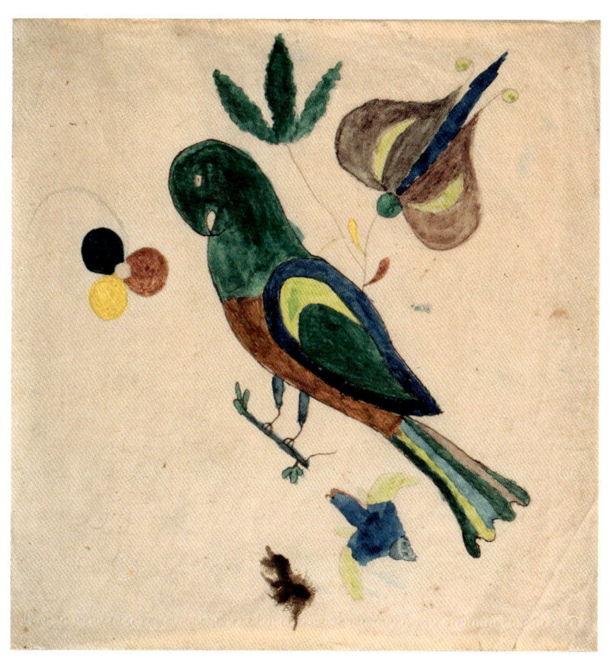

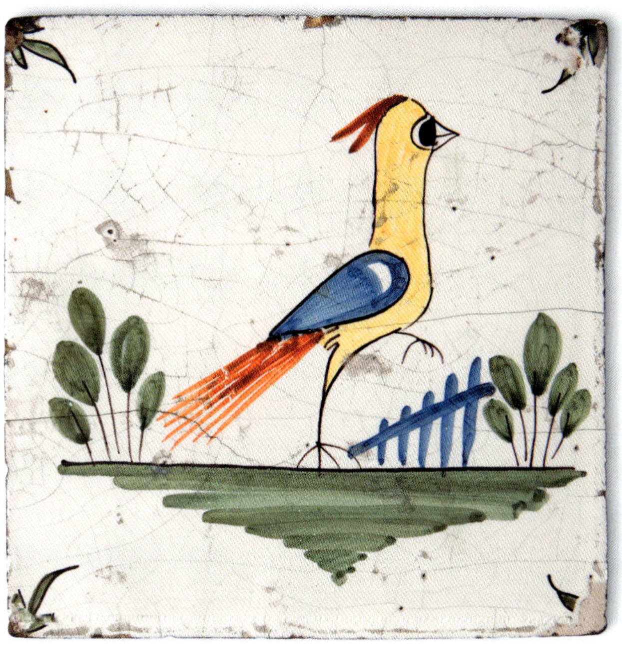

Parakeet, 19th century. // Decorative Tile. Ceramic.

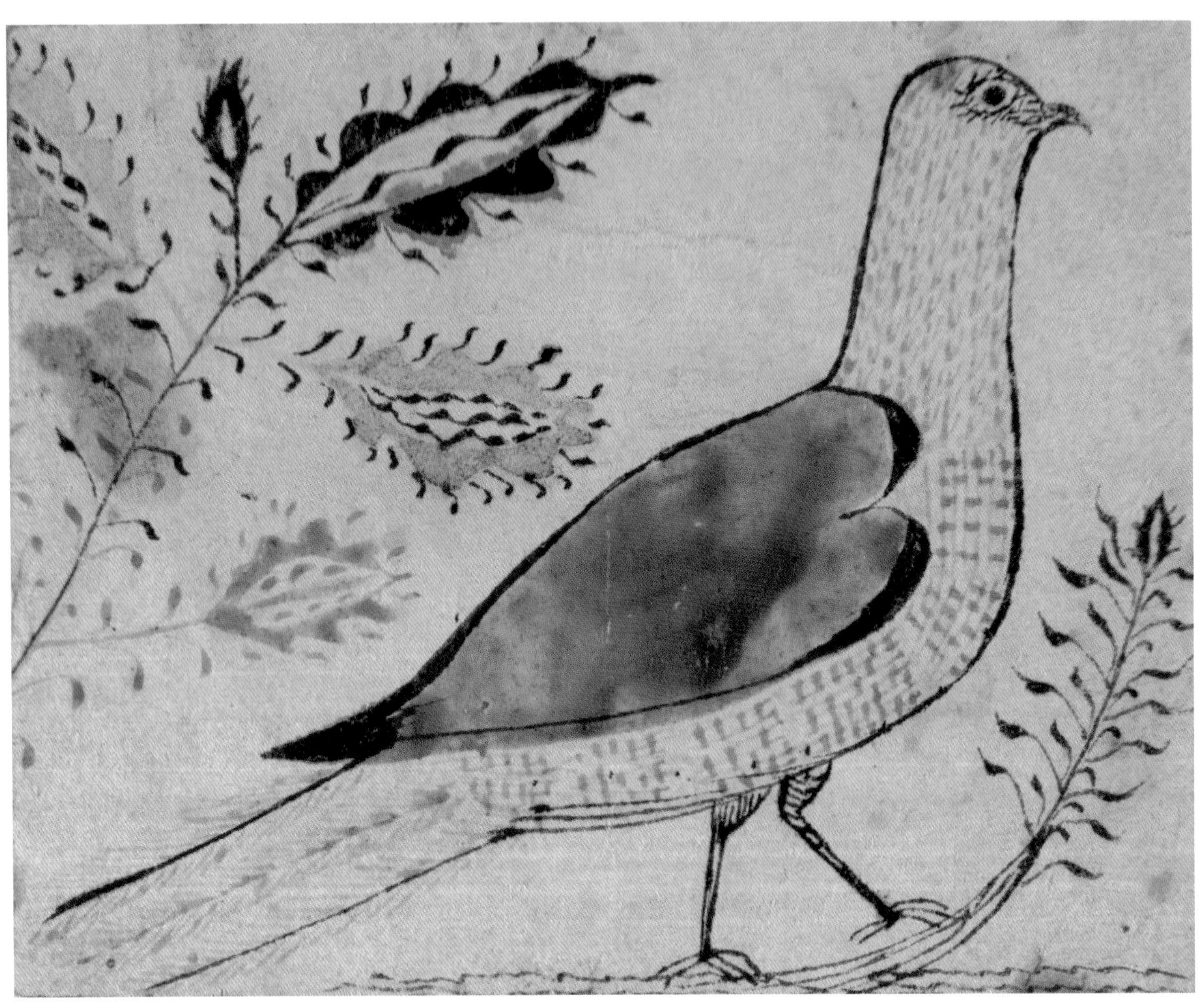

 Bird, 19th century.

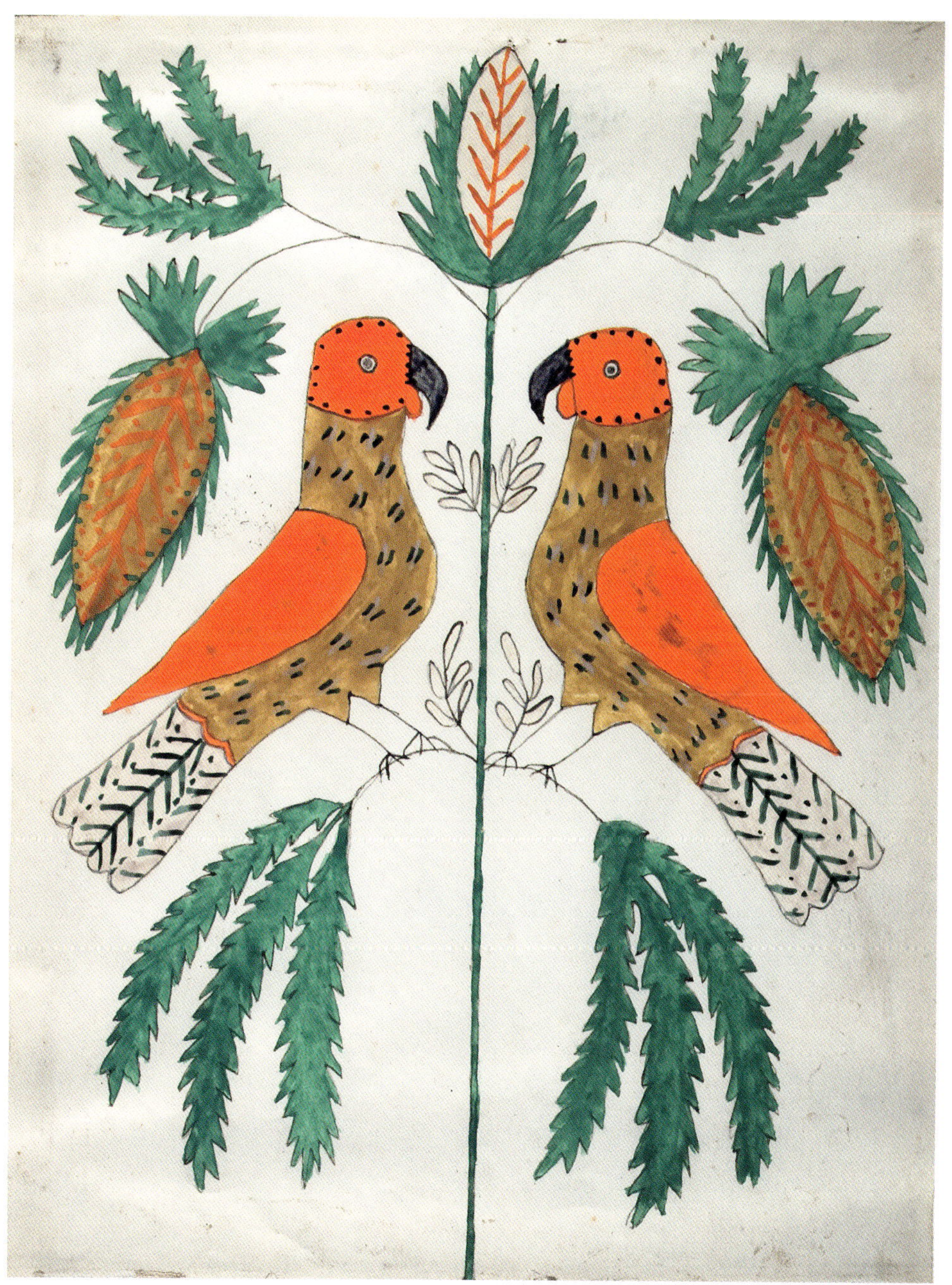

Two Red and Yellow Parrots Facing Each Other (Green Leaves), 19th century.

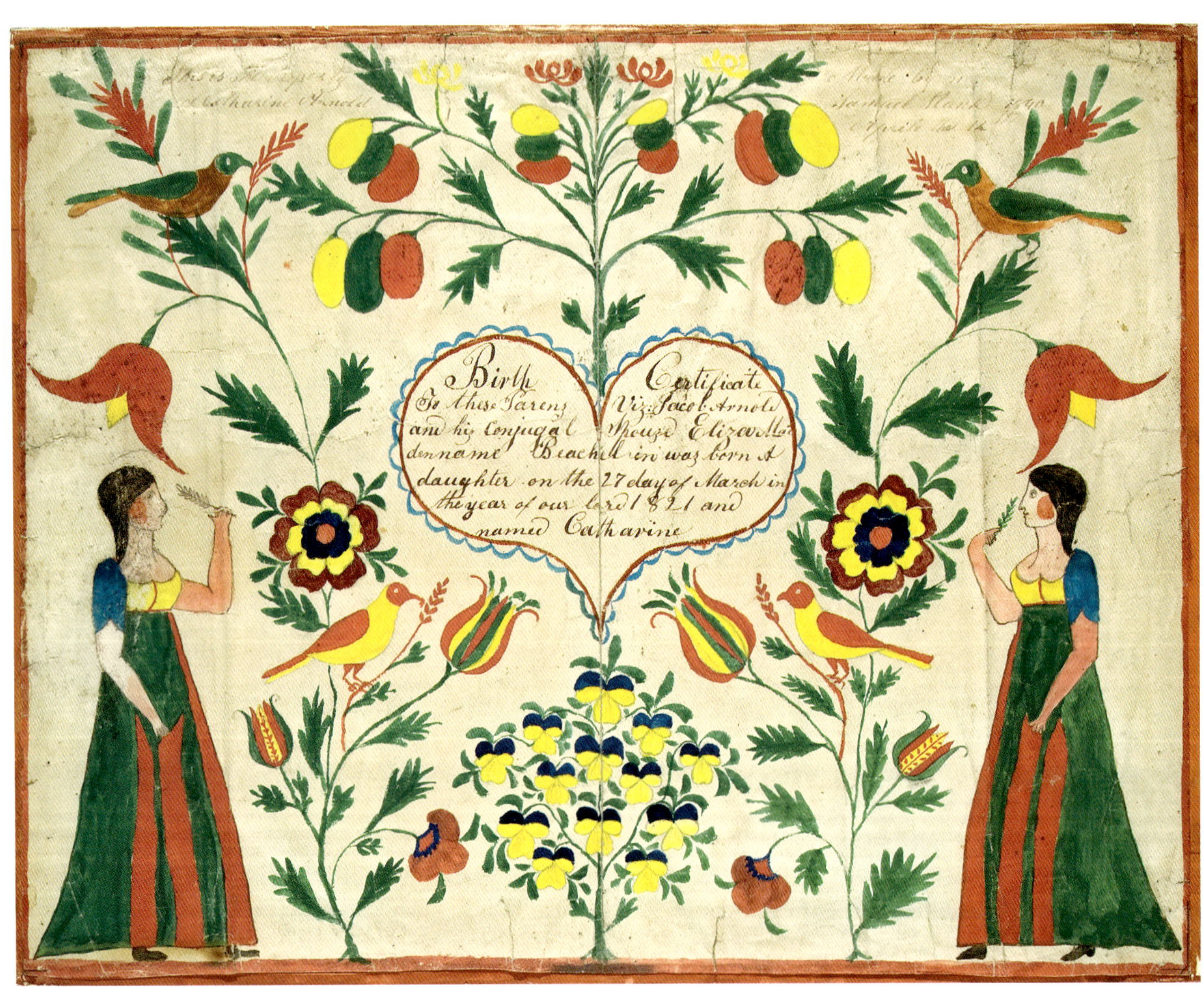

 Samuel Slank. *Birth Certificate*, 1840. // Plate. Tin-glazed earthenware.

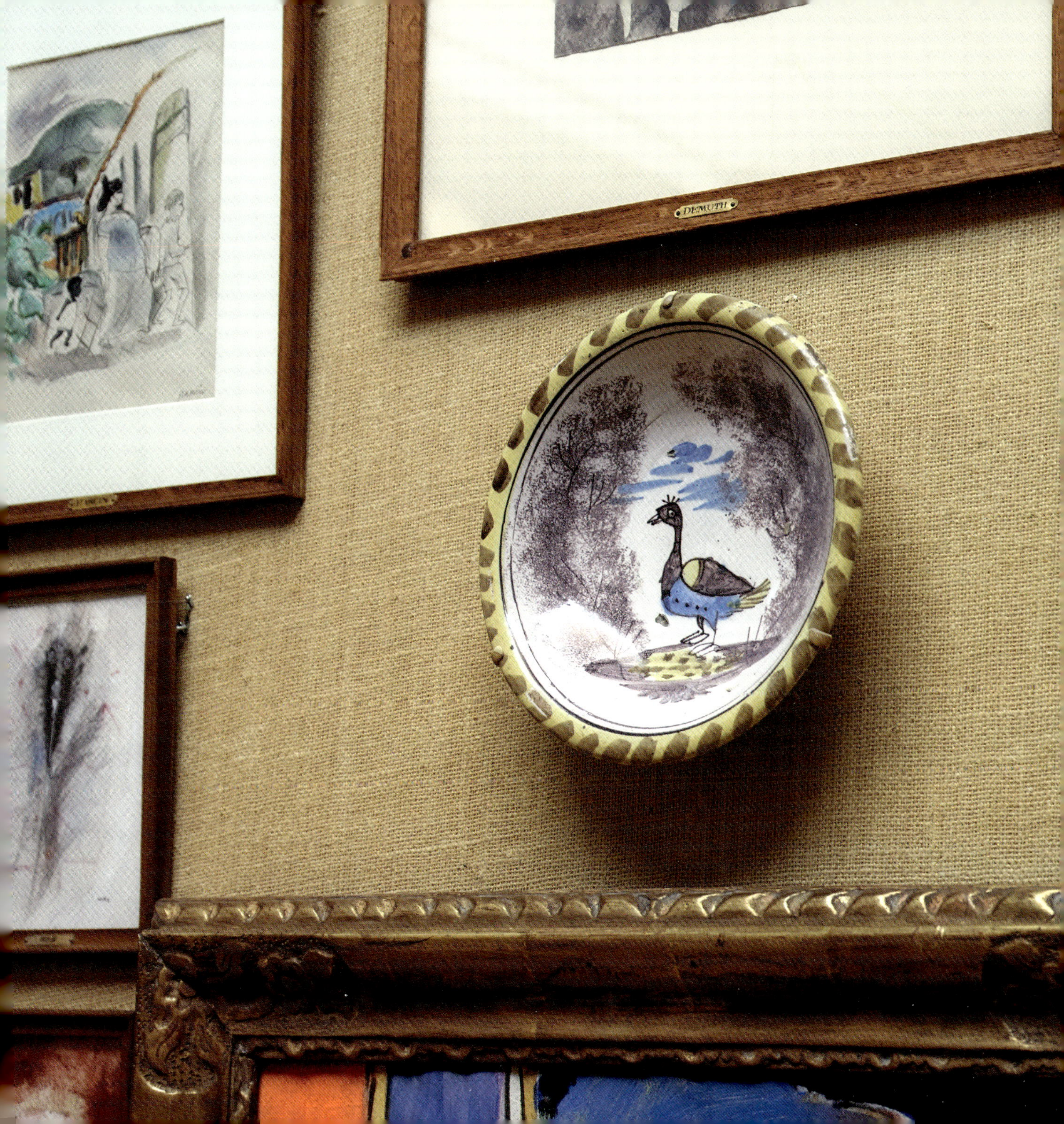
DEMUTH

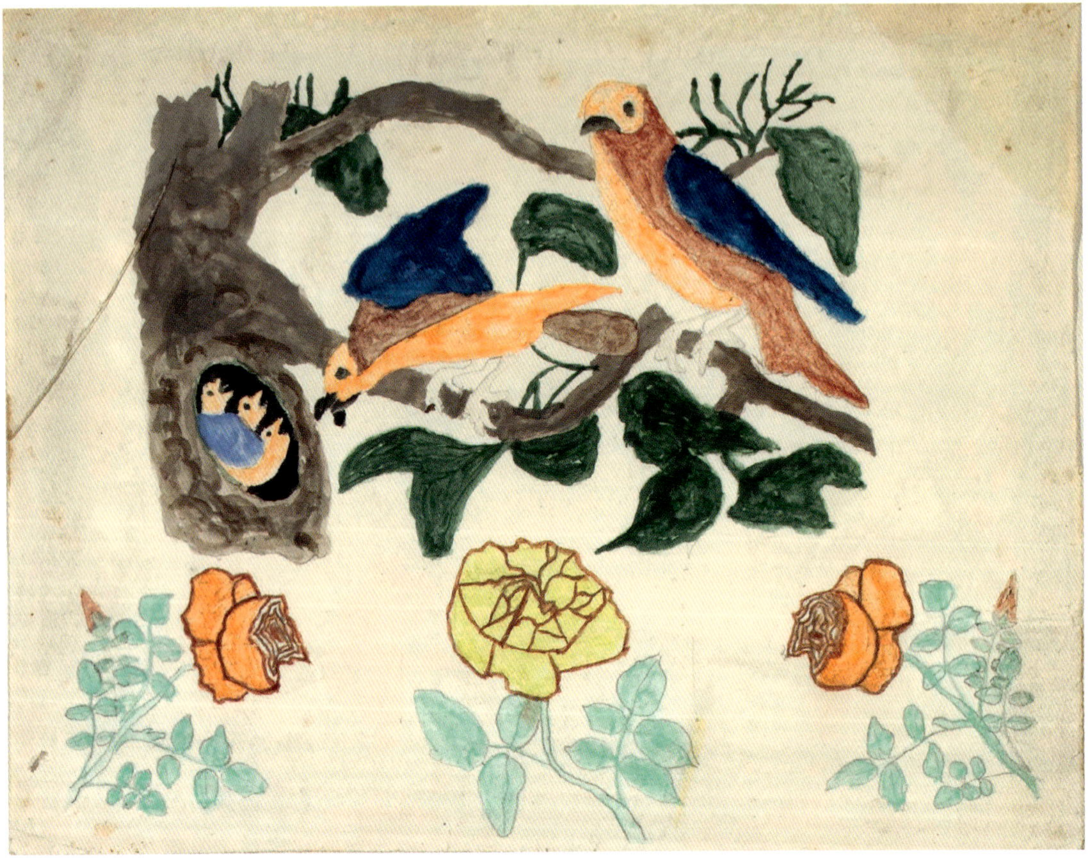

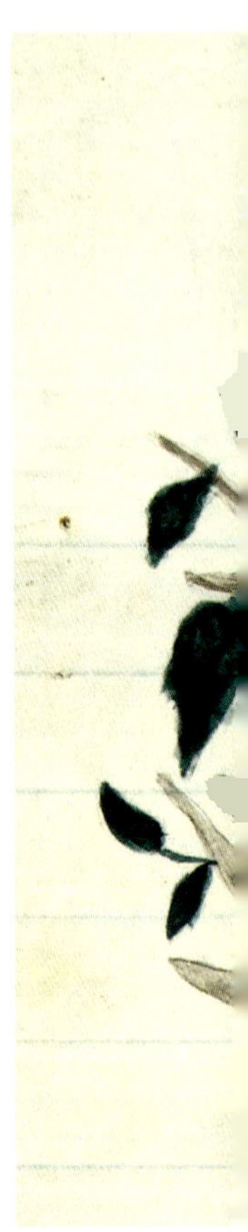

Three Roses and Bird's Family, 19th century.

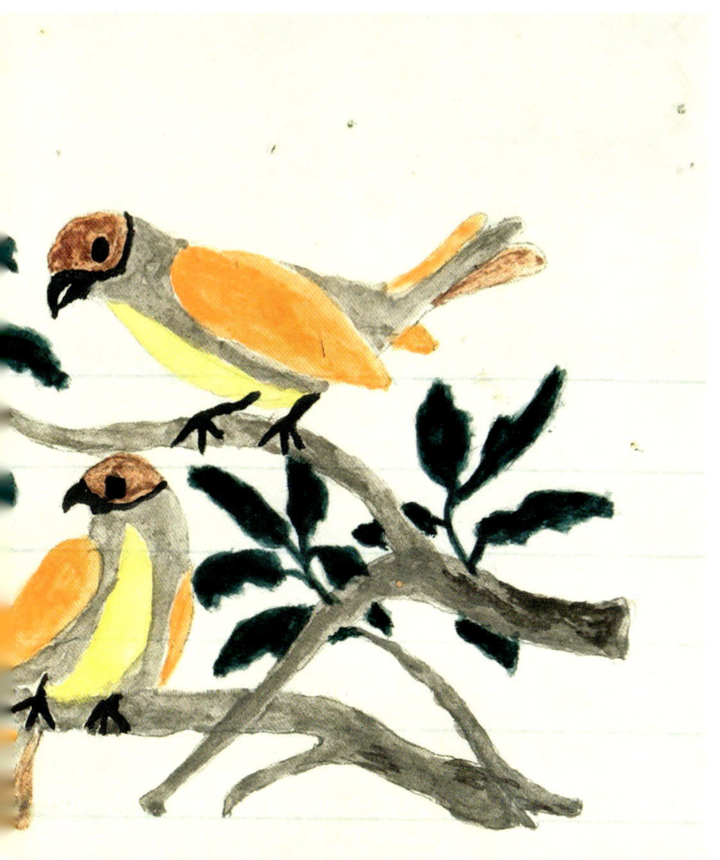

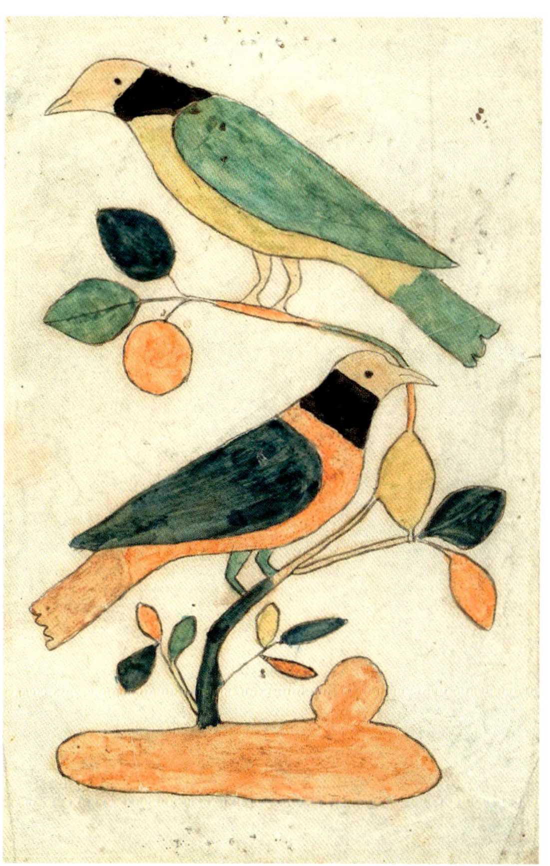

Two Birds, 19th century. // *Two Birds*, 19th century.

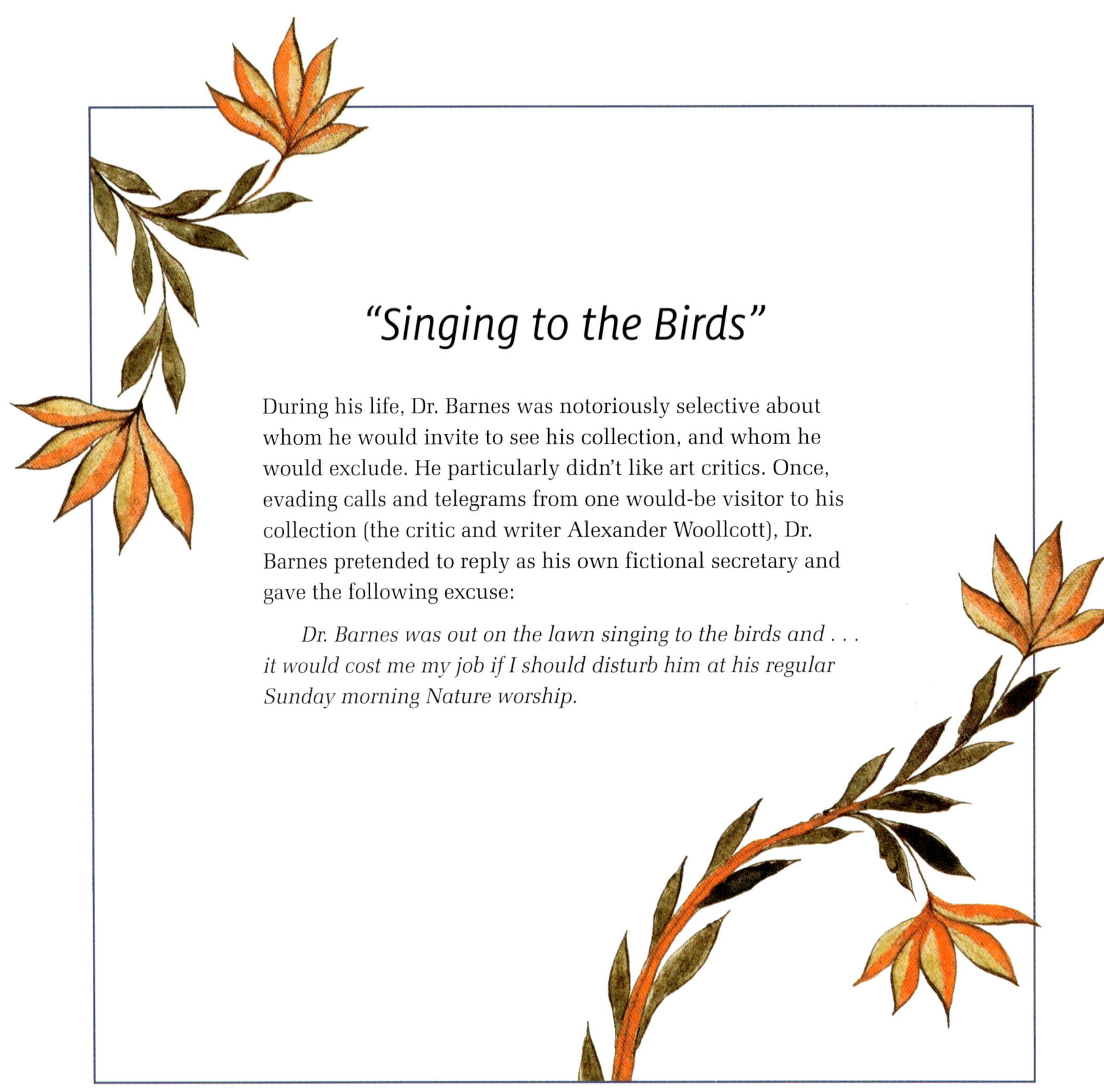

"Singing to the Birds"

During his life, Dr. Barnes was notoriously selective about whom he would invite to see his collection, and whom he would exclude. He particularly didn't like art critics. Once, evading calls and telegrams from one would-be visitor to his collection (the critic and writer Alexander Woollcott), Dr. Barnes pretended to reply as his own fictional secretary and gave the following excuse:

Dr. Barnes was out on the lawn singing to the birds and . . . it would cost me my job if I should disturb him at his regular Sunday morning Nature worship.

Bird Facing Left on Flowering Twig, 1882.

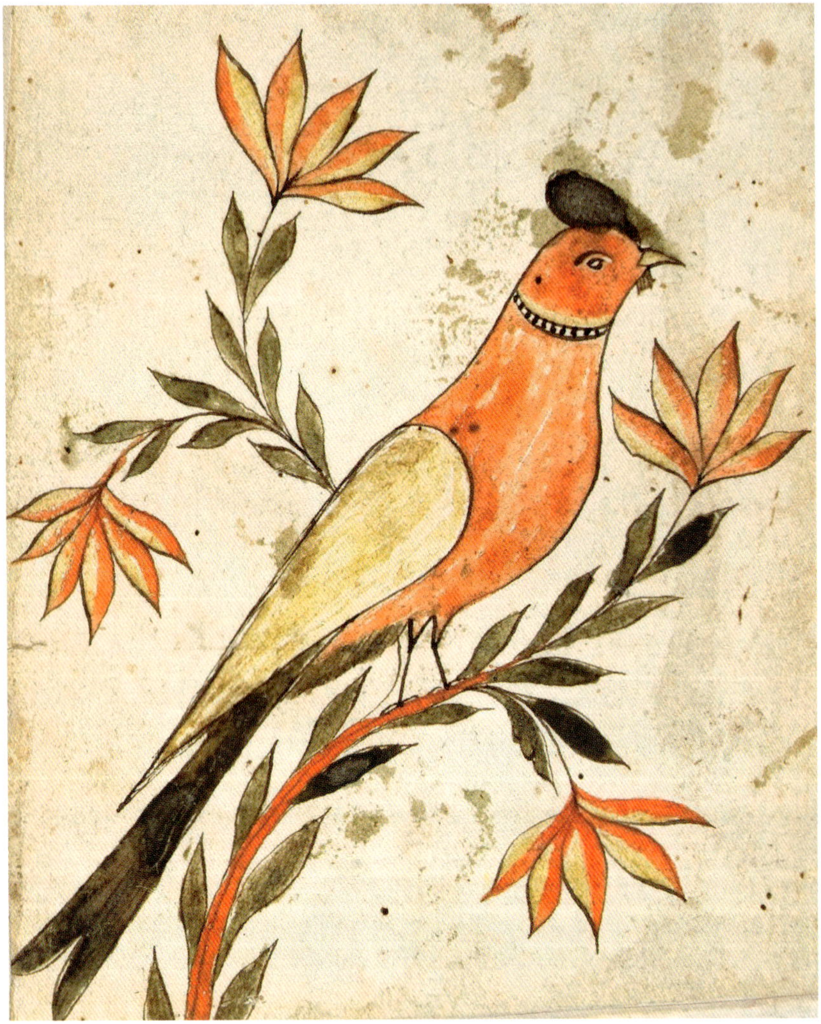

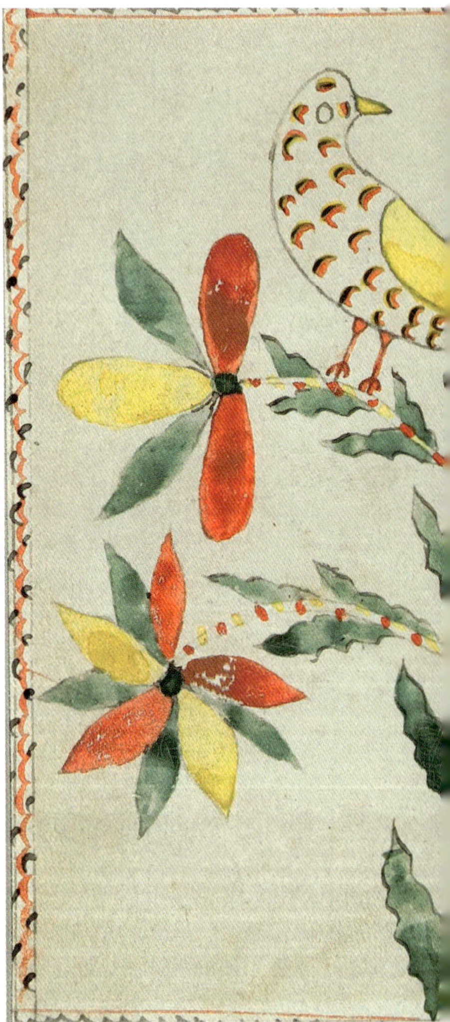

Bird Facing Right, 19th century.

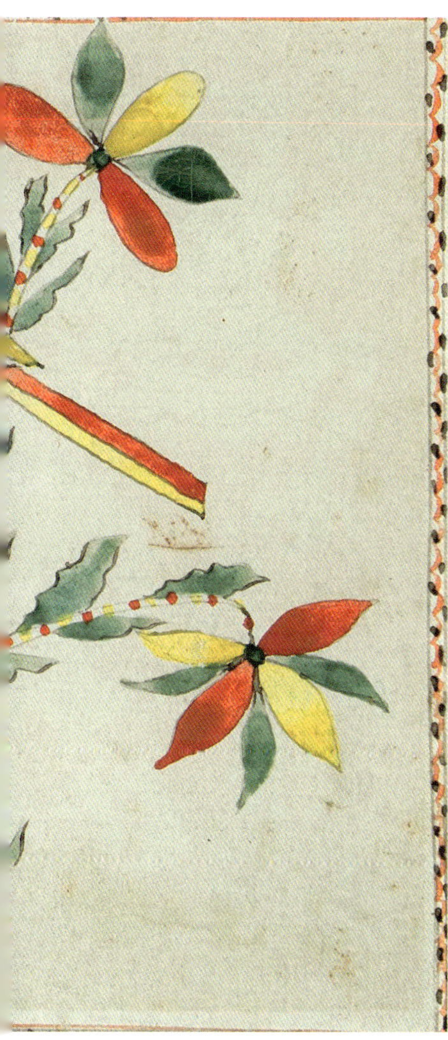

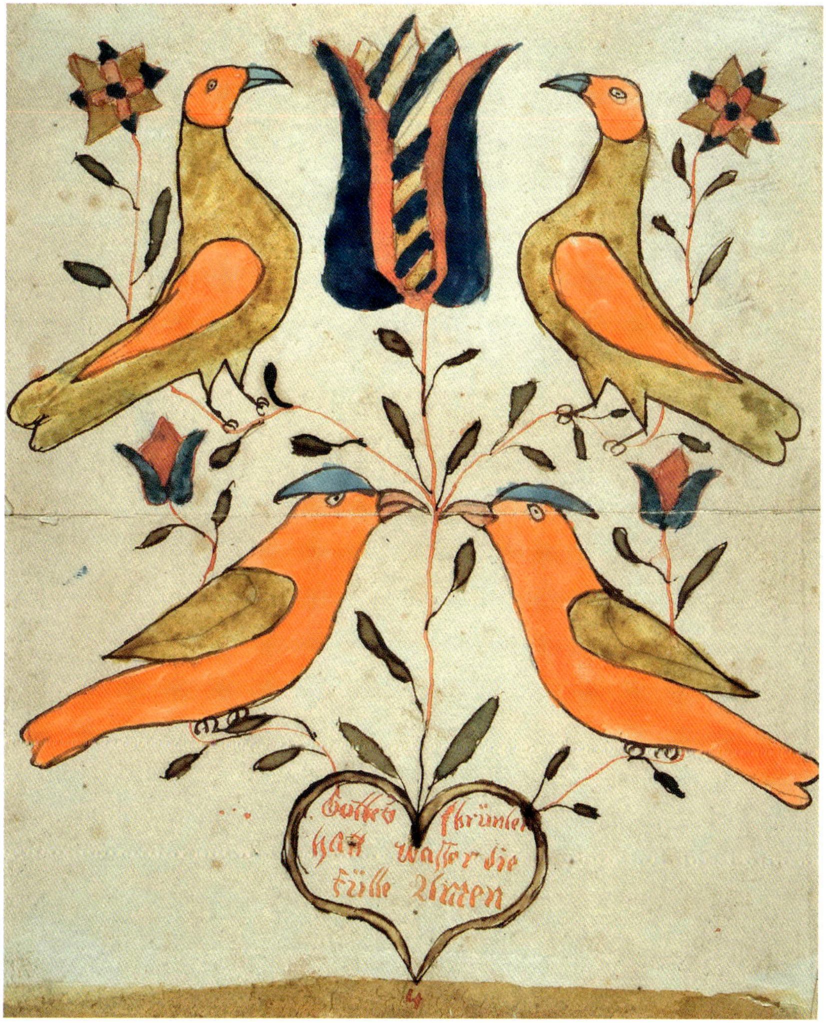

Tiny Yellow and Red Bird on Flowering Twig, 19th century. // *Four Birds, Tulip, and Heart*, 19th century.

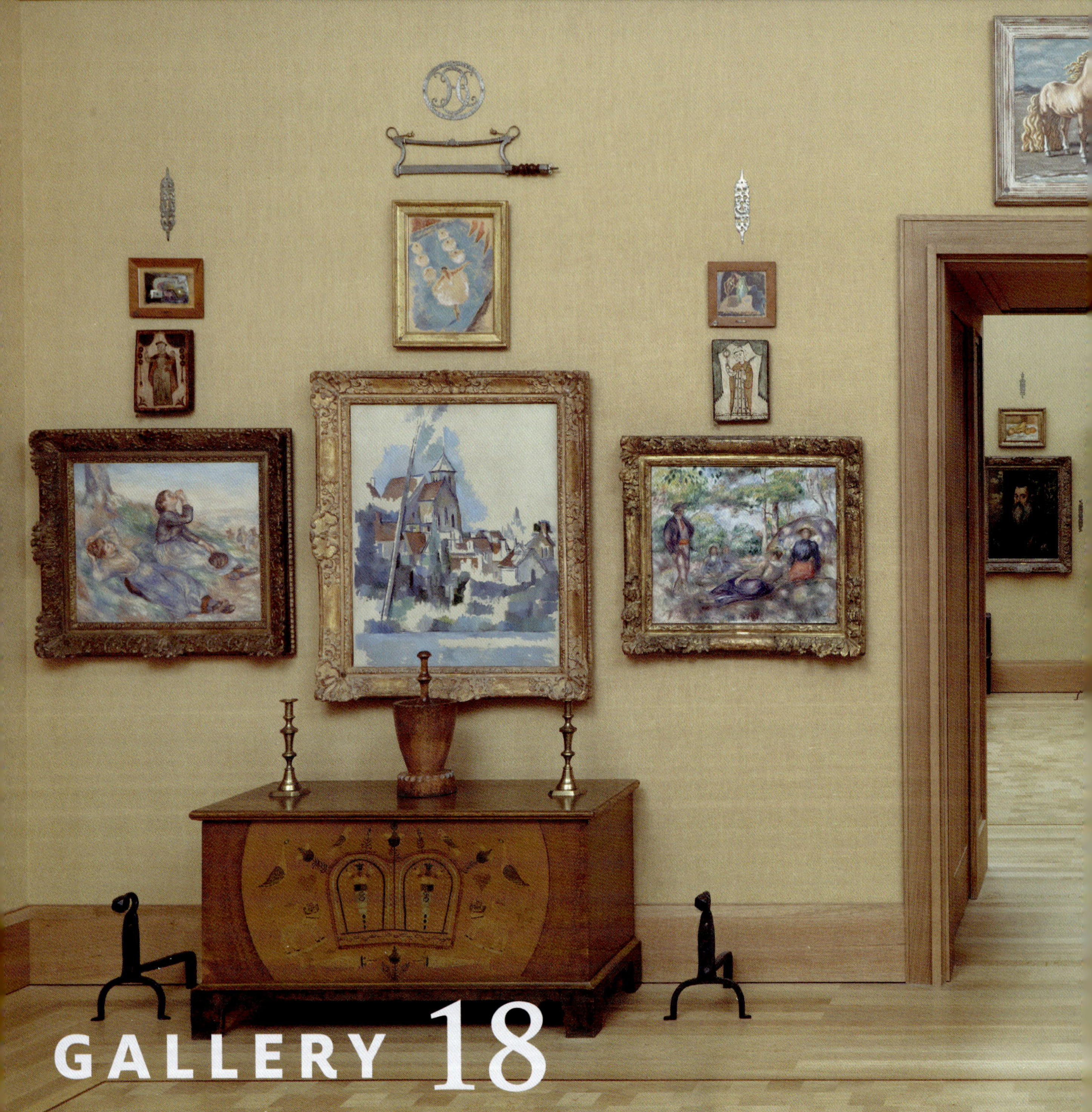

GALLERY 18

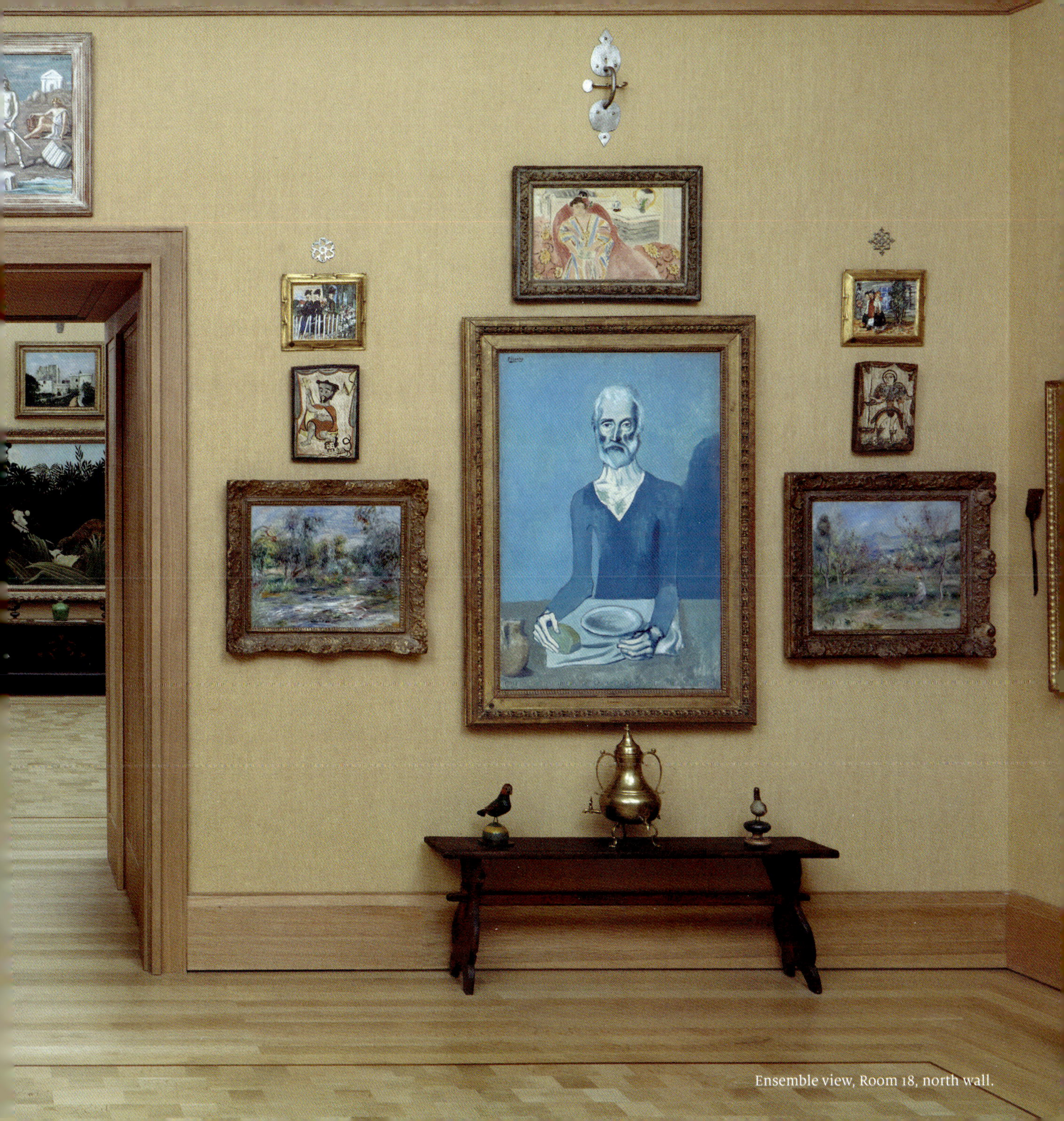

Ensemble view, Room 18, north wall.

Reflections and Repetitions

Gallery 18 holds two more carved wooden folk art birds, perched on a bench, similar to those in Gallery 14. These have distinctive shapes: one is a parrot and the other a goose. A careful investigation of the room reveals a pairing of these figures with a painted trunk at the same center position on the left side of the wall's ensemble: on the front of the trunk, long-necked geese flock together with birds with hooked, parrotlike bills. This symmetry indicates a playfulness on the part of Dr. Barnes, finding small similarities in objects to guide the placement of items within the rooms.

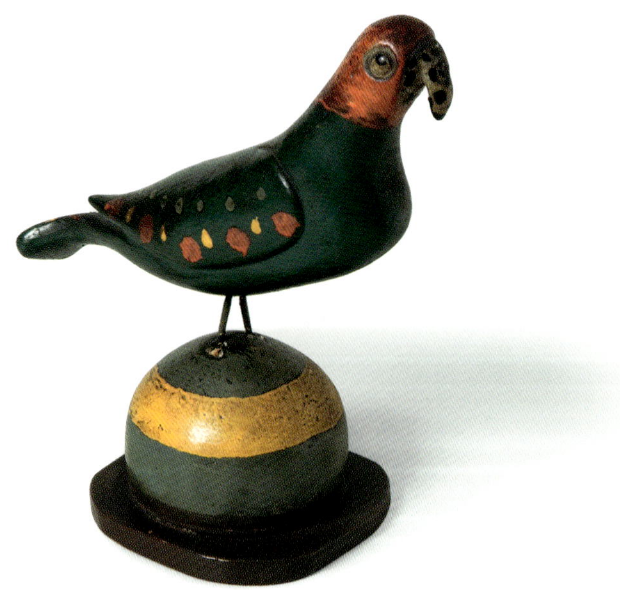

 Parrot, c. 1840.

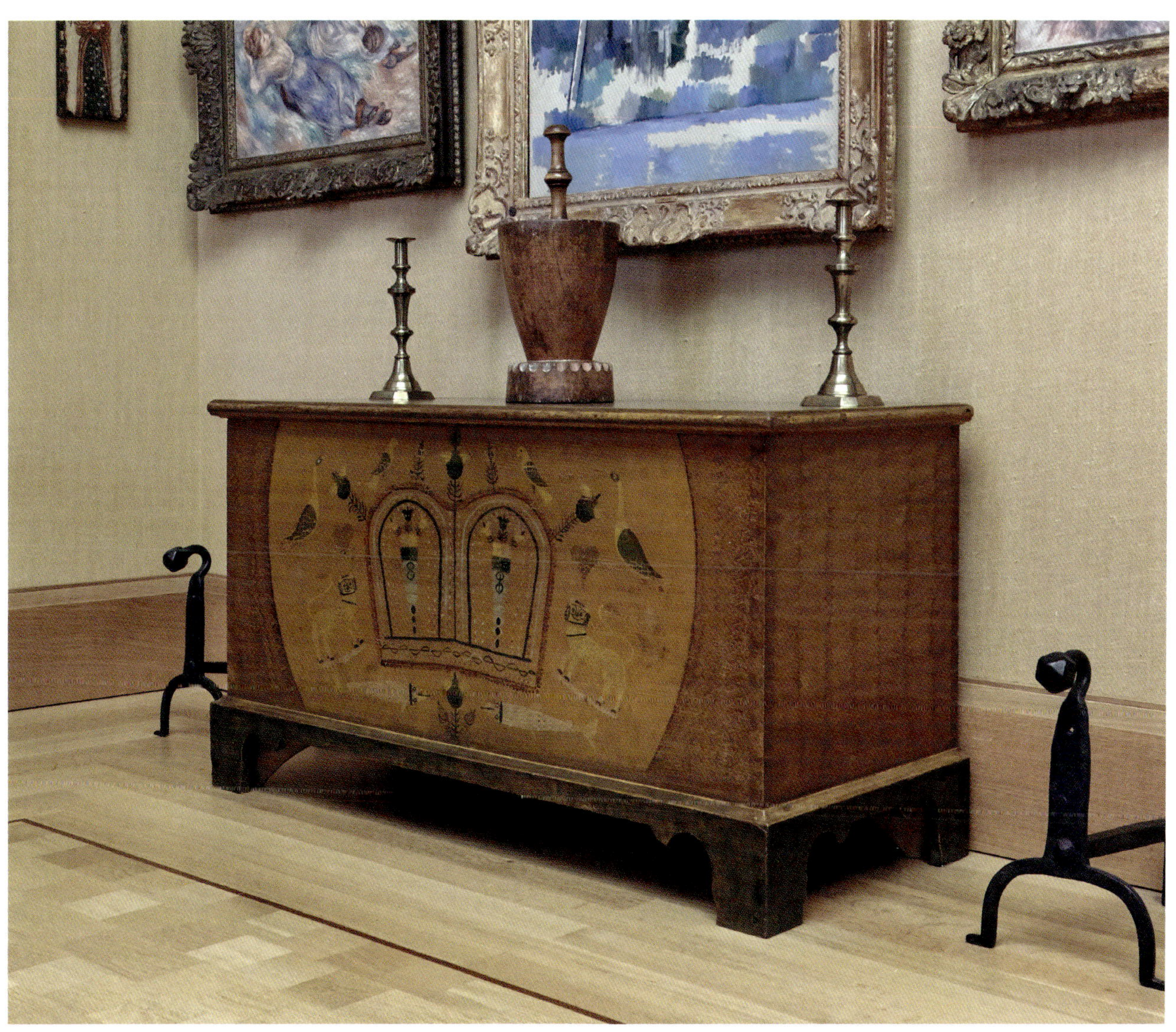

Chest, 18th century.

Additionally, through the doorway of this room, bracketed by these birds on either side, we look directly out on the wall of Gallery 14, the flock of birds, and the history lesson there. It's from this vantage point that Dr. Barnes leads us back to the traditions of art, even as we contemplate the Matisse and Picasso works shown in this room, continually connecting the past to the present.

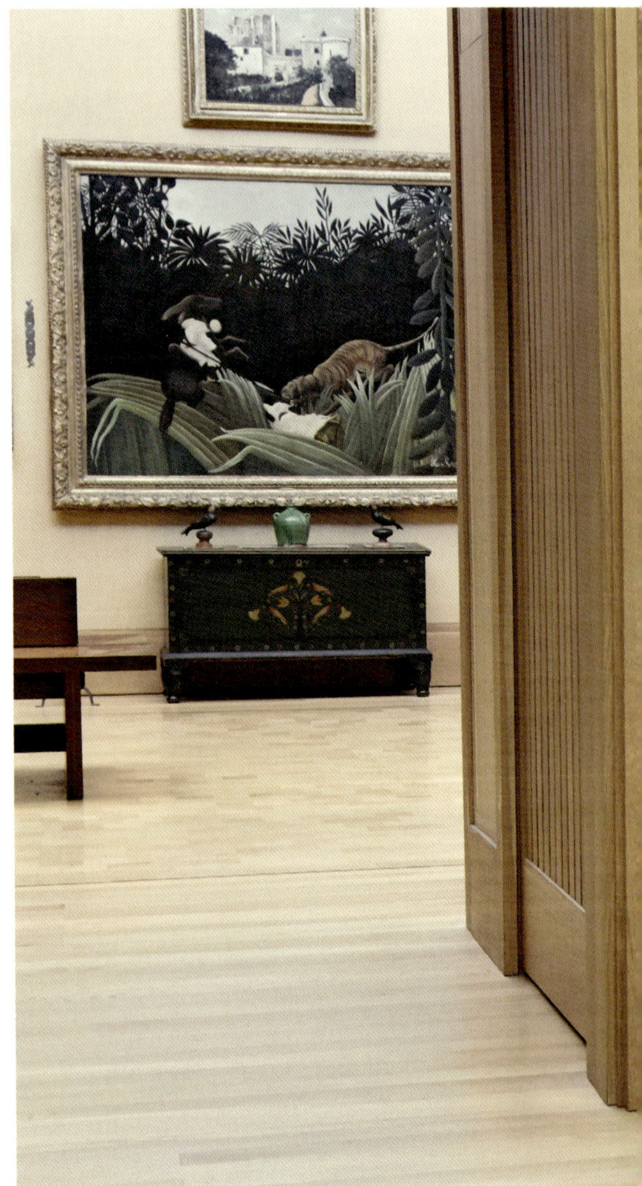

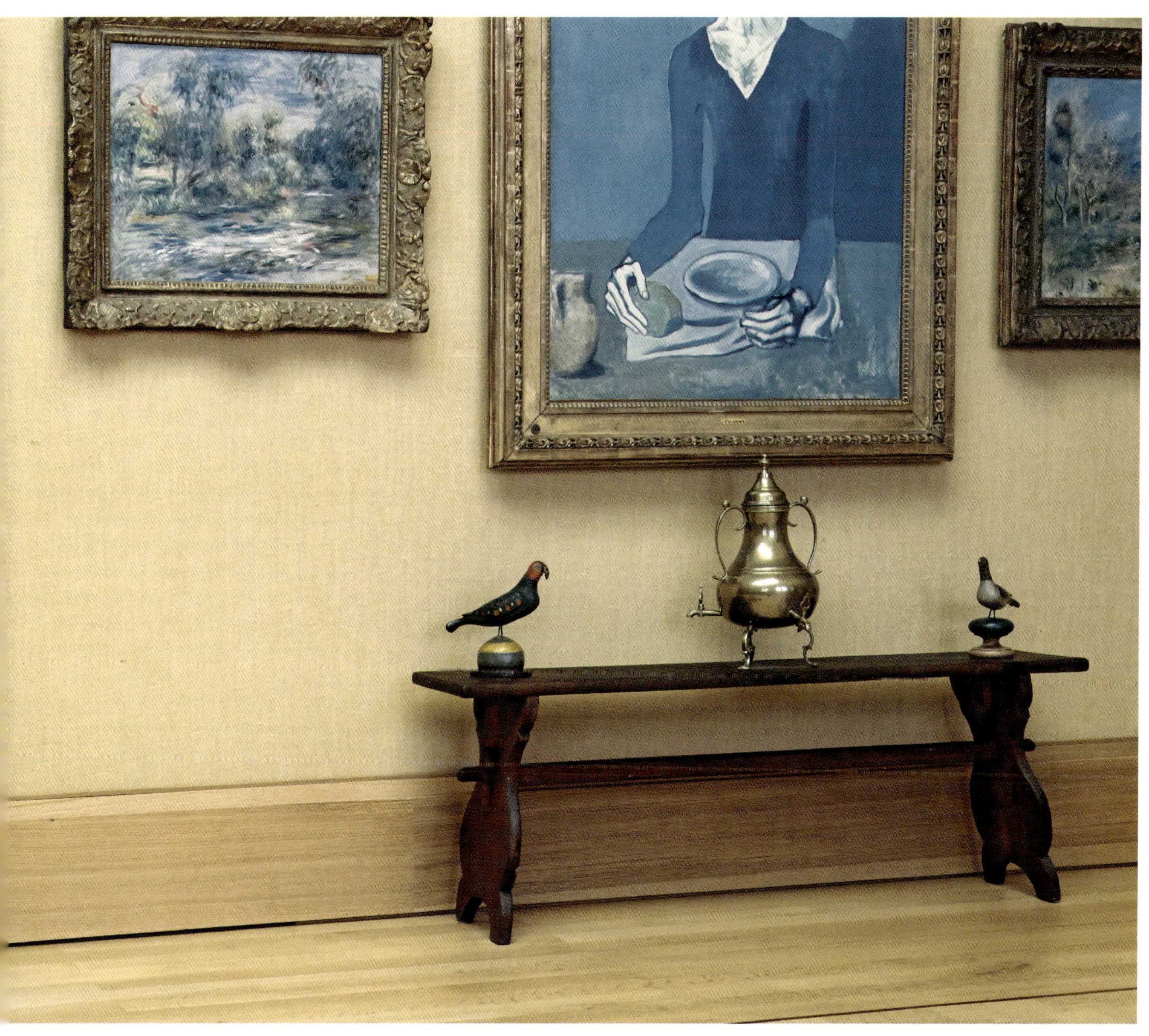

Ensemble view, Room 18, with Room 14 ensemble through doorway.

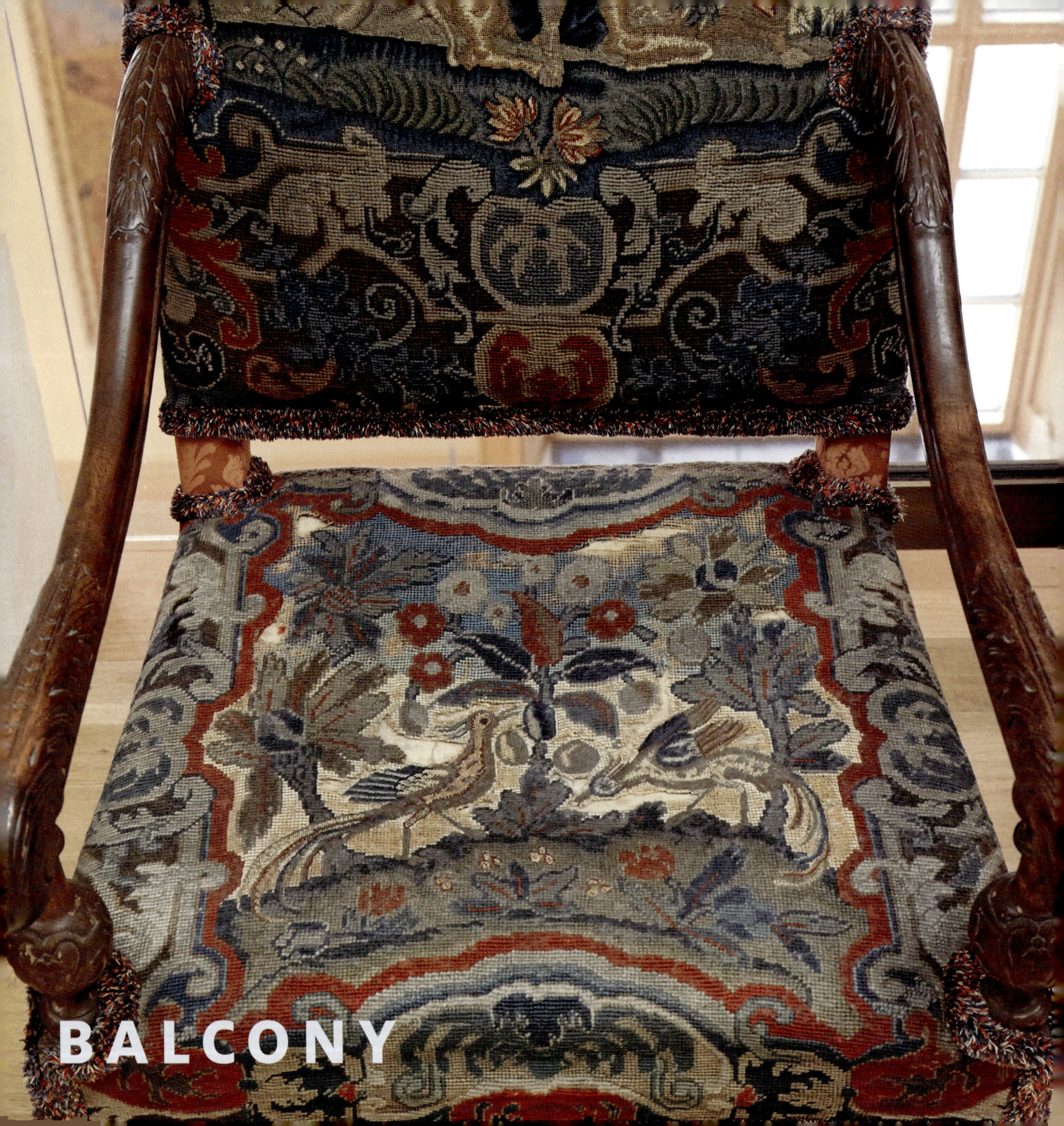
BALCONY

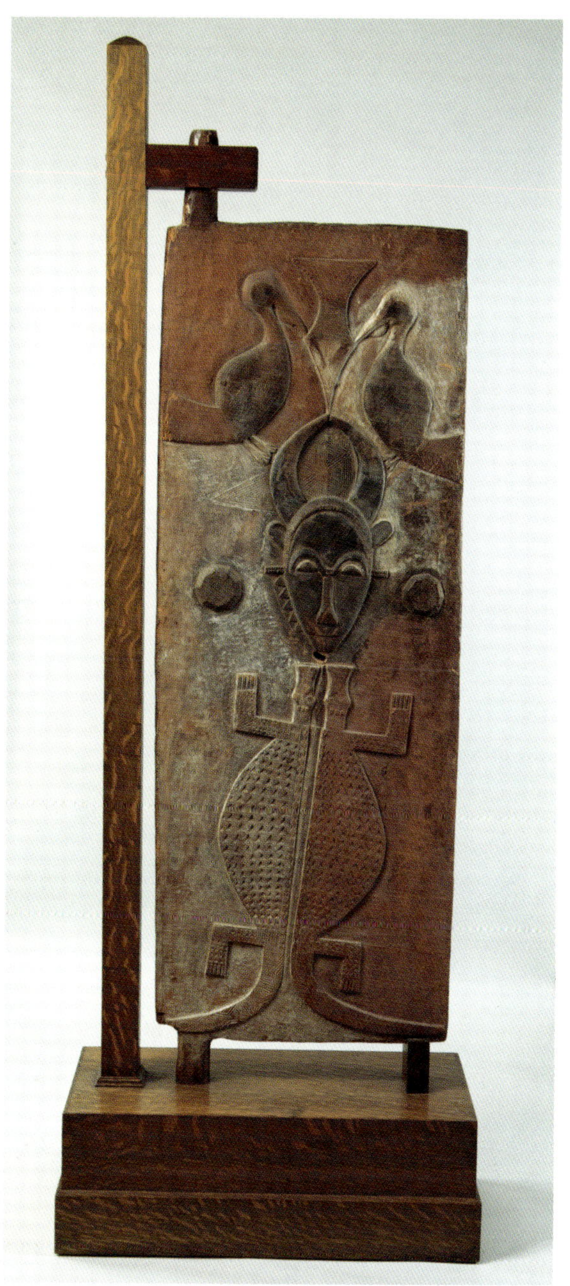

A Dividing Line

Between the two sides of the second floor, between Galleries 18 and 19, one crosses a balcony lined with English chairs upholstered in tapestry. The back of each chair shows a scene from classical mythology, while the seats are adorned with birds. The well-worn fabric shows the history of the chairs' functional service in the threadbare birds.

The balcony is punctuated halfway with a remarkable carved wooden door from the Baule people of western Africa, with a pair of elegant, incised birds.

Upholstered *Armchair*, late 19th–early 20th century, English. // *Door for an Inner Room*, late 19th Century.

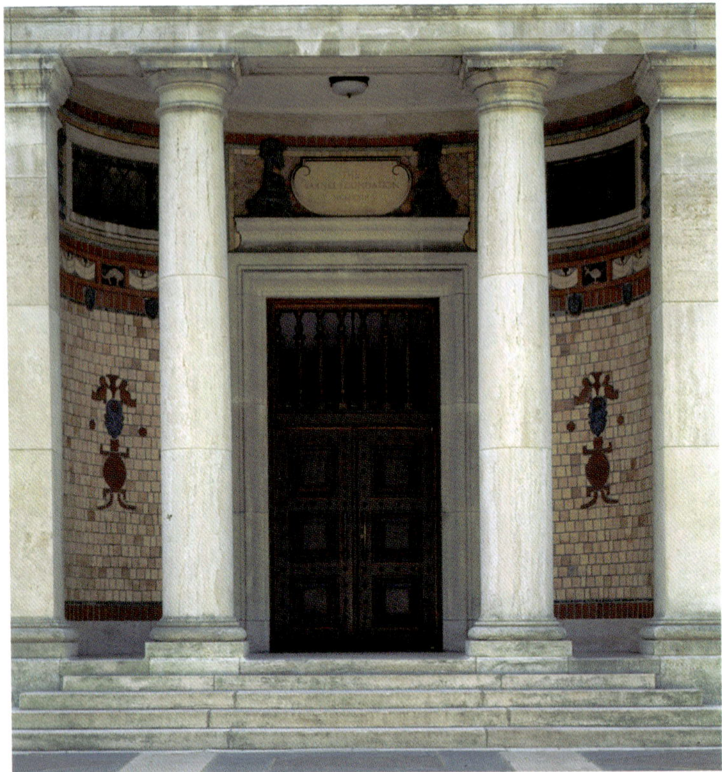

Dr. Barnes understood African art to be an essential influence of twentieth-century art. European painters such as Picasso and Modigliani collected wood carvings from Africa and incorporate design ideas from them into their own painting. Barnes was the first American collector to display African sculpture as fine art, rather than as anthropological artifact. Barnes found the wooden African sculptures he bought from the collector Paul Guillaume to express the formal elements he valued as clearly as European paintings.

Dr. Barnes not only placed this door with birds at the precise center point of his building, turned sideways to reveal both its figurative side and the abstract block pattern carved into its reverse, but he also commissioned this design to be prominently featured in tile work on the exterior of his original gallery building in Merion, Pennsylvania. This mask with birds on its head served as an emblem for the convergences of art (African and European, traditional and modern) that we encounter inside the galleries.

 Gallery door of Barnes Foundation building in Merion, Pennsylvania.

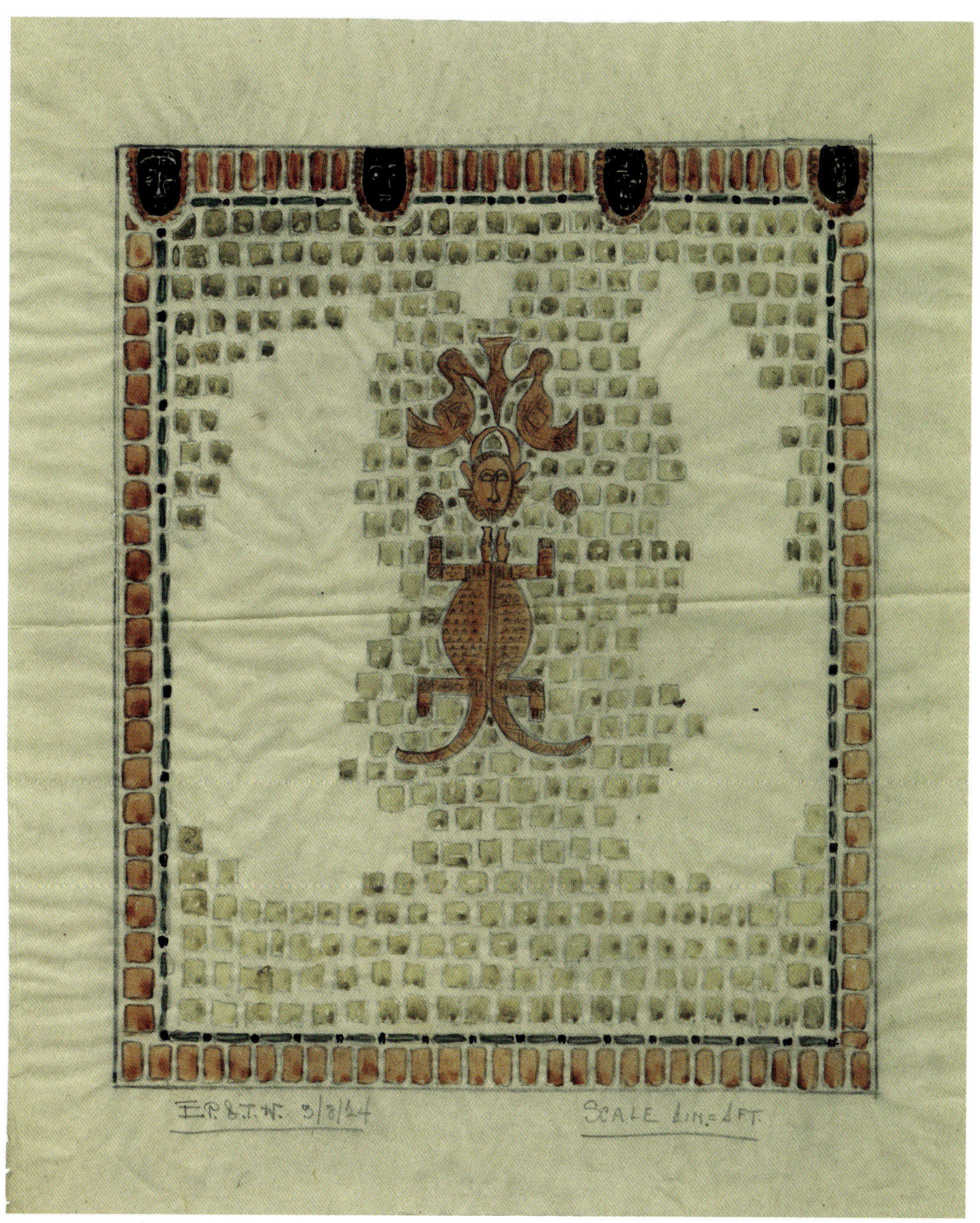

Design for Gallery portico by Enfield Pottery and Tile Works. // Following Pages: Native American pottery in the Barnes Foundation.

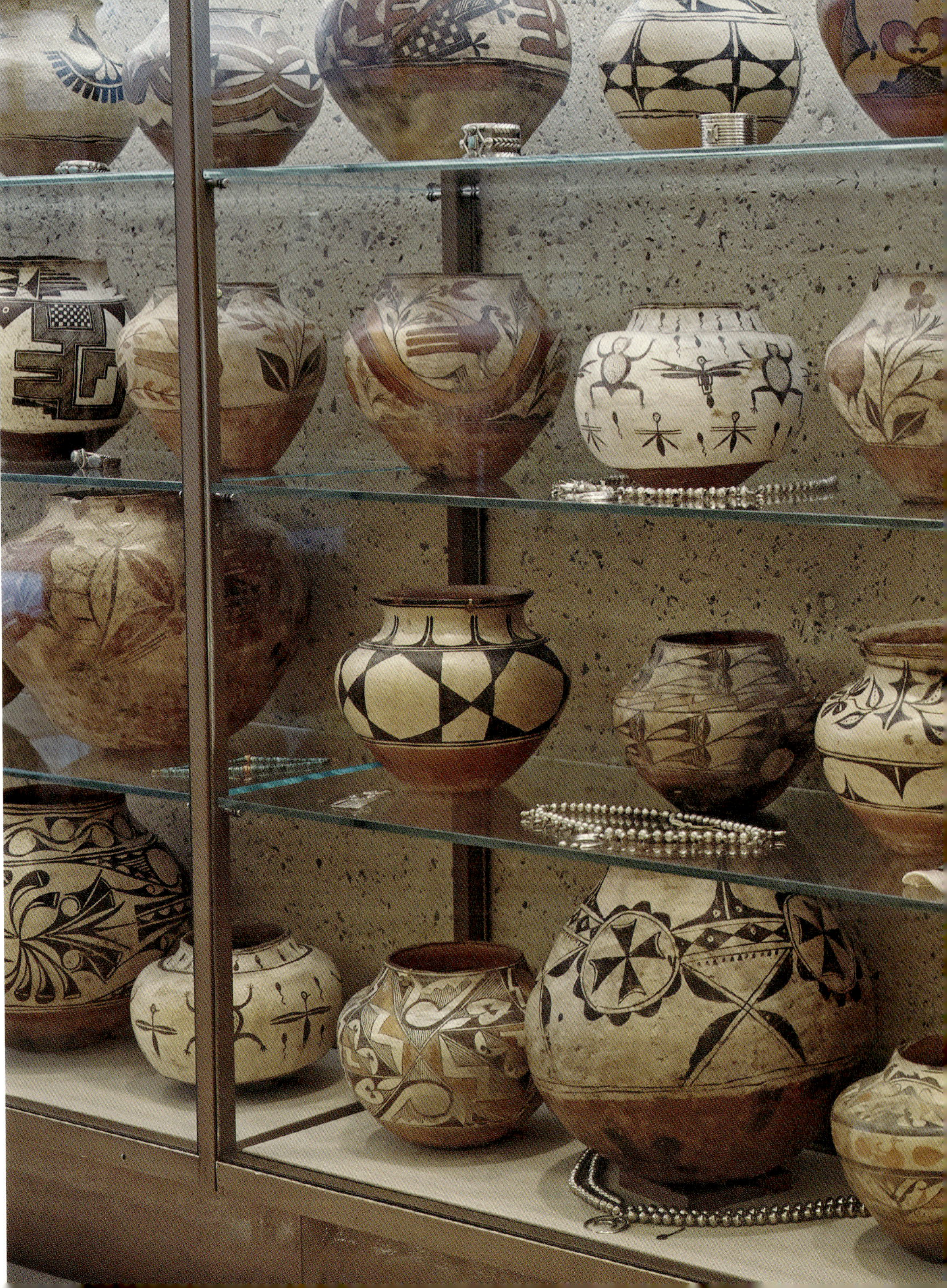

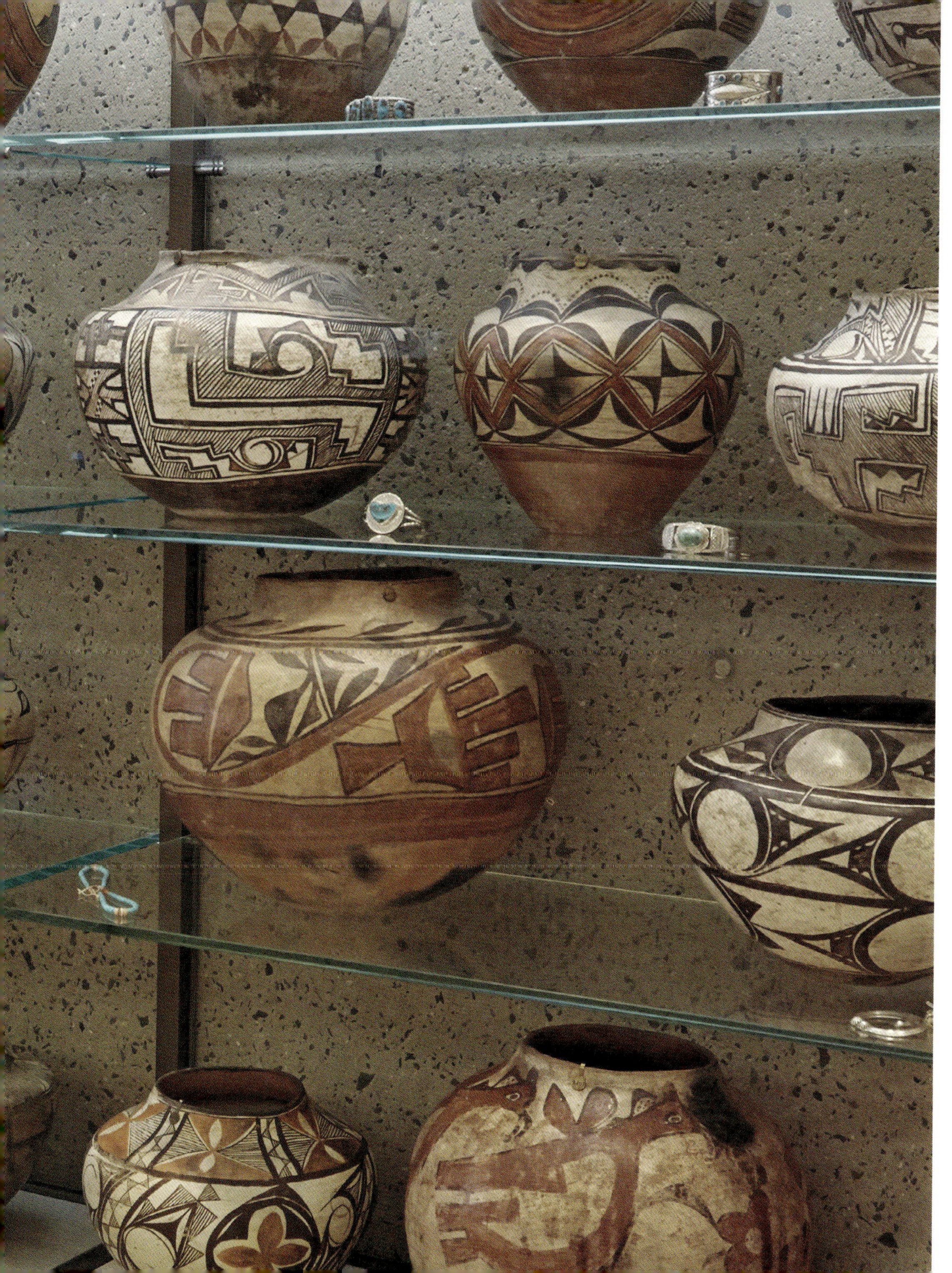

Native American Traditions

While the balcony spans the top floor of the collection and links the two symmetric halves of the building, another layer underlines the galleries from beneath: on the lower level of the collection stands a large display case well apart from everything else, filled with clay pots of various sizes.

In the winter of 1929–1930, Dr. Barnes and his wife, Laura Leggett Barnes, traveled to New Mexico for the benefit of her health. While Mrs. Barnes recuperated, Dr. Barnes explored and found new works from the American Southwest to bring home. He bought a vast array of pottery from the Santa Fe region of New Mexico, including large storage jars from the Zia, Old Domingo, Santa Ana, and Acoma people. These are hand-coiled pots, with designs applied in colored slips (clay thinned with water and brushed on like paint). A considerable number of these are decorated with birds, including chickens, ducks, pheasants, and the Zia bird (a roadrunner), which is a frequent motif on the pottery of the Zia Pueblo in New Mexico.

The bird and flower motifs on these pots recall the simple Pennsylvania German decorations in the preceding galleries, and Dr. Barnes's search for an American painting form that stands apart from European influence. The sheer volume of pottery, jewelry, rugs, and other pieces that he bought while on this brief sojourn to the Southwest indicates his delight on this encounter with Native American artwork. We can imagine him exuberantly embracing this undeniable "distinctively American form of painting" that he had been looking for, as he selected each of these pots with their expressive birds.

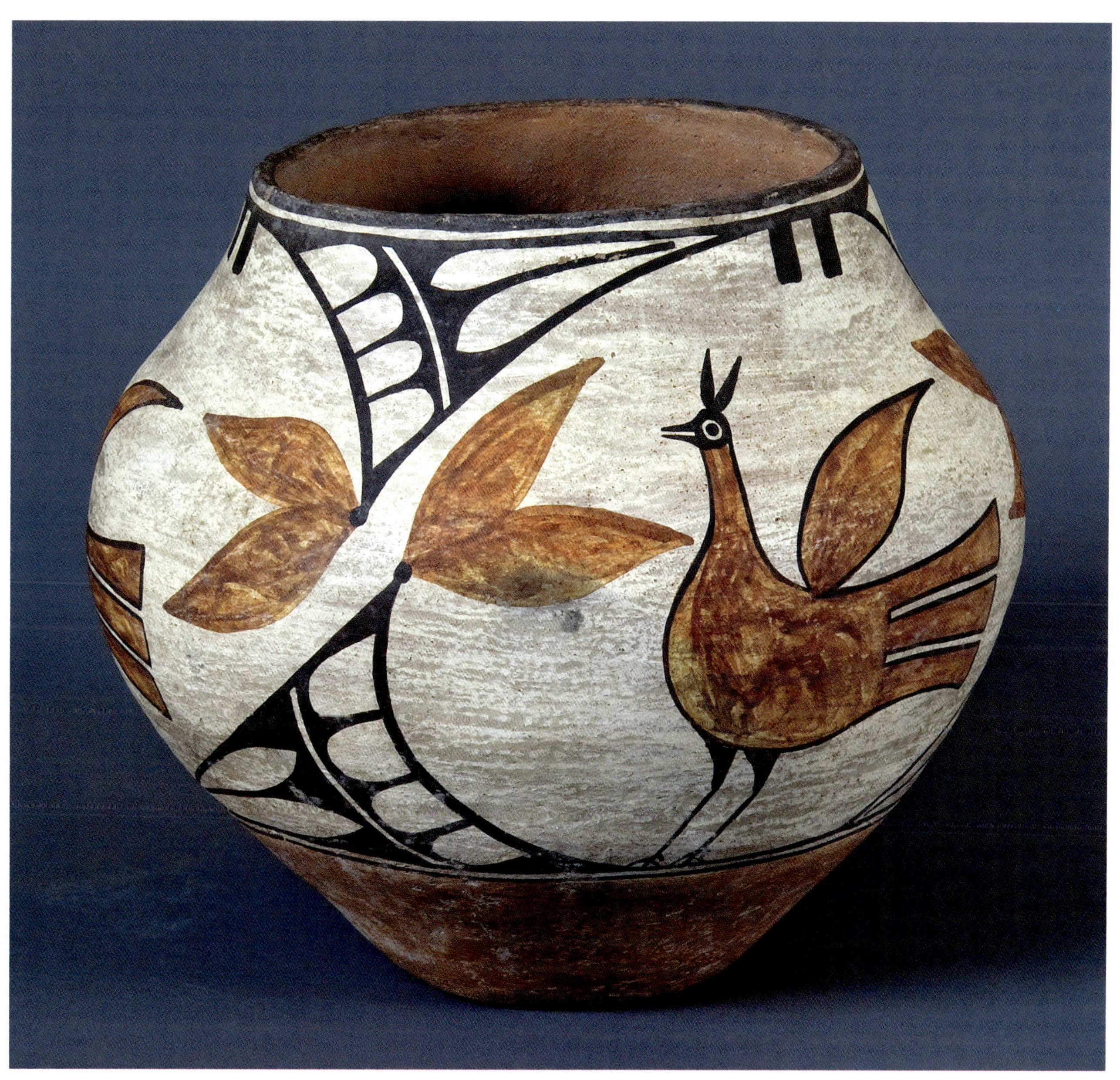

Water Jar, c. 1915–1920, Zia Pueblo.

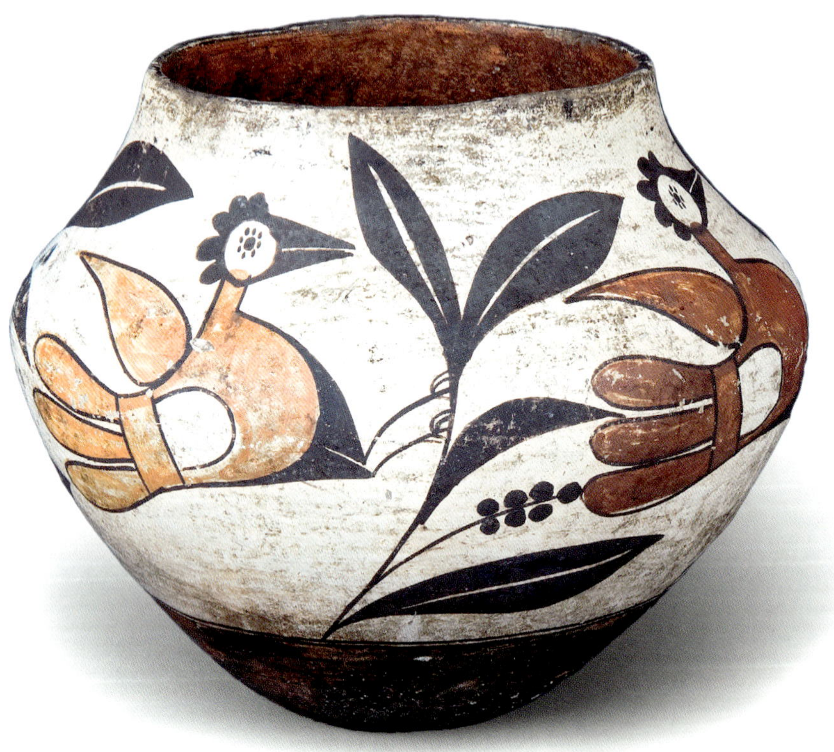

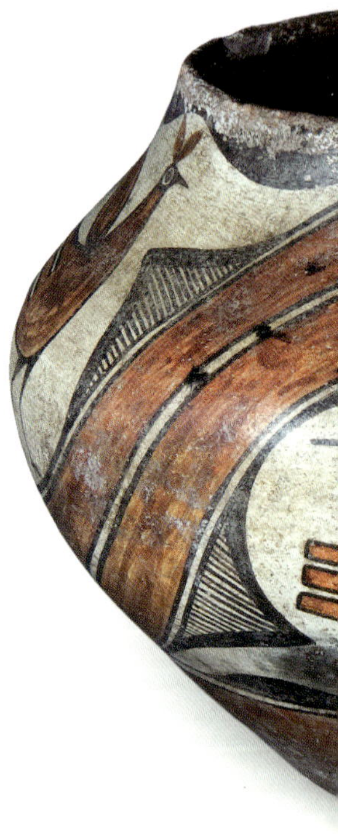

 Water Jar, c. 1885–1890, Acoma Pueblo.

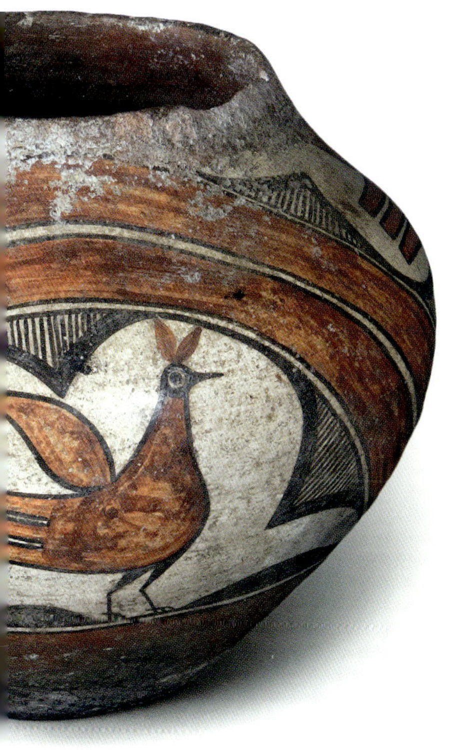

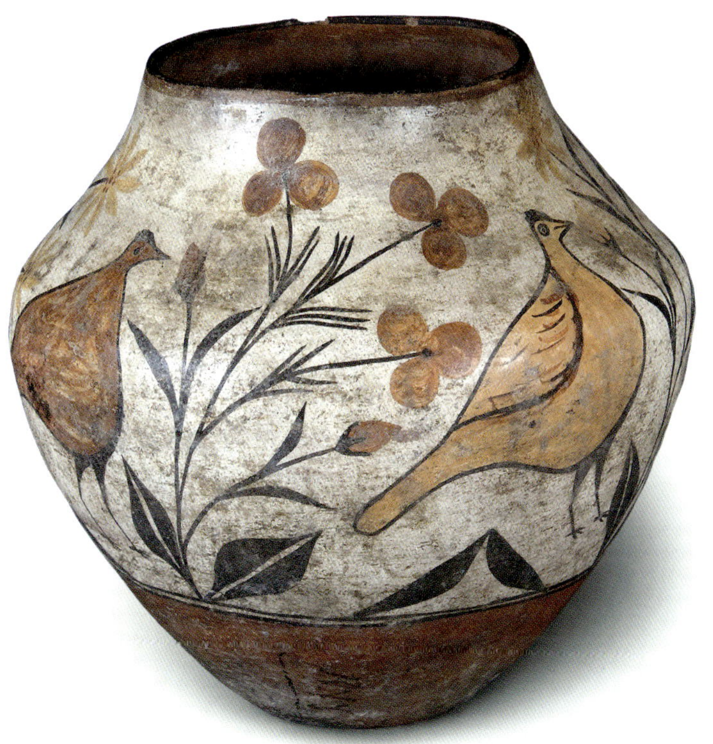

Water Jar, c. 1900–1910, Zia Pueblo. // Water Jar, c. 1890–1900, Zia Pueblo.

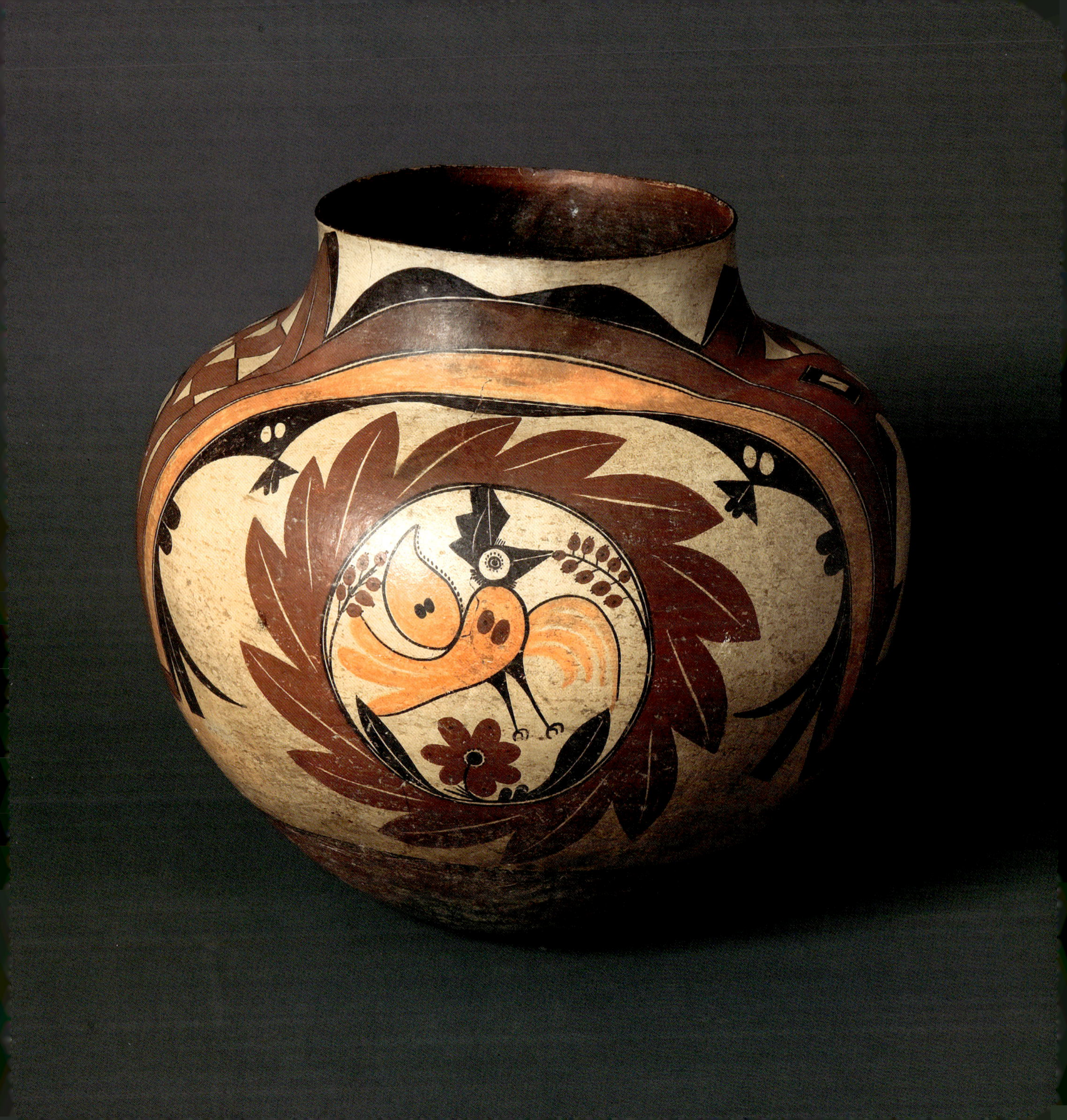

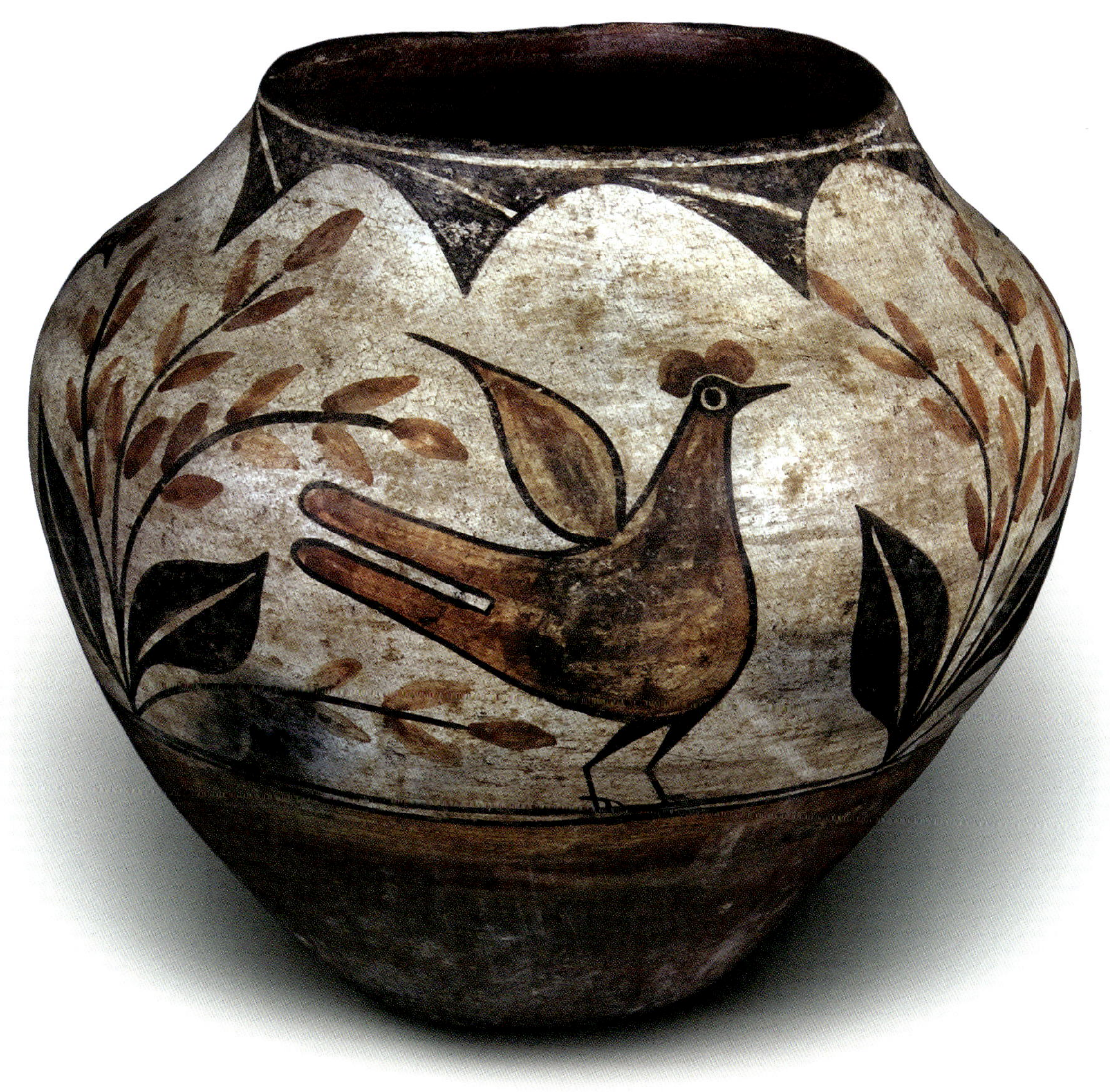

Attributed to Acoma Mary (Mary Histia). Storage Jar, c. 1900, Acoma Pueblo. // Water Jar, c. 1900–1910, Zia Pueblo.

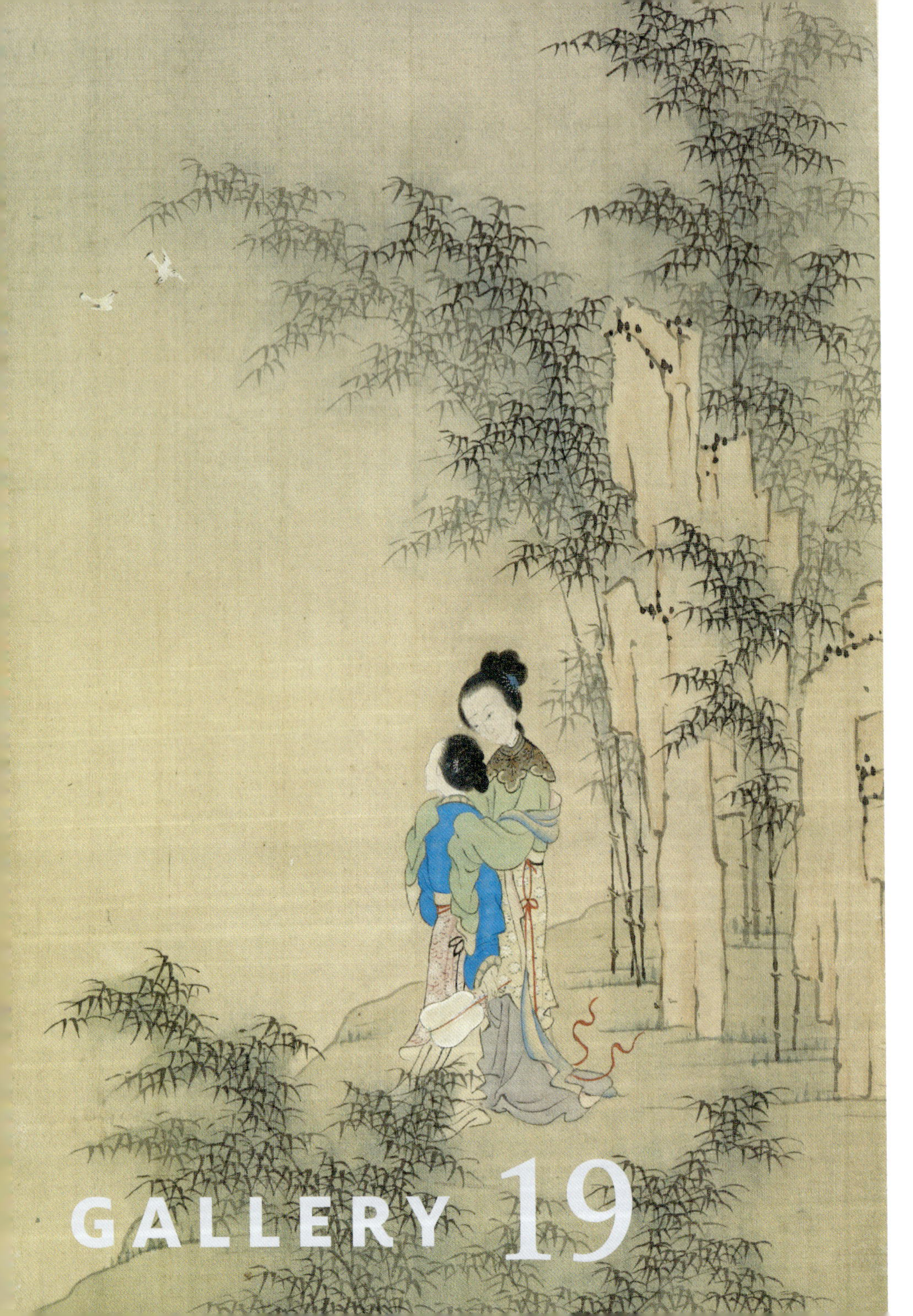
GALLERY 19

Size and Scale

Gallery 19 is a large, bright and spacious room, filled with some of the largest paintings: works by Matisse, Modigliani, Soutine, and Picasso. However, it is also home to some of the tiniest birds in the collection: a small Chinese silk painting shows miniscule white songbirds fluttering in the greenery above a pair of figures. Though diminutive, the meticulous details of their coloring and form show keen attentiveness on the part of the painter.

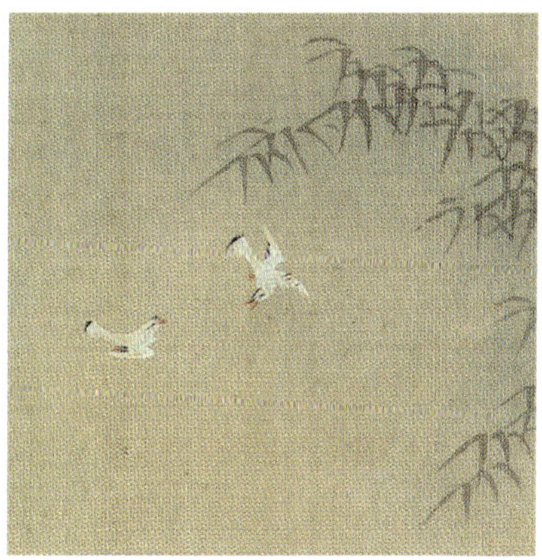

After Qiu Ying. *Two Figures Embracing in Landscape*, late 19th century.

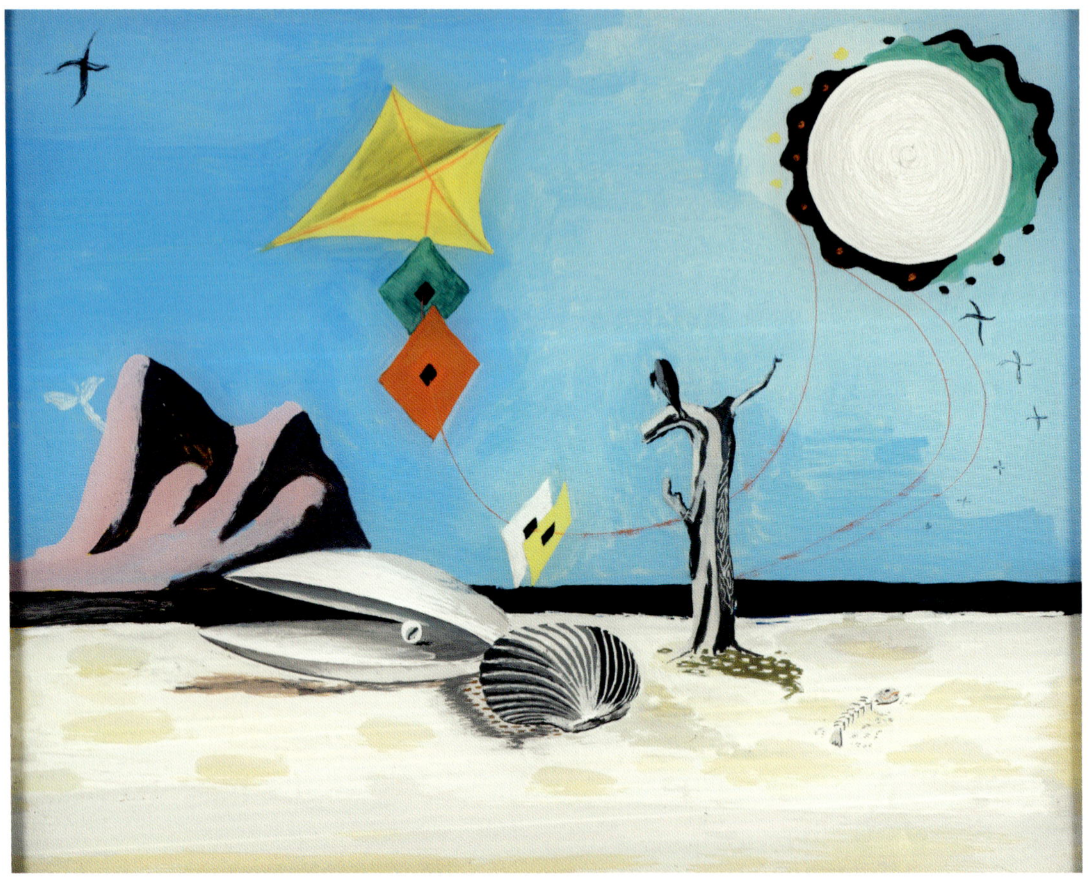

Small, too, are the birdlike marks in Angelo Pinto's beach scene and *Icarus* on the same wall. Pinto was a Philadelphia artist who began as a Barnes student but eventually became a close friend of the collector. Icarus, depicted here, was the character from Greek mythology who contrived wings of wax and feathers, but he flew too close to the sun and tumbled to the ground when the sun melted the wax. While not strictly a bird, his appearance here harmonizes with the other tiny birds in this large and lively gallery.

 Angelo Pinto. *Seashells*, c. 1944.

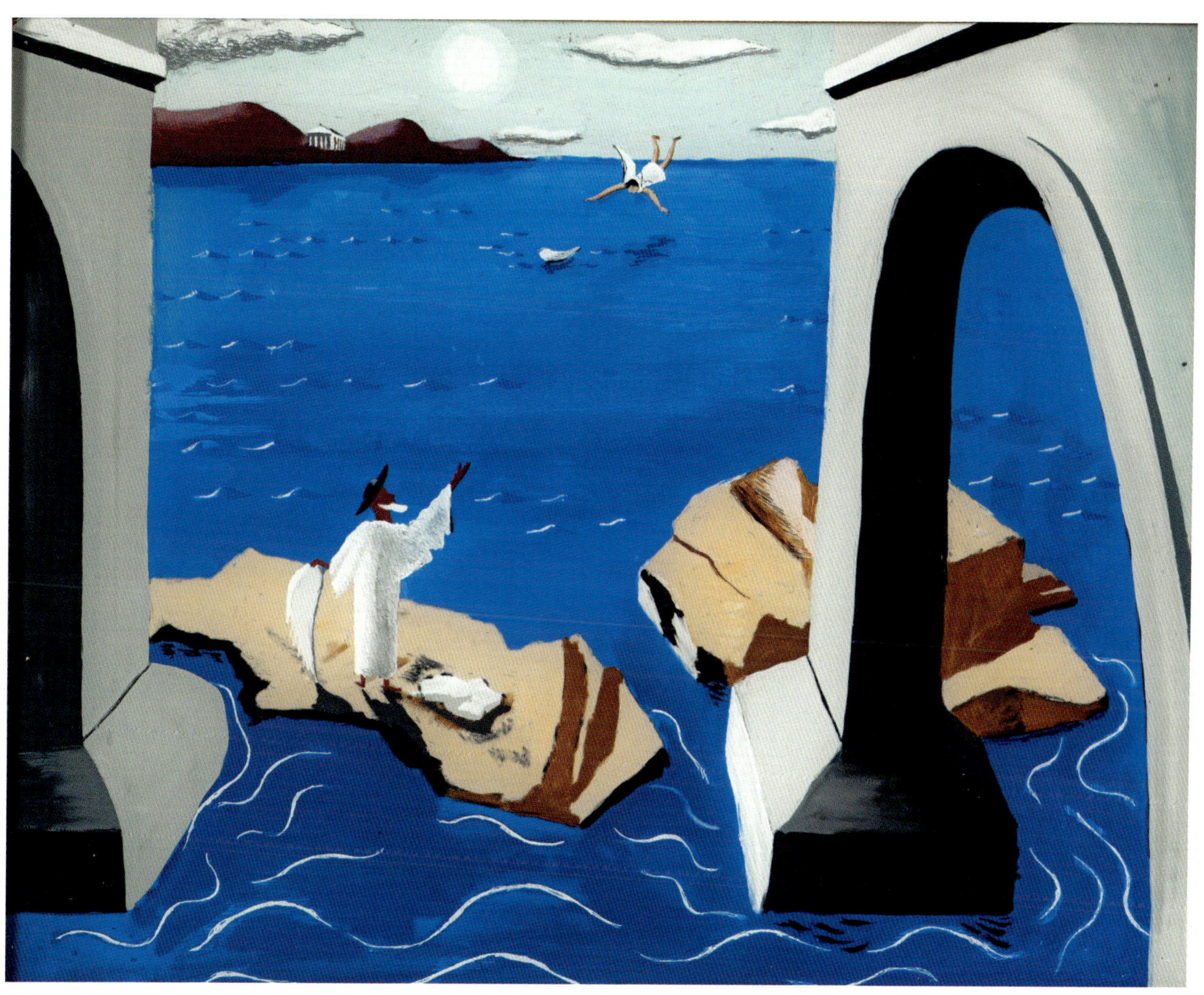

Angelo Pinto. *Icarus*, c. 1944.

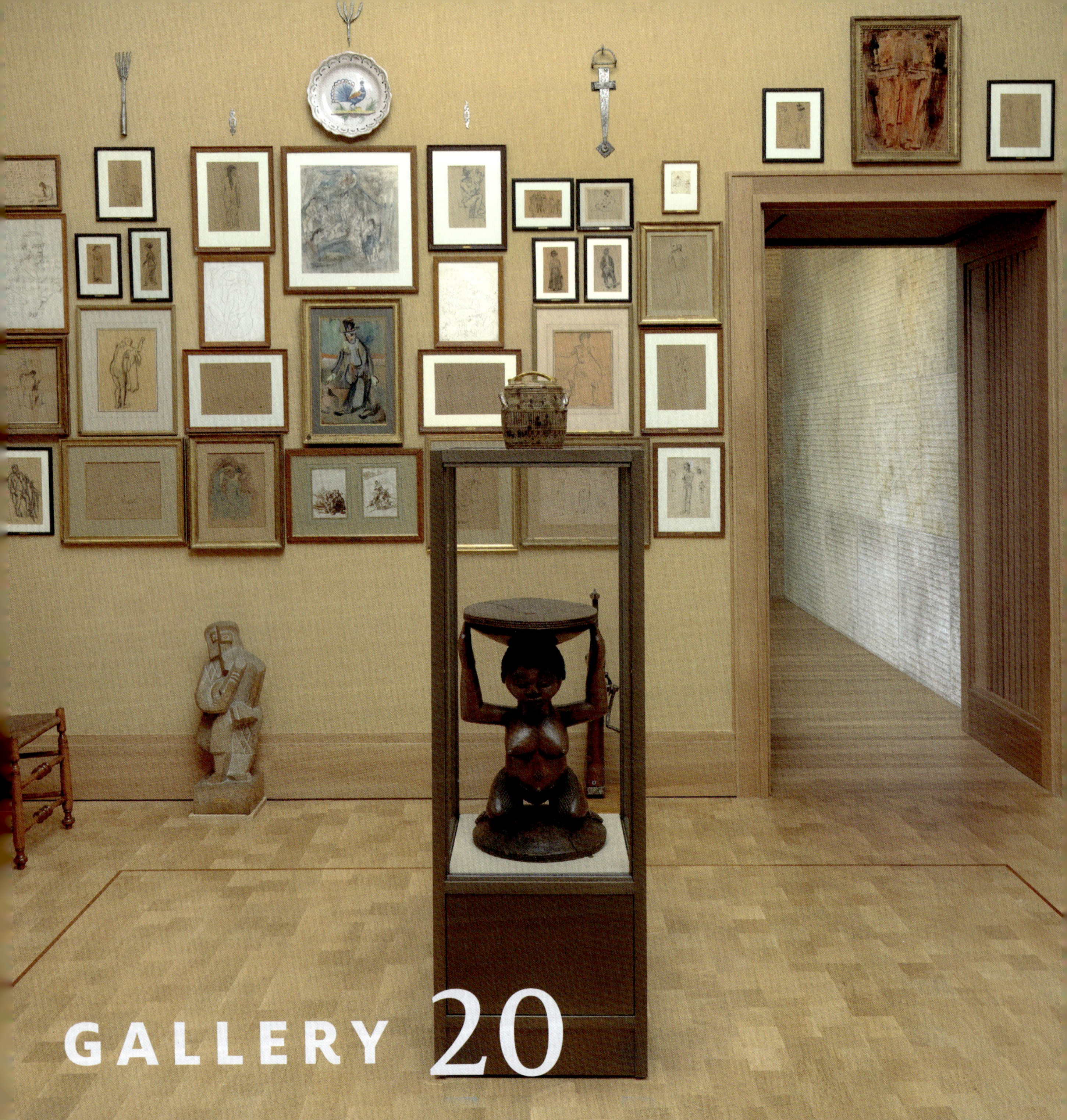

GALLERY 20

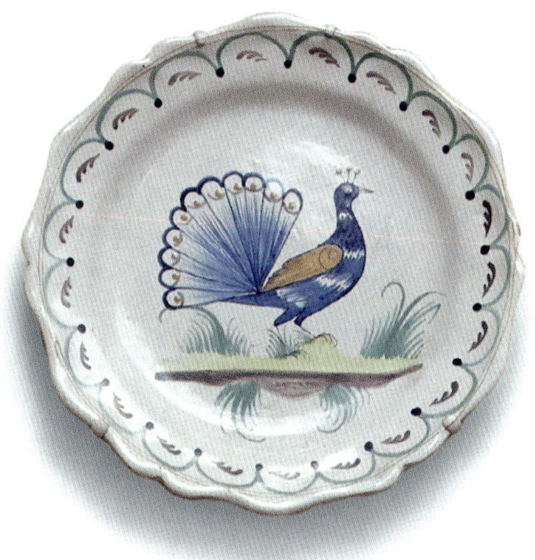

The Process of Making Art

Sketches and drawings fill Gallery 20, many from painters represented in other rooms of the collection: Picasso, Degas, Pascin, Cézanne, and Glackens. Hanging above these drawings like a capstone is this jaunty peacock, its tail spread full-fan across a ceramic pie plate, and the shape of its tail is repeated in metalwork just above it. Many of the drawings in this room are studies in which the painters observe elements later rendered in larger works. The pie pan may be a comment on artists' labor and the difficulty of the creative process: the many steps of work required to result in a finished product, just like the many preparatory sketches and subject studies that painters draw before creating a finished painting.

Ensemble view, Room 20, west wall. // Plate. Tin-glazed earthenware.

If the *Woman with Eggs* by Rousseau in Gallery 9 is the intended avian representation there, it would be unfair of us to overlook Edith Dimock's charming illustration here of women carrying their eggs to market. Dimock was the wife of Dr. Barnes's close friend, painter William Glackens. She was a watercolor artist and book illustrator, and a follower of the Ashcan School of painting. In the context of this room, these enormous baskets of eggs allude to both Dr. Barnes's wit, and to the theme of the room, by offering ample ingredients for metaphorical pie-making.

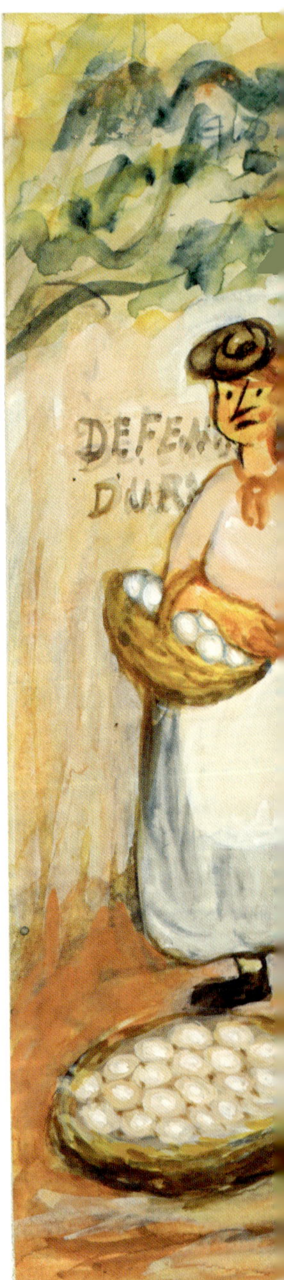

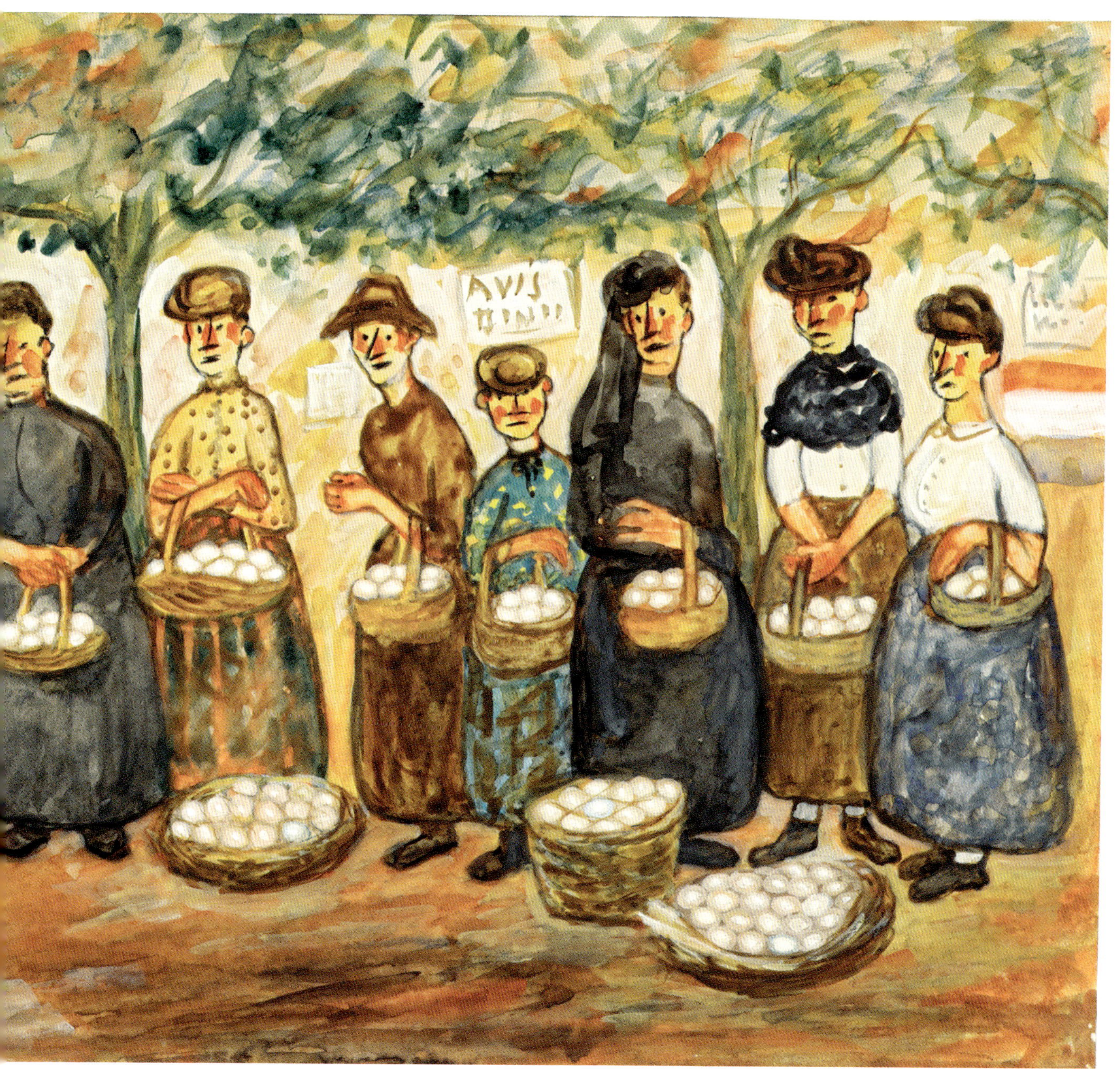

Edith Dimock. *Women with Eggs*, 1928.

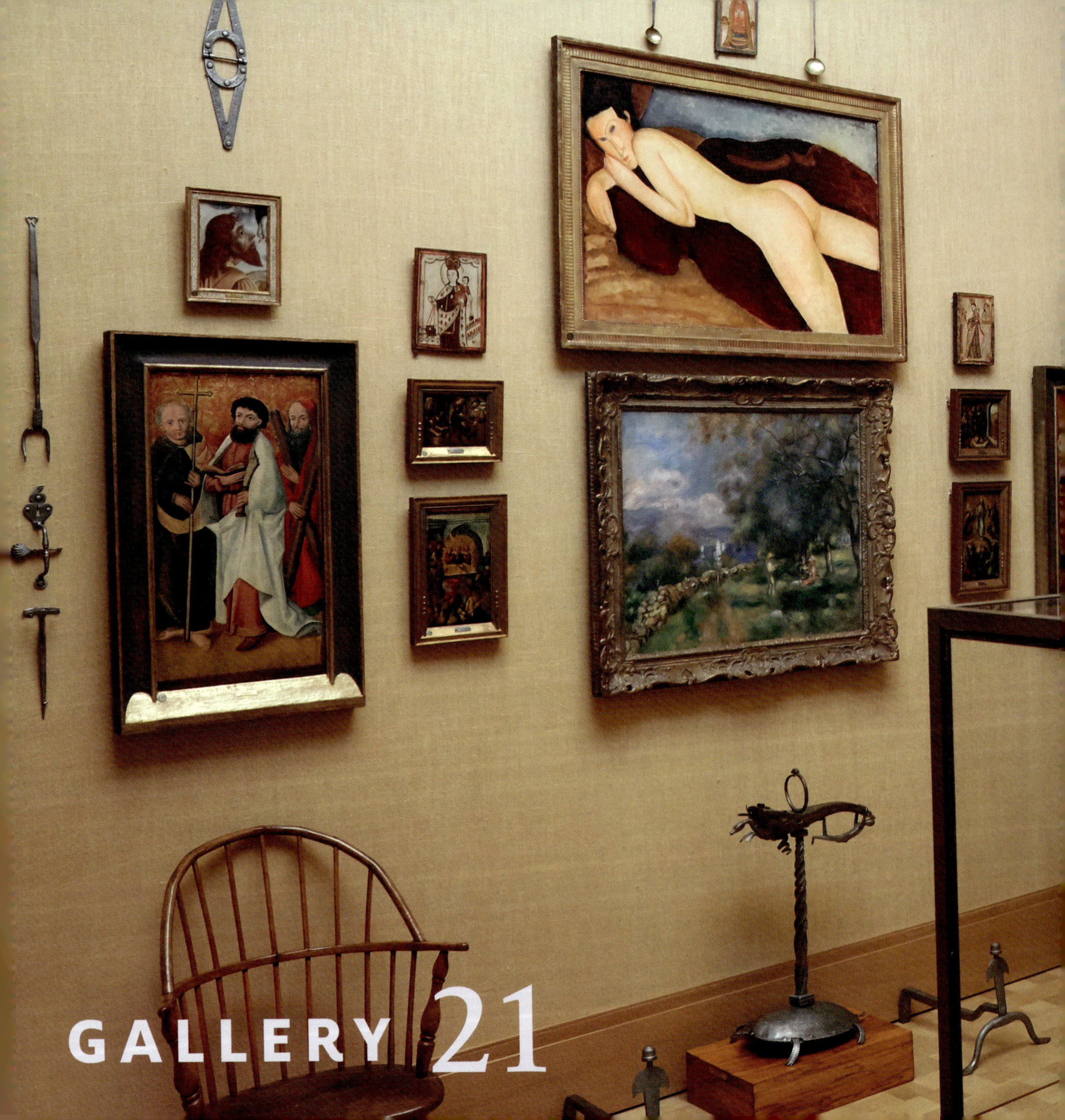

GALLERY 21

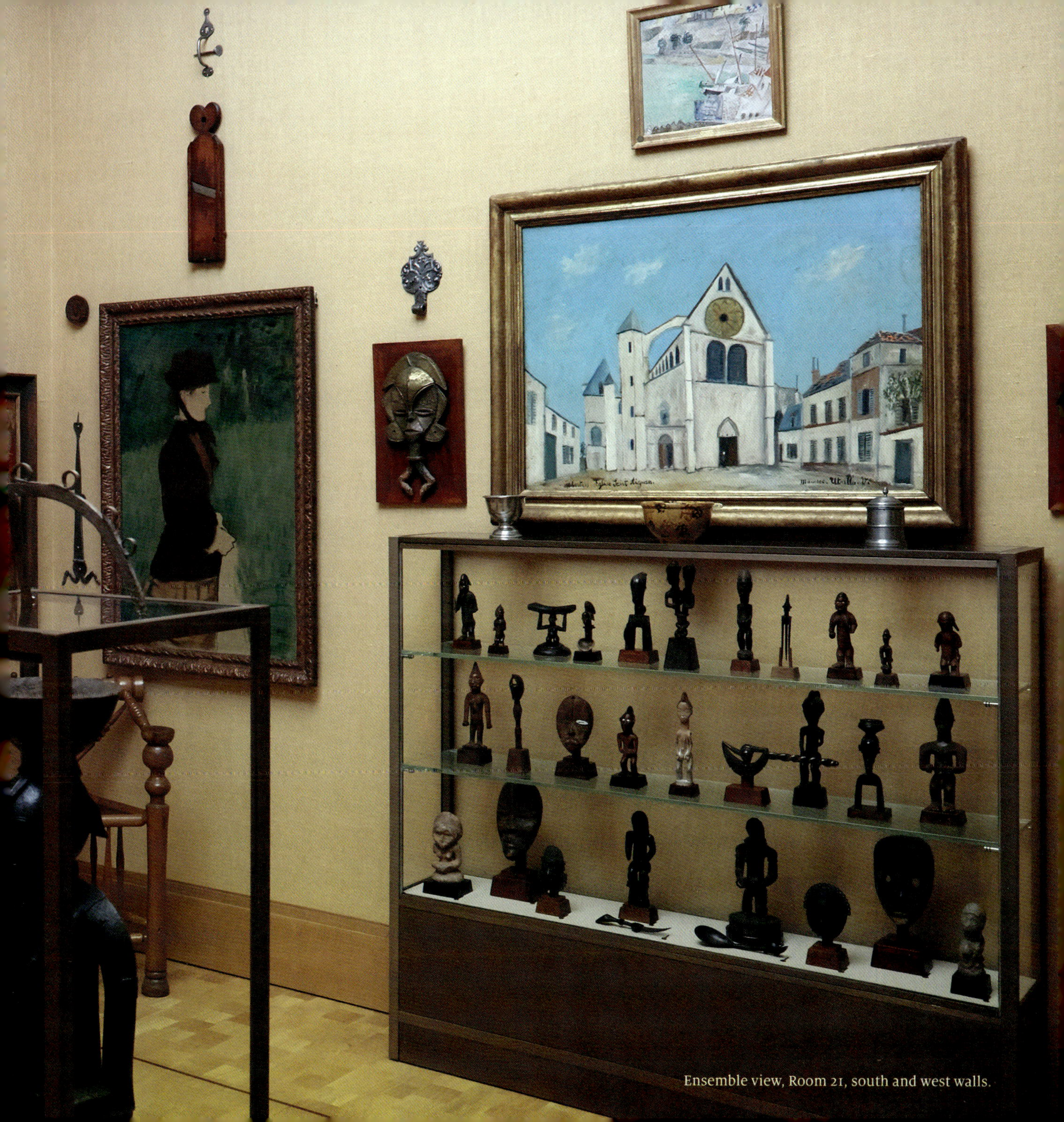

Ensemble view, Room 21, south and west walls.

The Legend of the Birds

It is here that the question of "a bird in every room" meets its greatest challenge. From top to bottom, around all four walls of this small room, only one winged creature can be found. That is the curious hybrid adorning a metal oil lamp: dragon-like, with a curled tail bearing a man oddly suspended from that, an ouroboros balanced upright on its back, and all of this balanced on the back of a turtle. This is one of the more remarkable oddities of the collection, with little known about its origin or inclusion in the collection. Left in solitary winged migration, this strange creature is the only potential "bird" to find its natural habitat in Gallery 21.

 Portable Oil Lamp. Iron.

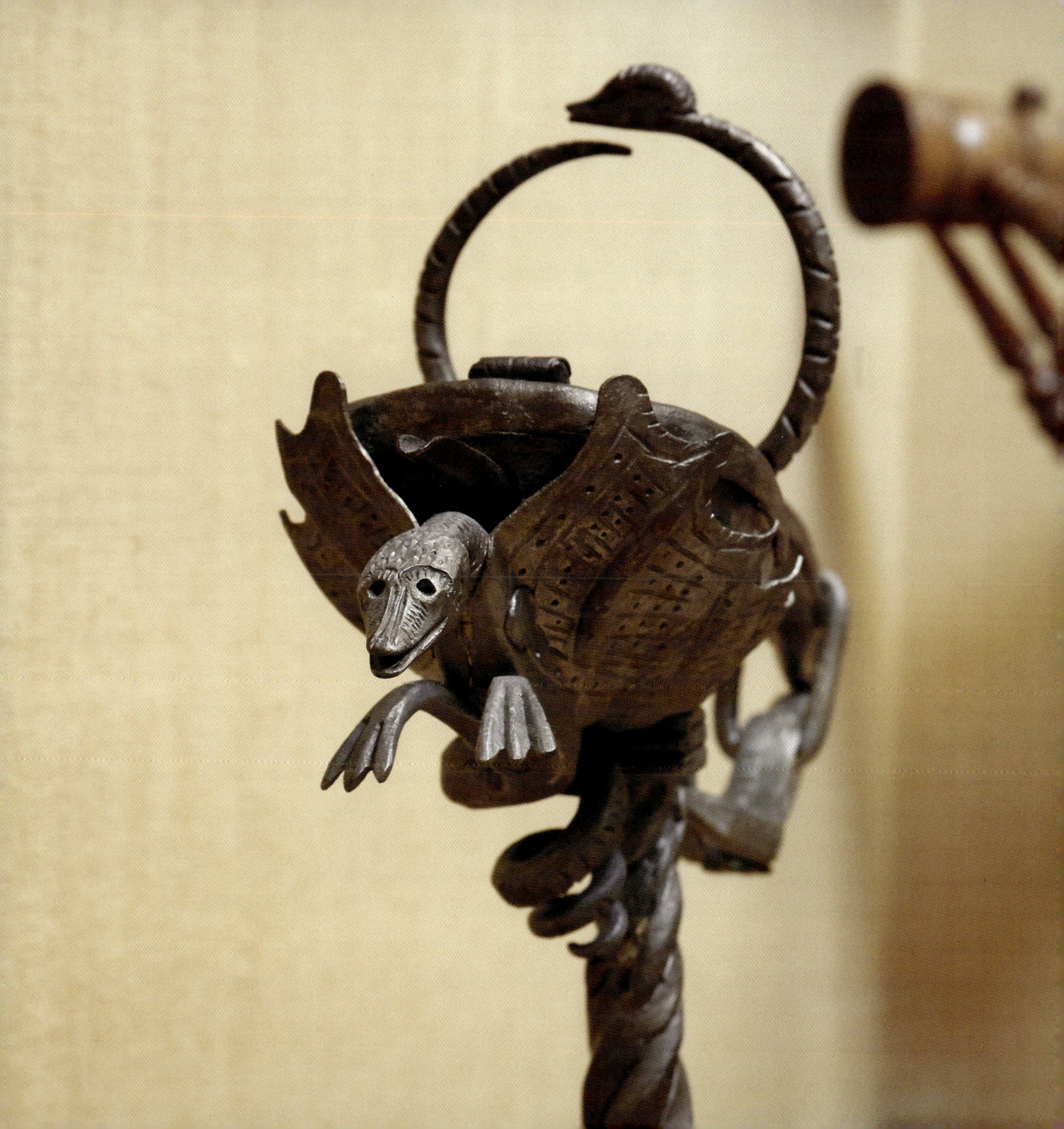

Interwoven Cultures

Gallery 22 reinforces Dr. Barnes's educational philosophy of interconnected representation through disparate cultures, with a bird perched on one of the African masks, a European goldfinch in a German oil painting, and small birds in a carved wooden Pennsylvania German butter mold.

The African mask is unusual because of its singular bird. Similar Baule masks would have been topped with a pair of symmetric birds, much like the wooden door on the Barnes balcony. This mask's notable crowning rooster is matched by another rooster: this one, a gift from one of his dealers, Étienne Bignou, is in metal, placed prominently in the center of the room.

GALLERY 22

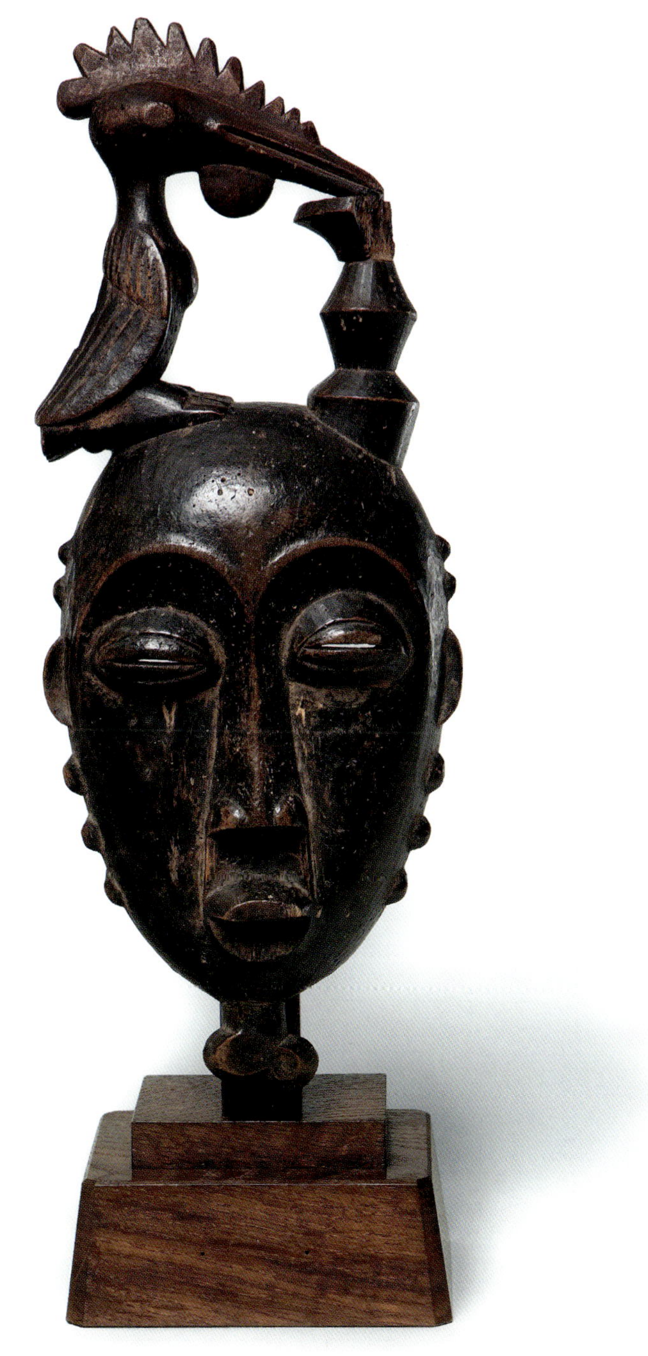

Owie Kimou. Portrait Mask (Mblo), late 19th century.

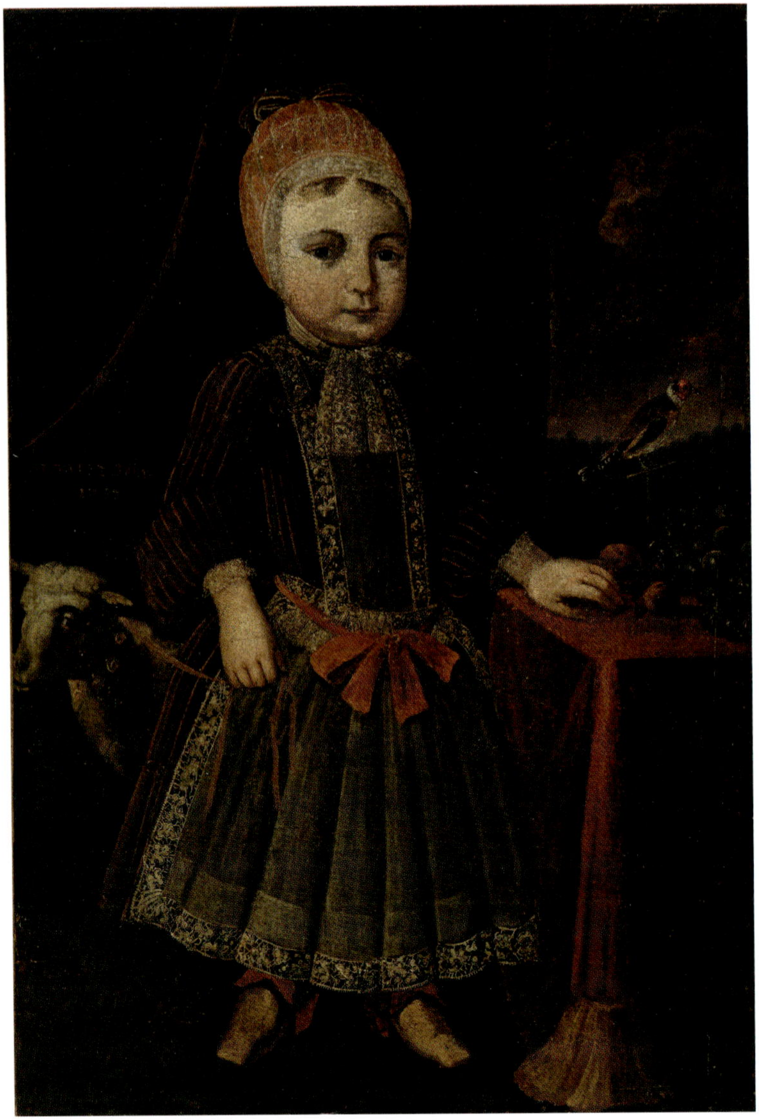

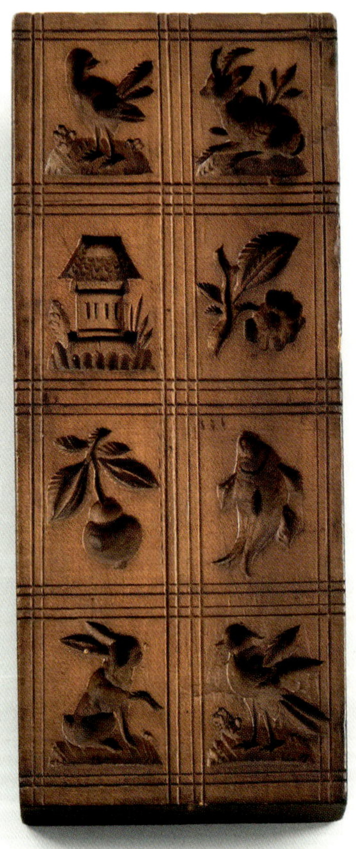

 Little Girl in Interior near Window, 1707. // Butter Mold. Wood.

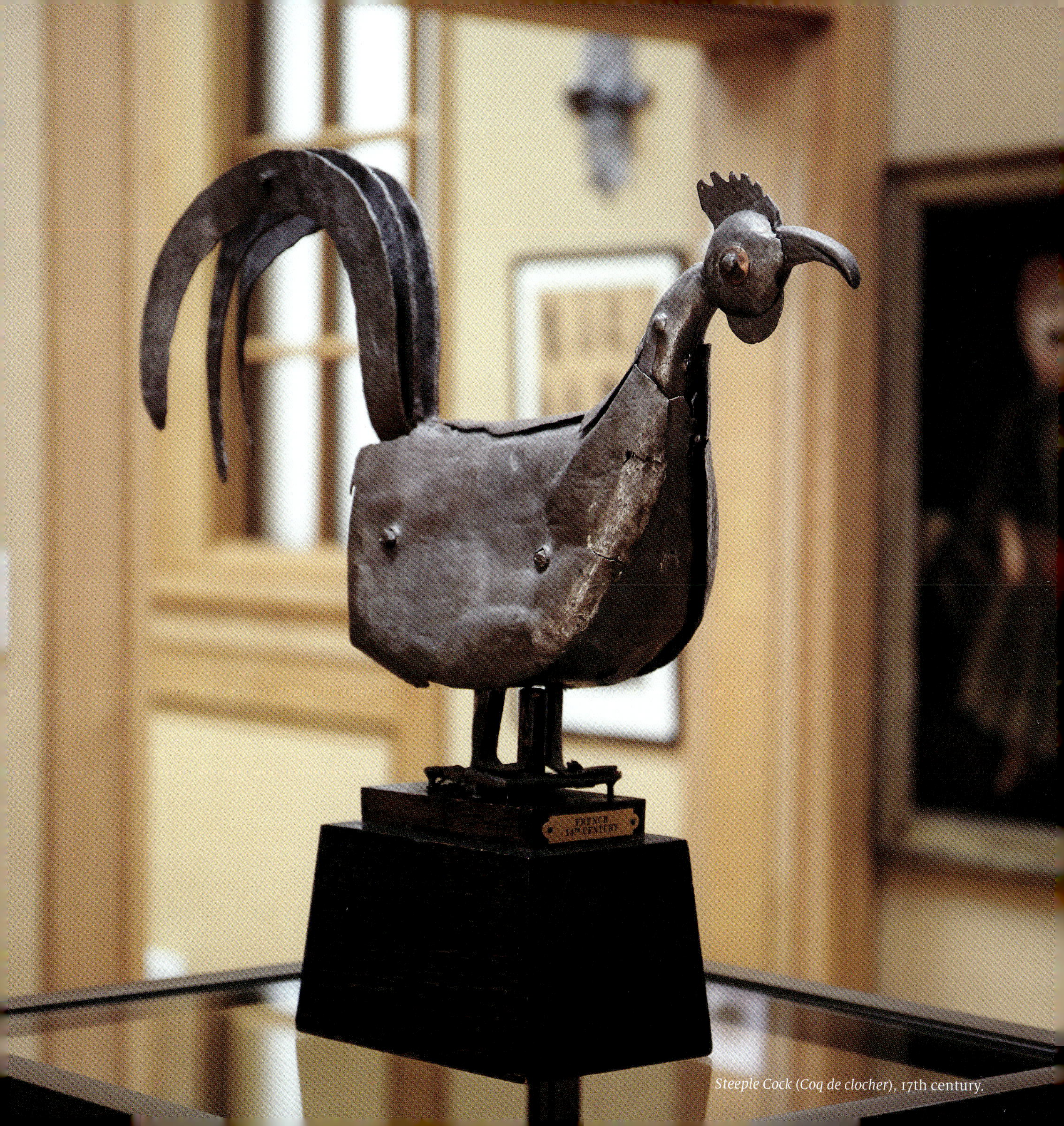

Steeple Cock (Coq de clocher), 17th century.

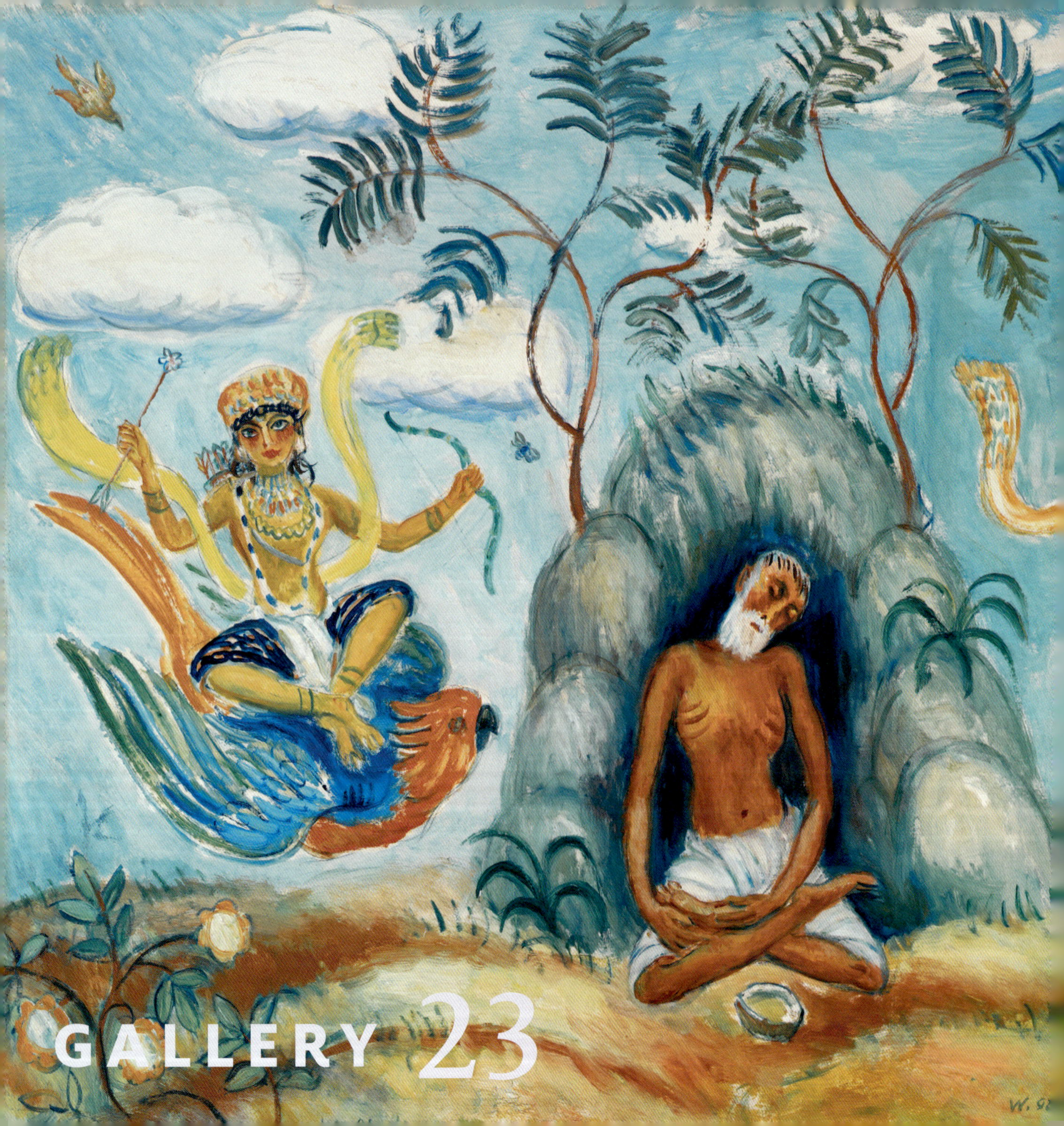
GALLERY 23

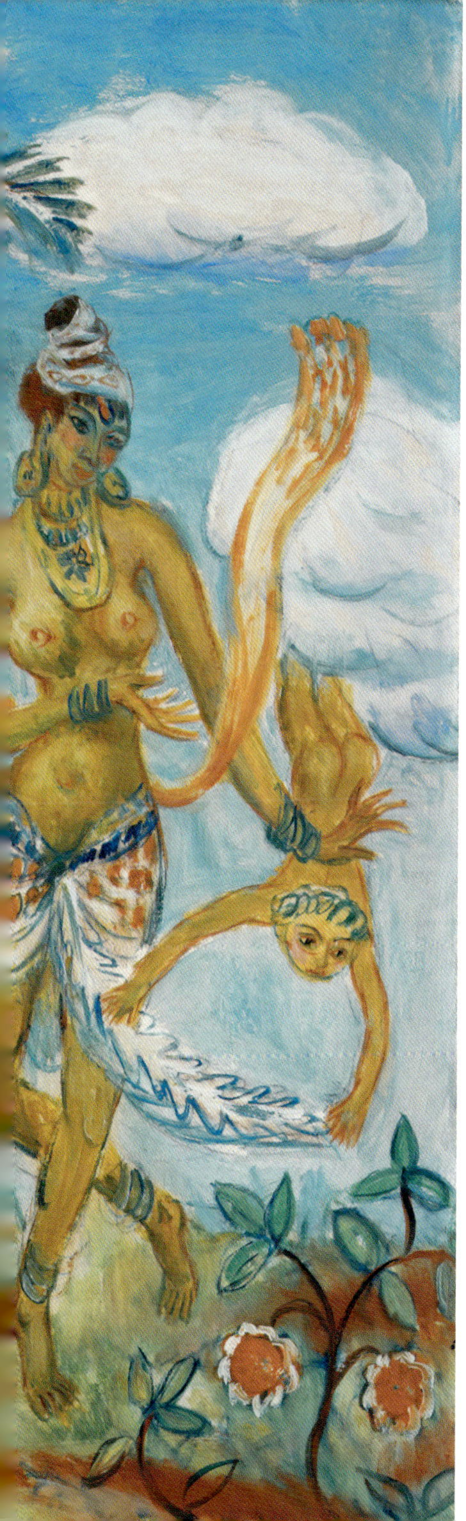

Bringing It All Together

Circling this final room, the birds here point the way to repetitions and reinforcement of the themes spotted on our tour so far:

- Decorative arts given pride of place alongside oil paintings
- Artworks from friends and familiars of the collector
- Inclusion of the work of common, everyday people alongside the most notable artists of their time
- Ironwork that reinforces painting compositions
- Traditions of art history reimagined in new modern movements in painting

William James Glackens. *Decoration*, c. 1914.

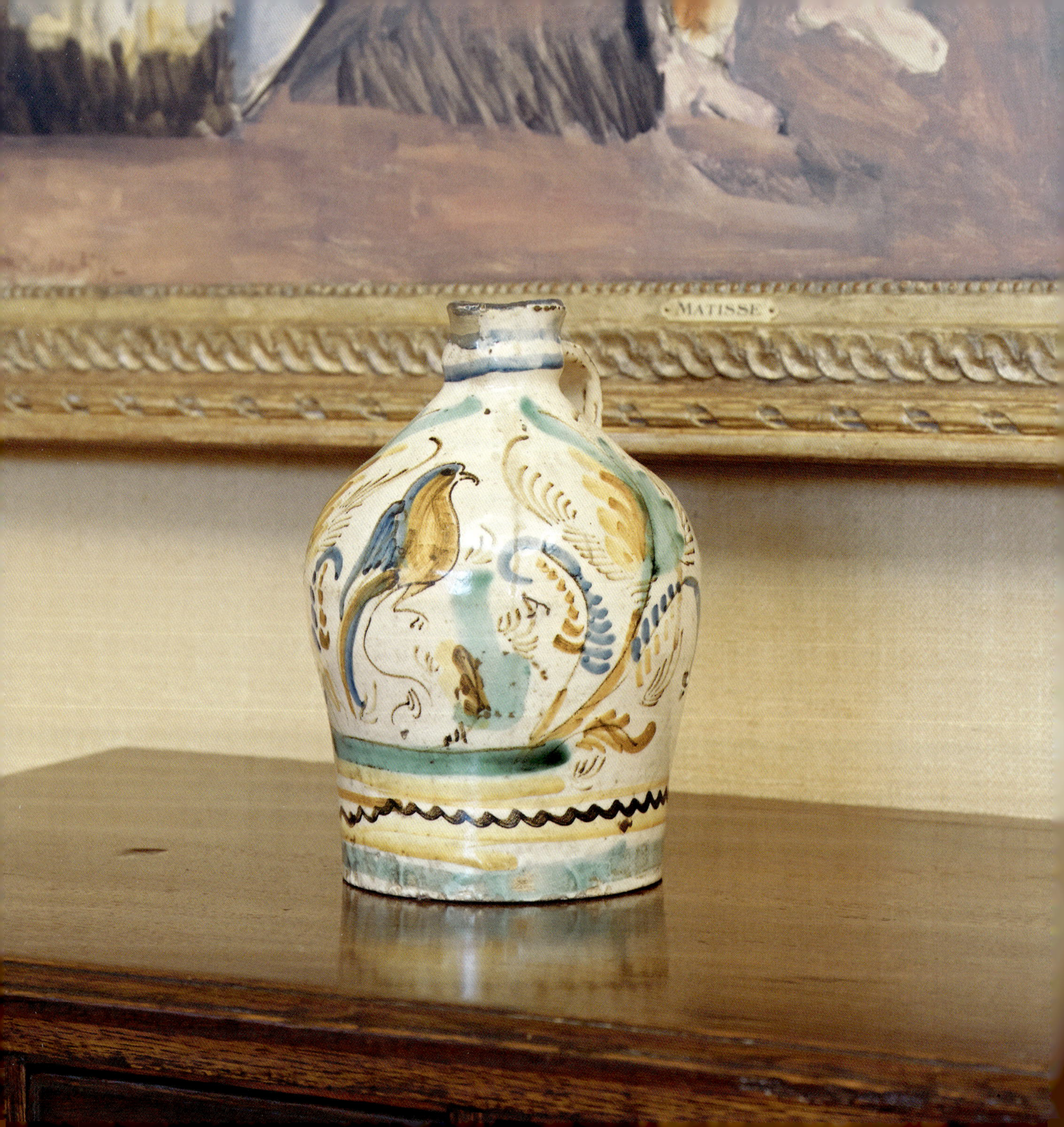
MATISSE

We see another simple jug with a bird in front of a large-scale painting by Matisse (a decorative bird by the painted opened window), and then a work by Dr. Barnes's close friend and former schoolmate William Glackens, who shared many of Dr. Barnes's ideas on art and education.

Next, we find quirky birds made of a lobster claw and seashell, which look more like souvenirs from a seaside boardwalk than fine art typically on display in a museum. They are the work of Thomas Maling, a scrimshaw artist from Maine. Maling made thousands of such figurative statues from pine cones, pine needles, acorns, and peach pits in addition to shells and lobster claws. He developed a friendship with Dr. Barnes, sending him a variety of samples of his work over time, "different articles which I wish to donate to your museum and some day about 50 years from now someone will enjoy them," he wrote to Dr. Barnes (Maling 1947).

An article from the *Boston Post Magazine* reported, of Maling, "It's said [Dr. Barnes] gets more kick out of them than out of the original paintings for which he has paid fabulous prices." Though hyperbolic, Dr. Barnes did write to Maling numerous times with great warmth and affection, reassuring him of the value of his work as an artist, and of the enjoyment his creations gave to his students and staff.

"Your package of artistic creations made out of lobster claws was a real delight. They leave no doubt that you are a genuine artist in being able to create things that give pleasure to other people and joy to yourself in making them. It will be a pleasure for me to show your works of art to our students, not only for their intrinsic artistic value, but because they are concrete proof of our teaching that art may arise in the most commonplace events of life and when one's expression is genuinely realized, that work of art takes its place with even the great paintings and great musical compositions."

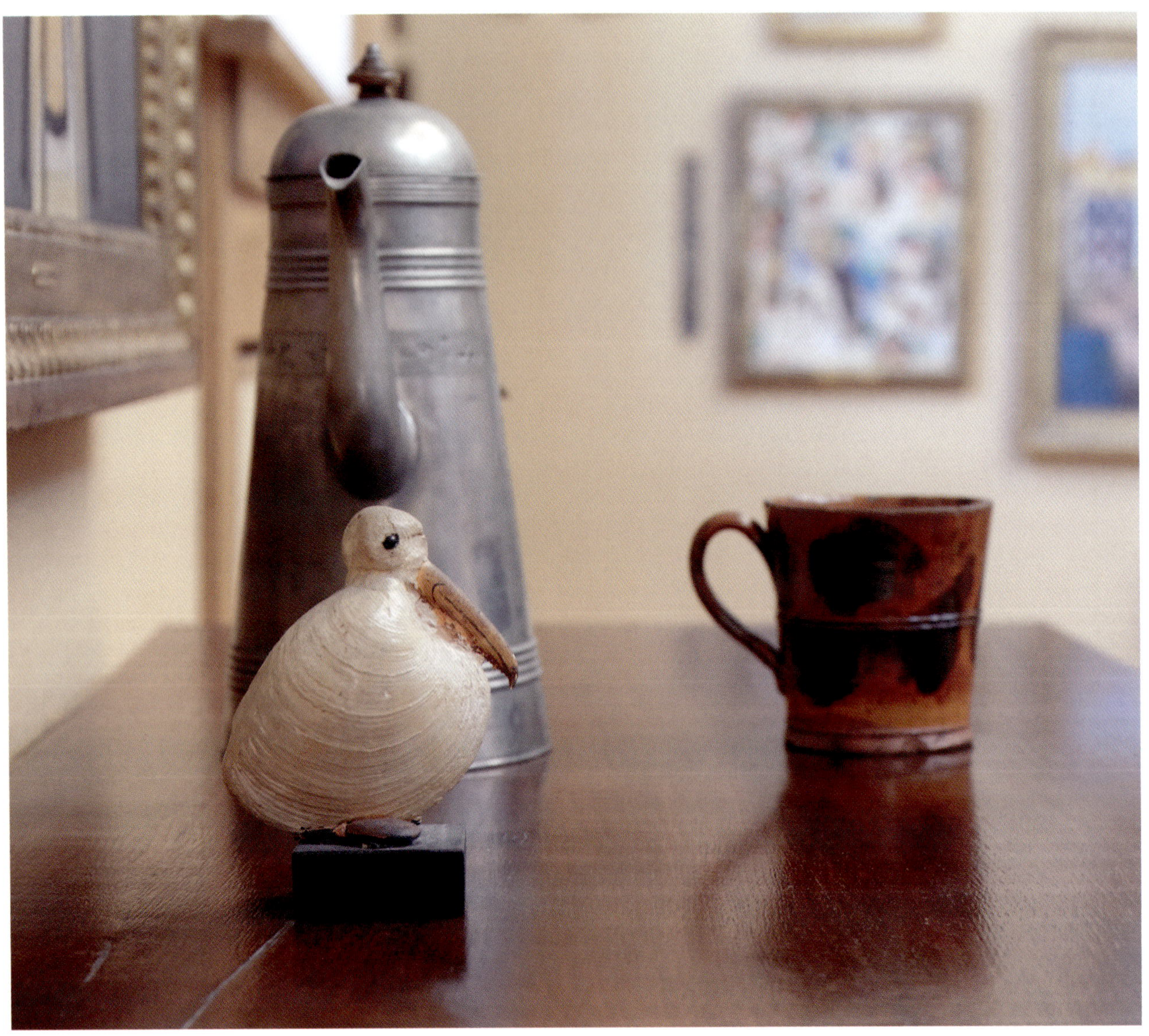

 Thomas G. Maling. Pelican.

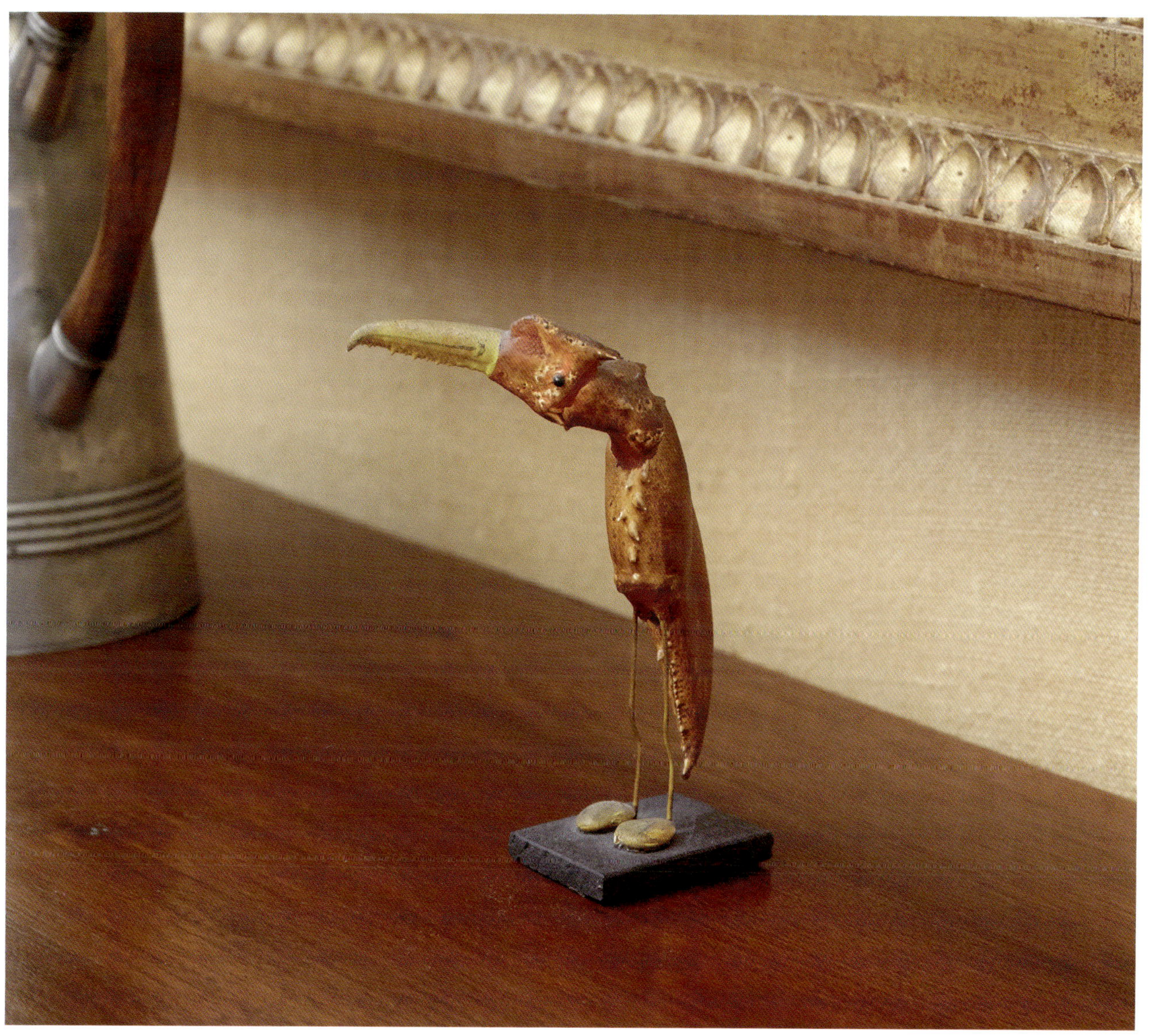

Thomas G. Maling. Bird.

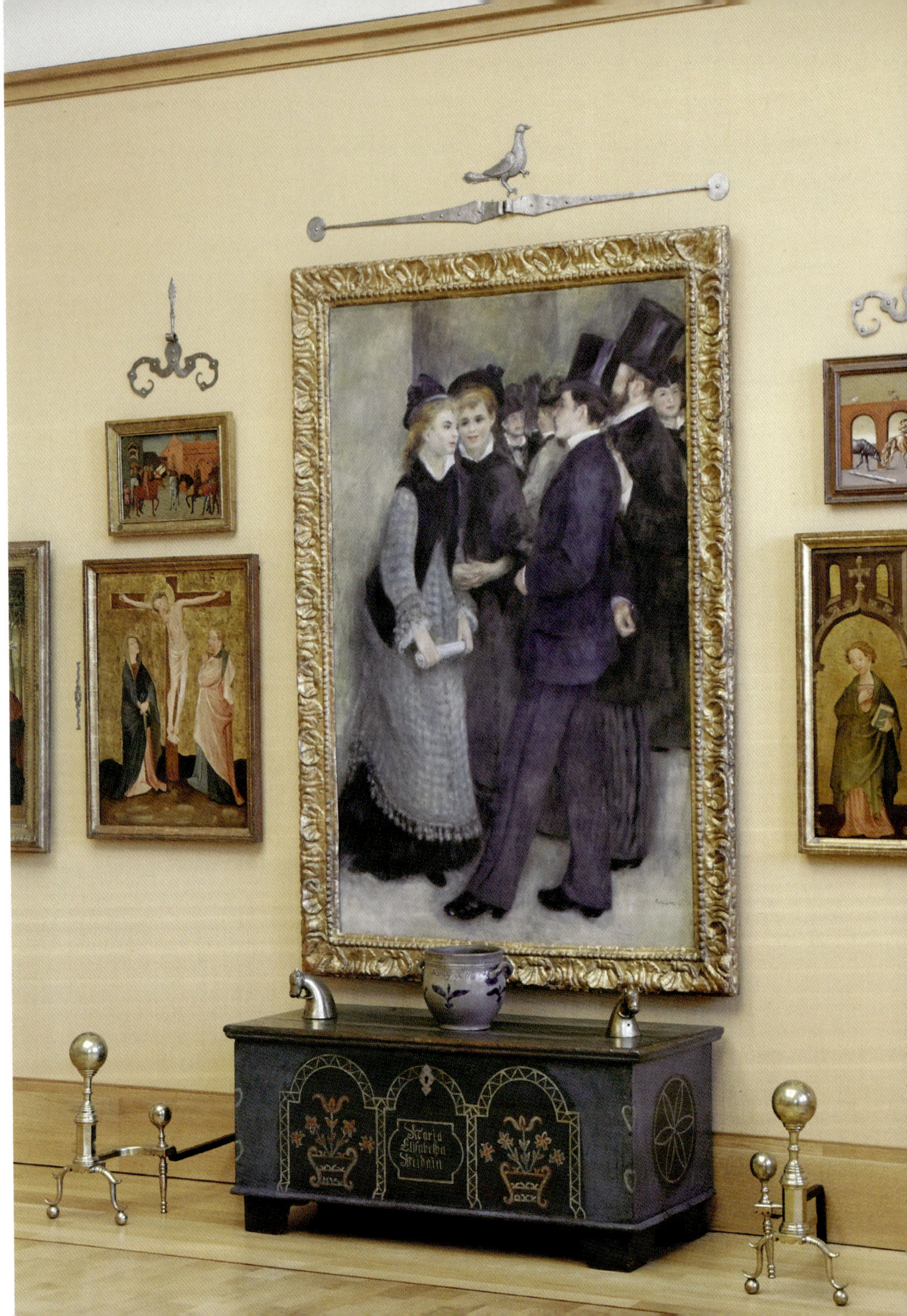

Continuing to the next wall, we find a particularly detailed metal bird stepping over a "threshold" drawn by a pair of long hinges that outlines the Renoir painting below it, *Leaving the Conservatory*. This bird echoes the painting, where the man's forward stride diagonally blocks the viewer, excluding us from his conversation with the women on the left. This angle, drawing the eye between painting and ironwork, is another frequent method Dr. Barnes used to create connections between objects and paintings.

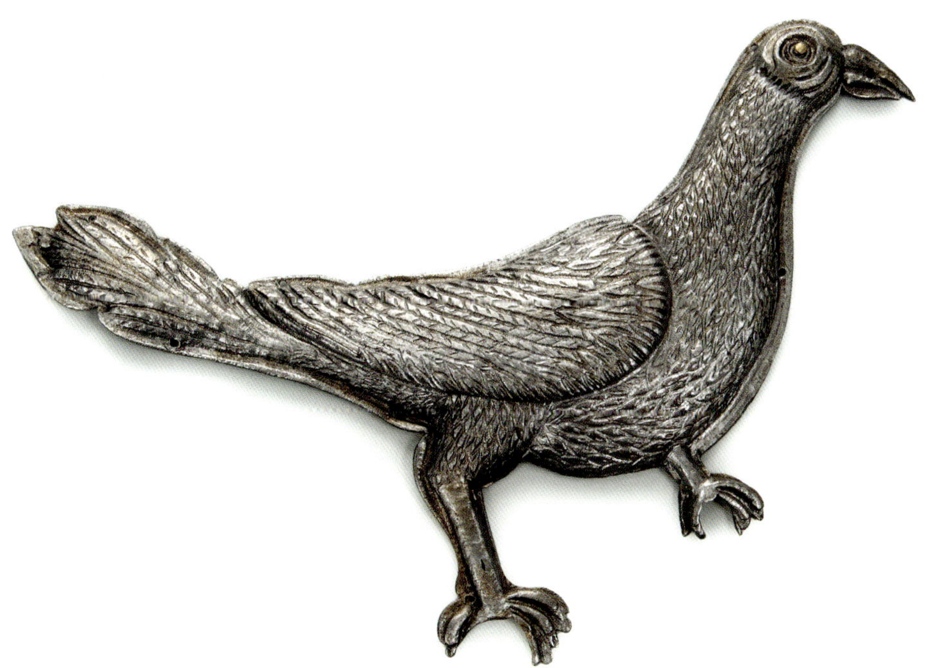

Ensemble view, Room 23, east wall. // Bird, 17th–18th century.

Finally, exiting the gallery, just to the right of the doorway before we go, we find a curious bird by Giorgio de Chirico. De Chirico's metaphysical painting (*pittura metafisica*) was based on poetry, philosophy, and mythology and inspired many artists in the surrealist movement. This piece, titled *The Mysterious Swan*, harkens back to Cézanne's *Leda*, found in the very first gallery. Like Cézanne, de Chirico adapted ideas from classical art and the Old Masters into his imagery, reinventing tradition in a new way of painting. So it is that a tour of the Barnes Foundation galleries in numerical order both begins and ends with a painting of a mythic apparition of a swan lifted from the classics, and painted in the hand of an artist at the forefront of inventing new methods of expression.

Giorgio de Chirico. *The Mysterious Swan*, 1934.

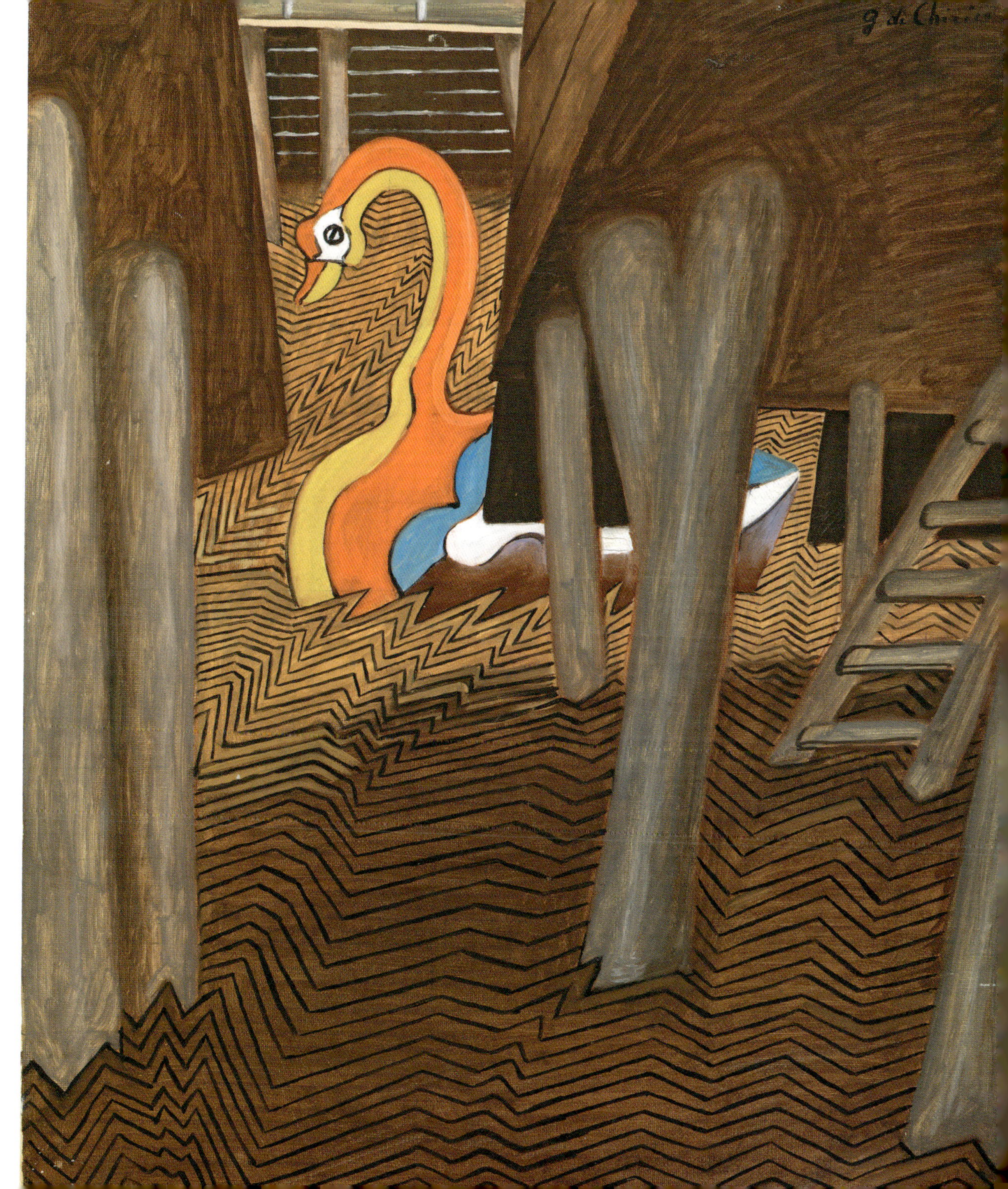

The More We Look, the More We See

Did Dr. Barnes intend to place a bird in every room of his famed collection? Did he specifically want *birds* to underscore his educational philosophy and draw the viewers' eyes to points he was trying to make in arranging the works in his collection? We may never know for sure. Deliberate or not, his methods in arranging artwork and decorative objects were consistent enough from room to room, and the birds an oft-repeated inclusion, so that any avid birdwatcher attentive to their subject will uncover in their pursuit the principles and ideas that Barnes did intend his students to discover in studying his collection. While contemplating similarities and differences among cultural traditions, formats, media, and artistic eras, we uncover an expanded visual vocabulary that enhances the way we view the world outside the collection as well.

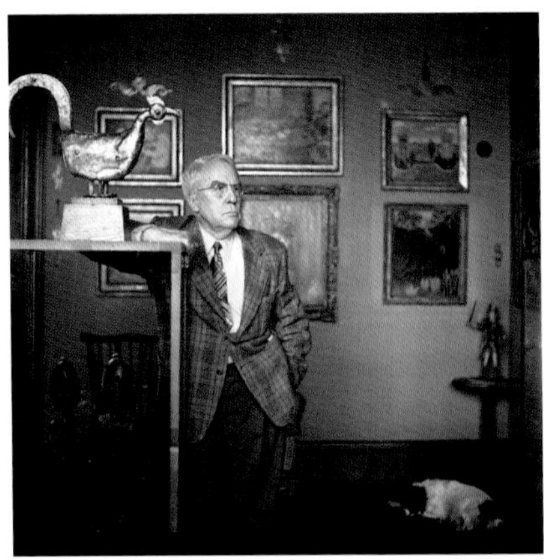

"All we hope to do at the Foundation is to help people learn to see not only pictures but every other object and situation in life."

—Dr. Albert C. Barnes

 Angelo Pinto. Photograph. Albert C. Barnes next to the *Coq du Clocher* (01.22.43), c. 1946.

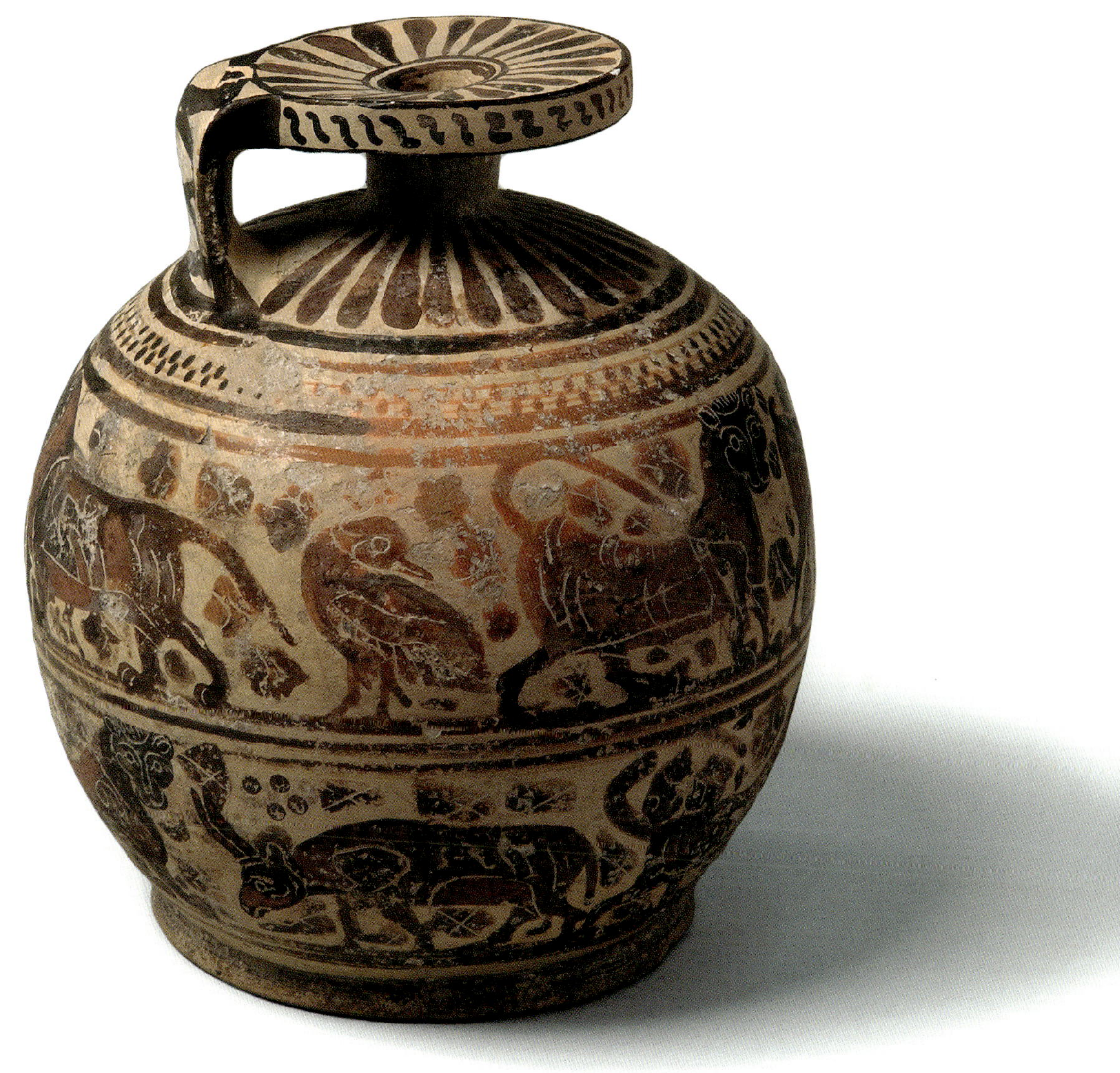

Corinthian Round Aryballos, possibly 6th century BCE, possibly Greek.

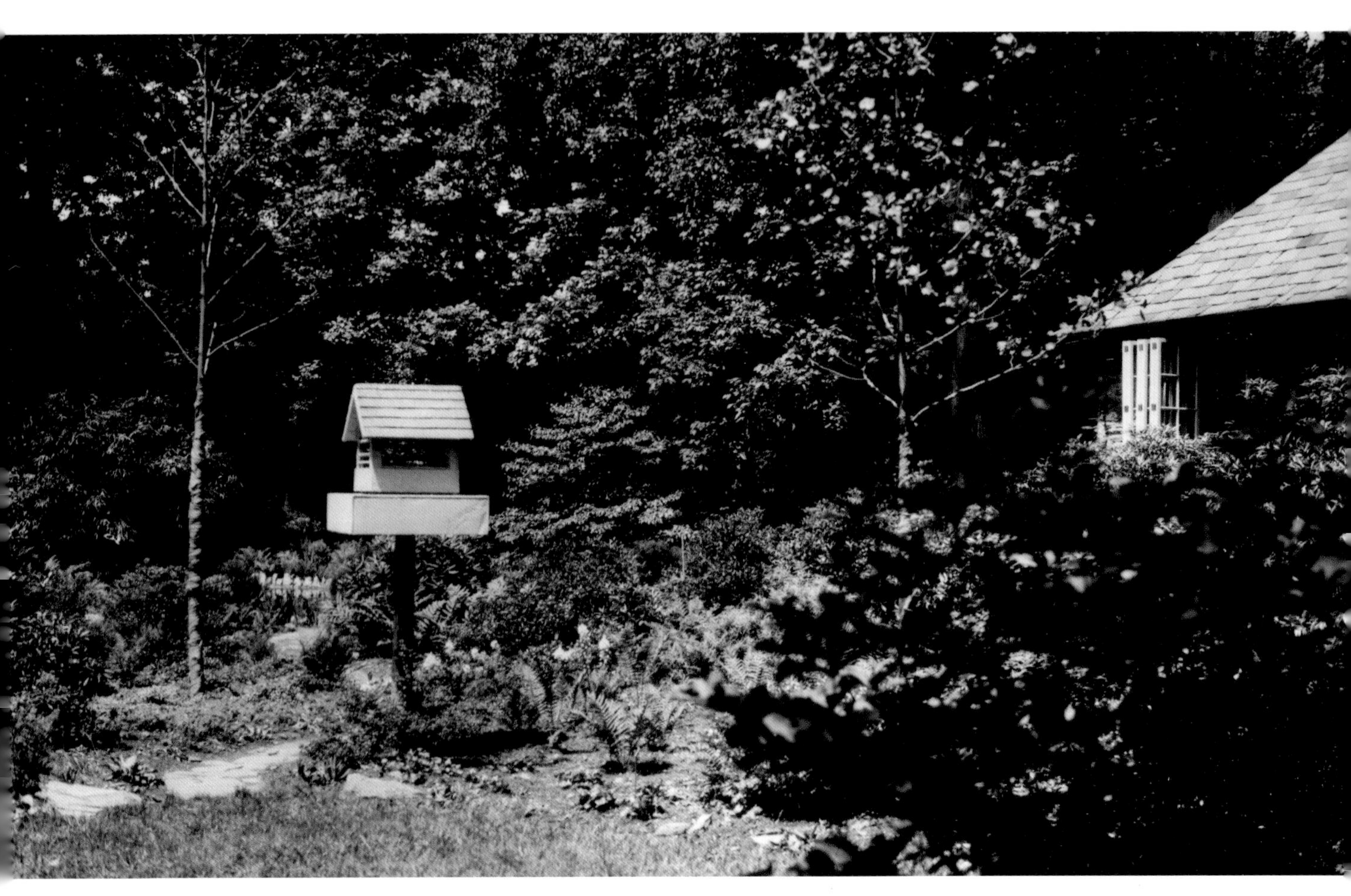

 Nicholas Valle. Photograph. Birdhouse near the teahouse in Merion, 1933.

Author's Note

Because of the placement of artwork in the galleries, it is tempting to ascribe to Dr. Barnes ideas that may or may not have been intentional. Because his philosophy of education encouraged students to use the ensembles to find new artistic correlations and to draw their own conclusions (what he called the "objective method"), it inevitably elicited guesses, hesitation, and sometimes wild theories. During his lifetime, Dr. Barnes regularly rearranged the walls in the galleries, making room for works added to the collection, filling in spaces for paintings sold or traded, or simply presenting new compositions for the ever-changing classes taught at the foundation. The galleries were, for many years, in constant fluctuation. The process of installation stopped only at the time of his death in 1951, and since that time, the works have stayed in the same relative positions, the ensembles frozen for all time, right along with their lessons, juxtapositions, and witticisms. While Barnes wrote often about the painters and individual works in his collection, he didn't leave a formal description or decoder for interpreting the rooms wall by wall. In most cases, we will never know exactly why he placed the works as they are. The conjecture about "a bird in every gallery" comes from oral tradition, and nowhere in his writings did Dr. Barnes state that such an inclusion was explicit, or for what purpose.

However, I believe the legend of the birds has value beyond its own proof or debunking. Dr. Barnes was attentive to the connections between fine art and the natural world, situating the building that housed his fine art collection on a 12-acre arboretum filled with tree specimens from around the world, with windows of the galleries looking out into the vivacious garden, connecting the painted landscapes on the walls to the seasonal landscape growing outside. His wife, Laura Barnes, was an avid birder and kept bird identification guides in her library. She hung birdhouses and feeders throughout the arboretum, all painted a distinctive shade of light blue, and designed a birdbath into her formal garden. It is reasonable to think that birds played some interest among many shared by the collecting couple. Moreover, Dr. Barnes wrote about his reverence for artists such as Renoir and Cézanne, who, he said, "treated the familiar, everyday events that make up our lives" and, by painting common and familiar things, created "a world richer, fuller, [and] more meaningful than that revealed to our own unaided perceptions" (Barnes 1925).

Similarly, birds, as a familiar, everyday motif, make an accessible starting point for taking in a large and often-bewildering collection. Regardless of intent, following this singular theme through the collection gives viewers a chance for "slow looking," for making the kinds of assessment Dr. Barnes and his cohorts taught students to make, and for appreciating art as a part of a richer, fuller, more meaningful experience.

Image Credits

Page 4: Ensemble view, Room 17, north wall.

Pages 6–7: Ensemble view, Room 1, west wall. Photo by Sean Murray.

Page 9: Paul Cézanne. *Leda and the Swan* (*Léda au cygne*), c. 1880, or possibly later. Oil on canvas, Overall: $23^{1}/_{2}$ × $29^{1}/_{2}$ in. (59.7 × 74.9 cm). BF36.

Page 10: Ensemble view, Room 2, north wall. Photo by Sean Murray.

Page 12: Unidentified maker, German. Door Knocker, 18th century. Iron, Overall: $21^{5}/_{16}$ × $6^{3}/_{8}$ × 4 in. (54.1 × 16.2 × 10.2 cm). 01.02.11.

Page 13: Unidentified maker, American. Jug, 1830–1850. Salt-glazed stoneware, Overall: 13 × $7^{3}/_{4}$ in. (33 × 19.7 cm). 01.02.08. Photo by Sean Murray.

Page 14: Karl Priebe. *Miss Chalfont*, 1947. Case in on cardboard, Overall: 12 × $12^{5}/_{8}$ in. (30.5 × 32.1 cm). BF1144. In Copyright. ©2019 Estate of Karl Priebe.

Page 15: Unidentified maker. Andiron. Metal, Overall: $12^{13}/_{16}$ × $7^{1}/_{4}$ × $12^{1}/_{4}$ in. (32.5 × 18.4 × 31.1 cm). 01.02.52. Photo by Sean Murray.

Page 16: Unidentified maker, American. Handle, Iron, Overall: $13^{3}/_{16}$ × $2^{5}/_{8}$ × $1^{7}/_{8}$ in. (33.5 × 6.7 × 4.8 cm). 01.03.16. Photo by Sean Murray.

Page 17: Pierre Puvis de Chavannes. *Dramatic Poetry* (*Aeschylus*), c. 1896. Oil on canvas, Overall: $48^{7}/_{8}$ × $24^{7}/_{8}$ in. (124.1 × 63.2 cm). BF100.

Page 18: Nicolas Lancret, French, 1690–1743. *The Open Cage*, 18th century. Oil on canvas, Overall: $28^{3}/_{4}$ × $23^{5}/_{8}$ in. (73 × 60 cm). BF814.

Pages 20–21: Ensemble view, Room 4, north wall. Photo by Sean Murray.

Page 21: Unidentified maker, French. Door Decoration, 18th century. Iron, Overall: $8^{3}/_{4}$ × $12^{3}/_{8}$ × $^{1}/_{2}$ in. (22.2 × 31.4 × 1.3 cm). 01.04.07.

Page 22: George Benjamin Luks. *The Blue Churn*, c. 1908–1910. Oil on wood panel, Overall: $20^{1}/_{8}$ × $16^{1}/_{8}$ in. (51.1 × 41 cm). BF391.

Page 23: Charles Prendergast. *The Offering*, c. 1915–1917. Tempera, gold, and silver leaf on incised, gessoed panel, Overall: 21 × $16^{1}/_{16}$ in. (53.3 × 40.8 cm). BF467.

Page 24: Copy after Hieronymus Bosch, Netherlandish, c. 1450–1516. *Temptation of Saint Anthony*, mid-16th century. Oil on panel, Overall: $27^{1}/_{2}$ × $20^{3}/_{8}$ in. (69.9 × 51.8 cm). BF962.

Page 27: Copy after Bosch. *Temptation of Saint Anthony*, detail. Photo by Sean Murray.

Page 29: Unidentified maker, Spanish. Decorative Element, 16th–17th century. Iron, Overall: $7^{1}/_{2}$ × $^{7}/_{8}$ × $3^{1}/_{4}$ in. (19.1 × 2.2 × 8.3 cm). 01.05.55.

Pages 30–31: Ensemble view, Room 6, east wall. Photo by Sean Murray.

Page 32: Unidentified maker, American. Sea Chest, c. 1840. Painted and carved pine, Overall: 15 × $37^{1}/_{2}$ × 16 in. (38.1 × 95.3 × 40.6 cm). 01.06.17.

Page 33: Unidentified maker, possibly Spanish. Embroidery Scissors, 18th century. Iron, Overall: $4^{3}/_{8}$ × $1^{5}/_{8}$ × $^{3}/_{16}$ in. (11.1 × 4.1 × 0.5 cm). 01.06.10.

Page 34: Joan Miró. *Two Women Surrounded by Birds*, 1937. Watercolor, ink, and pastel on wove paper, Overall: 25 × $19^{1}/_{4}$ in. (63.5 × 48.9 cm). BF967. In Copyright. ©2019 Successió Miró / Artists Rights Society (ARS), New York / ADAGP, Paris.

Page 36: Ensemble view, Room 7, west and north walls. Photo by Sean Murray.

Page 38: Unidentified maker, American. Cookie Cutter, 19th century. Tin, Overall: $4^{1}/_{2}$ × 5 × $^{3}/_{4}$ in. (11.4 × 12.7 × 1.9 cm). 01.07.04.

Page 39: After El Greco (Domenikos Theotokopoulos), Greek, active in Spain. *Annunciation*, Possibly 17th century. Oil on canvas, Overall: $22^{7}/_{8}$ × $18^{3}/_{4}$ in. (58.1 × 47.6 cm). BF117.

Pages 40–41: Charles Prendergast. *Angels*, c. 1917. Tempera, graphite, silver and gold leaf on carved, incised gessoed panel, Overall (with frame): $25^{1}/_{2}$ × $33^{1}/_{2}$ in. (64.8 × 85.1 cm). BF520.

Page 42: Unidentified maker, European. Nutcracker, 19th century. Iron, Overall: 7 × $1^{3}/_{4}$ × $^{9}/_{16}$ in. (17.8 × 4.4 × 1.4 cm). 01.08.75.

Page 43: Ensemble view, Room 8, west wall. Photo by Sean Murray.

Pages 44–45: Ensemble view, Room 9, south and west walls. Photo by Sean Murray.

Page 47: Henri Rousseau. *Woman with Basket of Eggs* (*La Femme au panier d'oeufs*), probably 1905–1910. Oil on canvas, Overall: $13^{7}/_{8}$ × $10^{5}/_{8}$ in. (35.2 × 27 cm). BF544.

Pages 48–49: Unidentified maker, Spanish or French. Scissors, 18th–19th century. Iron, Overall: $5^{3}/_{16}$ × $2^{1}/_{16}$ × $^{1}/_{4}$ in. (13.2 × 5.2 × 0.6 cm). 01.10.03.

Page 50: Ensemble view, Room 10, east wall. Photo by Sean Murray.

Page 52: Henri Rousseau. *Monkeys and Parrot in the Virgin Forest* (*Singes et perroquet dans la forêt vierge*), c. 1905–1906. Oil on canvas, Overall: $22^{1}/_{8}$ × $18^{5}/_{8}$ in. (56.2 × 47.3 cm). BF397.

Page 55: Jean Hugo. *Mullion Cove*, April 1933. Oil on canvas (later mounted to panel), Overall: $8^{3}/_{4}$ × $10^{3}/_{4}$ in. (22.2 × 27.3 cm). BF1138. In Copyright. ©2019 Artists Rights Society (ARS), New York / ADAGP, Paris.

Page 57: Albert H. Nulty. *Pennsylvania Dutch Motif*, 1940s. Reverse painting on glass, Overall (sight): $6^{1}/_{2}$ × $4^{1}/_{2}$ in. (16.5 × 11.4 cm). BF2554. In Copyright. ©2019 Estate of Albert H. Nulty.

Page 58: Susan Cray. *New Jersey Cut-Out*, 1843. Cut-out wove paper with glossy black coating mounted on cream wove paper, Overall: 10 × 14 in. (25.4 × 35.6 cm). BF1182.

Page 60: Luigi Settanni. *Landscape in Brittany* (*Pont l'Abbé Figure*), 1939. Oil on canvas (later mounted to fiberboard), Overall: $18^{3}/_{4}$ × 26 in. (47.6 × 66 cm). BF979. In Copyright. ©2019 Estate of Luigi Settanni.

Page 61: Unidentified maker. Box. Wood, Overall: 8 × $9^{1}/_{2}$ × $7^{1}/_{2}$ in. (20.3 × 24.1 × 19.1 cm). 01.12.07. Photo by Sean Murray.

Pages 62–63: Ensemble view, Room 13, west and north walls. Photo by Sean Murray.

Page 64: Unidentified maker. Vise. Metal, Overall: $5^{3}/_{4}$ × 1 × $3^{9}/_{16}$ in. (14.6 × 2.5 × 9 cm). 01.13.26. Photo by Sean Murray.

Page 64: Willoughby Shade, American, b. 1820. Coffeepot, 1840s. Tin over sheet iron and brass, Overall: $10^{3}/_{4}$ × $6^{1}/_{4}$ × 10 in. (27.3 × 15.9 × 25.4 cm). 01.13.01.

Page 65: William Roberts, American, born in Wales, 1818–1888. Jug, 1869–1880. Stoneware, Overall: $14^{1}/_{2}$ × 9 in. (36.8 × 22.9 cm). 01.13.47.

Pages 66–67: Ensemble view, Room 14, north wall.

Page 69: Veronese (Paolo Caliari). *Baptism of Christ*, mid-16th century. Oil on canvas, Overall: 42 × $31^{1}/_{4}$ in. (106.7 × 79.4 cm). BF800.

Page 70: Gustave Courbet. *Woman with Pigeons*, mid-1860s. Oil on canvas, Overall: $31^{3}/_{8}$ × $23^{7}/_{8}$ in. (79.7 × 60.6 cm). BF824.

Page 72: Paul Cézanne. *Girl with Birdcage* (*Jeune fille à la volière*), c. 1888, or possibly later. Oil on canvas, Overall: $17^{7}/_{8}$ × $14^{7}/_{8}$ in. (45.4 × 38.1 cm). BF280.

Page 73: Unidentified maker. Parrot. Carved and painted wood, Overall: 7 × $3^{1}/_{8}$ × $7^{1}/_{8}$ in. (17.8 × 7.9 × 18.1 cm). 01.14.12.

Pages 74–75: Unidentified maker, American, Pennsylvania German. Chest, c. 1840. Painted pine, Overall: $23^{1}/_{2}$ × $41^{1}/_{2}$ × $18^{3}/_{4}$ in. (59.7 × 105.4 × 47.6 cm). 01.14.16.

Pages 76–77: Unidentified artist, Flemish. *Coronation of the Virgin*, second half of the 15th century. Oil on panel, Overall: 27 $^{1}/_{4}$ × 26 in. (69.2 × 66 cm). BF841.

Page 78: Unidentified artist, Korean. *Sage with Tiger*, 16th century. Black ink and pigments on a coarsely woven fabric, Overall: $33^{3}/_{8}$ × $16^{1}/_{2}$ × $^{5}/_{8}$ in. (84.8 × 41.9 × 1.6 cm). BF1081.

Page 79: Unidentified maker, Etruscan. Red-Figure Bird *Askos*, end of the 4th century BCE. Ceramic, Overall: 7 × $9^{3}/_{4}$ × $3^{3}/_{8}$ in. (17.8 × 24.8 × 8.6 cm). A50.

Page 80: Johann Adam Eyer. *Cover for a Book of Copy Models* (*Vorschriften-Büchlein*), 1784. Watercolor, pen and iron gall ink, and pen and red watercolor on laid paper, Overall: $8^{1}/_{8}$ × $6^{7}/_{16}$ in. (20.6 × 16.4 cm). BF936.

Page 82: Unidentified maker, Greek. Geometric Amphora, c. 770–750 BCE. Ceramic, Overall: $16^{5}/_{8}$ × $10^{1}/_{8}$ in. (42.2 × 25.7 cm). A59.

Page 83: Unidentified maker, Greek. Geometric Amphora, possibly 8th century BCE, or possibly modern. Ceramic, Overall: $16^{3}/_{8}$ × 10 in. (41.6 × 25.4 cm). A188.

Page 84: Unidentified artist. Statuette of a Human-Headed Ba-Bird, c. 300 BCE. Polychrome wood, Overall: $4^{1}/_{4}$ × $3^{7}/_{8}$ × $1^{1}/_{2}$ in. (10.8 × 9.8 × 3.8 cm). A6.

Page 85: Unidentified artist, Egyptian. Relief, 2350–2130 BCE. Limestone with traces of red pigment, Overall: $9^{1}/_{8}$ × 14 × $6^{1}/_{8}$ in. (23.2 × 35.6 × 15.6 cm). A161.

Page 86: Unidentified artist, Cypriote. *"Bird-Face" Goddess*, c. 1450–1200 BCE, Overall: $8^{3}/_{4}$ × $3^{1}/_{16}$ × $1^{5}/_{8}$ in. (22.2 × 7.8 × 4.1 cm). A31.

Page 86: Unidentified artist, American, Pennsylvania German. *Bird on Twig*, 19th century. Opaque water-based paint and iron gall ink on wove paper, Overall: 10 × 8 in. (25.4 × 20.3 cm). BF716.

Page 88: Jean Bourdichon. *The Pentecost* or *Descent of the Holy Spirit*, from a Book of Hours, 1470–1480. Tempera, granular gold paint, inscribed brown ink, pen and ink, and gilding on parchment, Overall: $5^{11}/_{16}$ × 4 in. (14.4 × 10.2 cm). BF795.

Pages 88–89: Charles Prendergast. *Two Figures on a Mule*, c. 1917–1920. Tempera, graphite, gold and silver leaf on incised, gessoed panel, Overall: 23 × $31^{1}/_{16}$ in. (58.4 × 78.9 cm). BF297.

Pages 90–91: Unidentified maker. Pitchers. Redware, Overall: $10^{1}/_{4}$ × $5^{3}/_{4}$ × $7^{1}/_{4}$ in. (26 × 16.8 × 18.7 cm) each. 01.16.34 and 01.16.38. Photo by Sean Murray.

Pages 92–94: Unidentified artist, American, Pennsylvania German. *House and Bird on a Tree*, 19th century. Watercolor on laid paper, Overall: $6^{7}/_{8}$ × $4^{7}/_{8}$ in. (17.5 × 12.4 cm). BF1162.

Page 95: Unidentified artist, American, Pennsylvania German. *Parakeet*, 19th century. Opaque water-based paint and pen and iron gall ink with graphite underdrawing on wove paper, Overall: $7^{7}/_{8}$ × $7^{5}/_{8}$ in. (20 × 19.4 cm). BF1161.

Page 95: Unidentified maker, American, Pennsylvania German. Decorative Tile. Ceramic, Overall: $5^{3}/_{4}$ × $5^{3}/_{4}$ × $^{3}/_{8}$ in. (14.6 × 14.6 × 1 cm). 01.17.29.

Page 96: Unidentified artist, American, Pennsylvania German. *Bird*, 19th century. Brush and blue ink and water-based paint on wove paper, Overall: 3 × $3^{11}/_{16}$ in. (7.6 × 9.4 cm). BF1159.

Page 97: Unidentified artist, American, Pennsylvania German. *Two Red and Yellow Parrots Facing Each Other (Green Leaves)*, 19th century. Opaque water-based paint and pen and iron gall ink with graphite underdrawing on wove paper, Overall: $10^{1}/_{16} \times 7^{5}/_{8}$ in. (25.6 × 19.4 cm). BF2089.

Page 98: Samuel Slank. *Birth Certificate*, 1840. Opaque water-based paint, iron gall ink, and graphite on wove paper, Overall (primary support): $12 \times 15^{3}/_{8}$ in. (30.5 × 39.1 cm). BF1165.

Page 99: Unidentified maker. Plate. Tin-glazed earthenware, Overall: $2^{1}/_{8} \times 8^{3}/_{4}$ in. (5.4 × 22.2 cm). 01.17.05.

Page 100: Unidentified artist, American, Pennsylvania German. *Three Roses and Bird's Family*, 19th century. Opaque water-based paint with graphite on wove paper, Overall: $6 \times 7^{5}/_{8}$ in. (15.2 × 19.4 cm). BF414.

Pages 100–101: Unidentified artist, American, Pennsylvania German. *Two Birds*, 19th century. Opaque water-based paint with graphite on ruled blue wove paper, Overall: $3^{3}/_{4} \times 4^{3}/_{8}$ in. (9.5 × 11.1 cm). BF1158.

Page 101: Unidentified artist, American, Pennsylvania German. *Two Birds*, 19th century. Water-based paint, gum glaze, and pen and iron gall ink on wove paper, Overall: $6^{1}/_{4} \times 4^{1}/_{4}$ in. (15.9 × 10.8 cm). BF605.

Page 103: Unidentified artist, American, Pennsylvania German. *Bird Facing Left on Flowering Twig*, 1882. Water-based paint with graphite underdrawing on wove paper, Overall: $4^{7}/_{8} \times 4^{1}/_{8}$ in. (12.4 × 10.5 cm). BF1160.

Page 104: Unidentified artist, American, Pennsylvania German. *Bird Facing Right*, 19th century. Water-based paint with pen and iron gall ink on wove paper, Overall: $4^{3}/_{4} \times 3^{7}/_{8}$ in. (12.1 × 9.8 cm). BF2083.

Pages 104–105: Unidentified artist, American, Pennsylvania German. *Tiny Yellow and Red Bird on Flowering Twig*, 19th century. Water-based paint with pen and ink on wove paper, Sight: $4^{5}/_{16} \times 4$ in. (11 × 10.2 cm). BF769.

Page 105: Unidentified artist, American, Pennsylvania German. *Four Birds, Tulip, and Heart*, 19th century. Watercolor, opaque water-based paint, iron gall ink, red ink, and graphite on handmade wove paper, Overall: $8 \times 6^{5}/_{8}$ in. (20.3 × 16.8 cm). BF1038.

Pages 106–107: Ensemble view, Room 18, north wall.

Page 108: Unidentified maker, American or French. Parrot, c. 1840. Carved and painted pine, Overall: $8^{3}/_{8} \times 4^{1}/_{4} \times 8$ in. (21.3 × 10.8 × 20.3 cm). 01.18.13.

Page 109: Unidentified maker, American, Pennsylvania German, Center County. Chest, 18th century, Pennsylvania. Painted pine, Overall: $27^{1}/_{2} \times 50^{1}/_{2} \times 21^{1}/_{2}$ in. (69.9 × 128.3 × 54.6 cm). 01.18.08. Photo by Sean Murray.

Pages 110–111: Ensemble view, Room 18, with Room 14 ensemble through doorway. Photo by Sean Murray.

Page 112: Unidentified maker, English. Upholstered Armchair, late 19th–early 20th century. Walnut and fabric, Overall: $48 \times 23^{1}/_{2} \times 19^{1}/_{2}$ in. (121.9 × 59.7 × 49.5 cm). 01.24.13.

Page 113: Unidentified maker, Baule. Door for an Inner Room, late 19th century. Wood, pigment, Overall: $61^{1}/_{2} \times 20 \times 2$ in. (156.2 × 50.8 × 5.1 cm). Mount: $76 \times 13^{3}/_{4} \times 27^{3}/_{4}$ in. (193 × 34.9 × 70.5 cm). A238.

Page 114: Gallery door of Barnes Foundation building in Merion, Pennsylvania.

Page 115: Design for Gallery portico by Enfield Pottery and Tile Works, Paul Cret correspondence, 1924 Barnes Foundation Archives.

Pages 116–117: Native American pottery in the Barnes Foundation. Photo by Sean Murray.

Page 119: Unidentified maker, Zia Pueblo. Water Jar, c. 1915–1920. Polychrome earthenware, Overall: $9^{1}/_{4} \times 10^{3}/_{4}$ in. (23.5 × 27.3 cm). A358.

Page 120: Unidentified maker, Acoma Pueblo. Water Jar, c. 1885–1890. Polychrome earthenware, Overall: $7^{1}/_{4} \times 8^{3}/_{4}$ in. (18.4 × 22.2 cm). A408.

Pages 120–121: Unidentified maker, Zia Pueblo. Water Jar, c. 1900–1910. Polychrome earthenware, Overall: $8^{1}/_{2} \times 11^{1}/_{4}$ in. (21.6 × 28.6 cm). A394.

Page 121: Unidentified maker, Zia Pueblo. Water Jar, c. 1890–1900. Polychrome earthenware, Overall: $9^{7}/_{8} \times 10^{3}/_{8}$ in. (25.1 × 26.4 cm). A379.

Page 122: Attributed to Acoma Mary (Mary Histia), Native American, 1881–1973, Acoma Pueblo. Storage Jar, c. 1900. Polychrome earthenware, Overall: $15^{3}/_{4} \times 17^{3}/_{4}$ in. (40 × 45.1 cm). A383.

Page 123: Unidentified maker, Zia Pueblo. Water Jar, c. 1900–1910. Polychrome earthenware, Overall: $9^{3}/_{4} \times 11^{1}/_{4}$ in. (24.8 × 28.6 cm). A367.

Pages 124–125: After Qiu Ying, Chinese, c. 1494–1552. *Two Figures Embracing in Landscape*, late 19th century. Chinese black ink and heavily applied pigments on silk, Overall: $11 \times 7^{3}/_{8}$ in. (27.9 × 18.7 cm). BF2515.

Page 126: Angelo Pinto. *Seashells*, c. 1944. Reverse painting on glass, Sight: $7^{3}/_{4} \times 9^{3}/_{4}$ in. (19.7 × 24.8 cm). BF1002. In Copyright. ©2019 Estate of Angelo Pinto.

Page 127: Angelo Pinto. *Icarus*, c. 1944. Reverse painting on glass, Sight: $7^{3}/_{4} \times 9^{7}/_{8}$ in. (19.7 × 25.1 cm). BF744. In Copyright. ©2019 Estate of Angelo Pinto.

Page 128: Ensemble view, Room 20, west wall.

Page 129: Unidentified maker. Plate. Tin-glazed earthenware, Overall: $1^{1}/_{4} \times 14$ in. (3.2 × 35.6 cm). 01.20.25. Photo by Sean Murray.

Pages 130–131: Edith Dimock. *Women with Eggs*, 1928. Watercolor, gouache, and black crayon on thick wove paper, Overall: $9^{1}/_{8} \times 12^{1}/_{2}$ in. (23.2 × 31.8 cm). BF784. In Copyright. ©2019 Estate of Edith Dimock.

Pages 132–133: Ensemble view, Room 21, south and west walls. Photo by Sean Murray.

Page 135: Unidentified maker, possibly German, North African, or Turkish.

Portable Oil Lamp. Iron, Overall: $28\frac{1}{2} \times 11\frac{3}{8} \times 17\frac{1}{2}$ in. (72.4 × 28.9 × 44.5 cm). 01.21.37. Photo by Sean Murray.

Page 137: Unidentified maker, Baule. Portrait Mask (Mblo), late 19th century. Wood, pigment, Overall: $12\frac{7}{8} \times 5\frac{1}{2} \times 3\frac{1}{8}$ in. (32.7 × 14 × 7.9 cm). A160.

Page 138: Unidentified artist, German. *Little Girl in Interior near Window*, 1707. Oil on canvas, Overall: $36\frac{3}{4} \times 25\frac{5}{8}$ in. (93.3 × 65.1 cm). BF821.

Page 138: Unidentified maker. Butter Mold. Wood, Overall: $7\frac{7}{8} \times 3 \times \frac{11}{16}$ in. (20 × 7.6 × 1.7 cm). 01.22.29.

Page 139: Unidentified artist, French. Steeple Cock (*Coq de clocher*), 17th century. Iron with inlaid copper eyes, Overall (with mount): $17\frac{13}{16} \times 5\frac{1}{4} \times 21$ in. (45.2 × 13.3 × 53.3 cm). 01.22.43. Photo by Sean Murray.

Pages 140–141: William James Glackens. *Decoration*, c. 1914. Oil and tempera on canvas, Overall: $17\frac{1}{2} \times 23$ in. (44.5 × 58.4 cm). BF256.

Page 142: Unidentified maker. Jug. Earthenware, $9\frac{1}{4} \times 6\frac{1}{8} \times 6\frac{3}{8}$ in. (23.5 × 15.6 × 16.2 cm). 01.23.04.

Page 144: Thomas G. Maling. *Pelican*. Clam shell, Overall: $4\frac{7}{8} \times 2 \times 3\frac{7}{8}$ in. (12.4 × 5.1 × 9.8 cm). 01.23.43. Photo by Sean Murray.

Page 145: Thomas G. Maling. *Bird*. Lobster claw, Overall: $6 \times 2\frac{1}{2} \times 4\frac{1}{8}$ in. (15.2 × 6.4 × 10.5 cm). 01.23.45. Photo by Sean Murray.

Page 146: Ensemble view, Room 23, east wall. Photo by Sean Murray.

Page 147: Unidentified maker, French. Bird, 17th–18th century. Iron, Overall: $7 \times 10\frac{1}{4} \times \frac{1}{4}$ in. (17.8 × 26 × 0.6 cm). 01.23.26.

Page 149: Giorgio de Chirico. *The Mysterious Swan*, 1934. Oil on canvas, Overall: $23\frac{7}{8} \times 19\frac{3}{4}$ in. (60.6 × 50.2 cm). BF410.

Page 150: Angelo Pinto. Photograph. Albert C. Barnes next to the *Coq du Clocher* (01.22.43), c. 1946. Barnes Foundation Archives, Philadelphia, PA. Reprinted with permission.

Page 151: Unidentified maker. Corinthian Round *Aryballos*, possibly 6th century BCE. Ceramic, Overall: $6\frac{1}{8} \times 5\frac{3}{4}$ in. (15.6 × 14.6 cm). A112.

Page 152: Nicholas Valle. Photograph. Birdhouse near the teahouse in Merion, 1933. Photograph Collection, Barnes Foundation Archives, Philadelphia, PA. Reprinted with permission.

Page 159: Unidentified maker, European. Keyhole Escutcheon, 19th century. Copper, Overall: $5 \times 4\frac{7}{8} \times \frac{1}{8}$ in. (12.7 × 12.4 × 0.3 cm). 01.22.15.

Page 160: Unidentified maker. *Coq de Clocher*, 18th century. Iron, Overall: $26\frac{1}{8} \times 15\frac{1}{2} \times 1\frac{7}{8}$ in. (66.4 × 39.4 × 4.8 cm). 01.18.106.

Bibliography

Albert C. Barnes to Alexander Woollcott, 23 March 1941, President's Files, Albert C. Barnes Correspondence, Barnes Foundation Archives, Philadelphia.

Albert C. Barnes to Stuart Davis, 1 April 1942, President's Files, Albert C. Barnes Correspondence, Barnes Foundation Archives, Philadelphia.

Albert C. Barnes to Charles F. Montgomery, 5 March 1948, President's Files, Albert C. Barnes Correspondence, BFA.

Barnes, Dr. Albert C. *The Art in Painting*. Merion, PA: Barnes Foundation Press, 1925.

Clarke, Christa. *African Art in the Barnes Foundation: the Triumph of L'Art Nègre and the Harlem Renaissance*. New York: Rizzoli, 2015.

Dawson, George. "Live Ants Aid Scrimshaw Artist." *Boston Post Magazine*, December 19, 1948.

Dolkart, Judith F., and Martha Lucy. *The Barnes Foundation: Masterworks*. New York: Rizzoli, 2012.

Lucy, Martha. *The Order of Things*. Philadelphia: Barnes Foundation, 2015.

Thomas Maling to Albert C. Barnes, 10 April 1947, President's Files, Albert C. Barnes Correspondence, BFA.

Wattenmaker, Richard J. *American Paintings and Works on Paper in the Barnes Foundation*. Merion: Barnes Foundation, 2010.

Acknowledgments

Gratitude goes to so many individuals at the Barnes Foundation who contributed to the bird collection in this book. Barbara Beaucar and Amanda McKnight, in the archives, with their extensive and intuitive knowledge of Barnes's letters and newspaper clippings, helped keep the birds from flying away from historical fact. Instructor Molly Walker contributed her thoughtful interpretations of room 20. Ken Avella and Tia Bianchini showed me new connections in room 11. Ed Dixon offered the family stories of Albert Nulty and the other examples of his work. Objects conservator and "dragon wrangler" Margaret Little's lively commentary while cleaning ironwork long ago brought in the dragons. Barbara Buckley, for all her and her team's many generosities. Kerry Annos conducted some intense hunting in the underbrush of the photo archives, and Olivia Verdugo spent time preening the finished design. Thanks to all of the staff and volunteers who took excursions to the galleries in search of overlooked birds to add to our cumulative Barnes artistic birdwatching "life list." My heartfelt thanks go to Joe Langman for seeing the promise in the birds, and to the Schiffer team who brought it all together, particularly editors Sandra Korinchak and Helena Neufeld, and Molly Shields for her keen design instincts. Above all, thanks to Dan Ellerbroek, with whom birdwatching is a sheer pleasure, both in art museums and in the natural world outside.

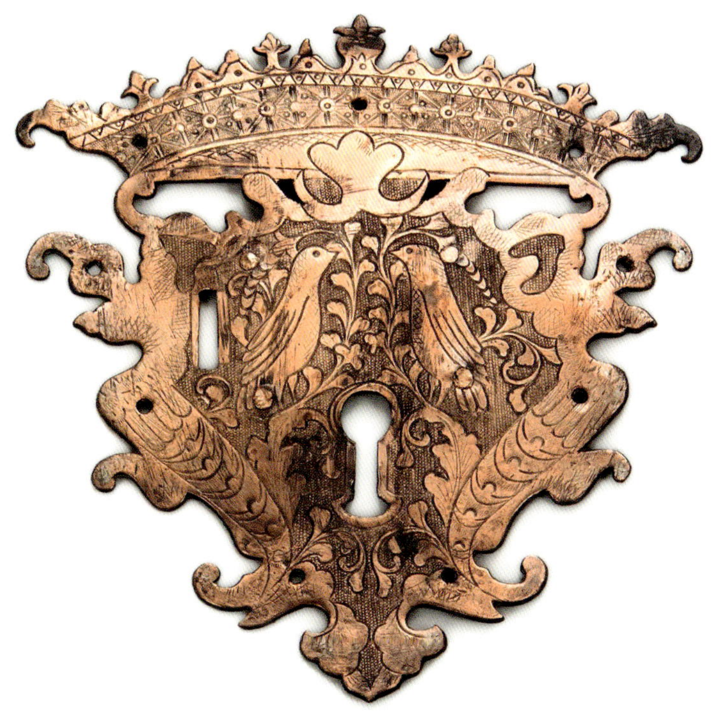

Keyhole Escutcheon, 19th century, European.

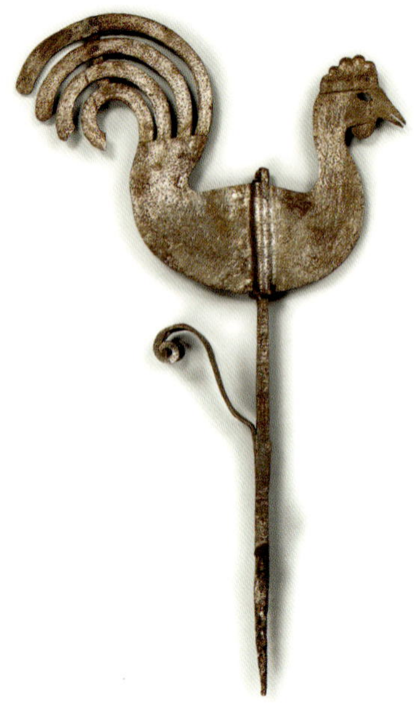

Julie Steiner has worked at the Barnes Foundation in Philadelphia for more than a decade. She writes and teaches on a variety of fine art topics, as well as on retail and product development, perpetually investigating ways to make art history accessible to wider audiences and to create meaningful personal connections to fine art. Julie has a degree in art from Smith College and studied art history in Paris at the Sorbonne. She has worked in museums in education, curatorial, and operations departments and is the author of *A Short Biography of Paul Cézanne*.